Fictions of U.S. History

FRANCES RICHARDSON KELLER

Fictions of U.S. History

A Theory and Four Illustrations

INDIANA UNIVERSITY PRESS

Bloomington and Indianapolis

This book is a publication of

Indiana University Press
601 North Morton Street
Bloomington, Indiana 47404-3797 USA

http://iupress.indiana.edu

Telephone orders   800-842-6796
Fax orders   812-855-7931
Orders by email   iuporder@indiana.edu

The paper used in this publication meets the minimum
requirements of American National Standard for Information
Sciences—Permanence of Paper for Printed Library
Materials, ANSI Z39.48-1984.

Manufactured in the United States of America

Library of Congress Cataloging-in-Publication Data

Keller, Frances Richardson, date
    Fictions of U.S. history : a theory and four illustrations /
Frances Richardson Keller.
        p. cm.
Includes bibliographical references and index.
    ISBN 0-253-34076-4 (cloth : alk. paper)
    1. United States—Historiography.   2. United States—History—
Philosophy.   3. Fictions, Theory of.   4. Ideology—Social aspects—
United States.   5. Patriarchy.   I. Title.
    E175 .K45 2002
    973'.01—dc21
                                            2001004949

1 2 3 4 5   07 06 05 04 03 02

To
John Hope Franklin
&
William H. McNeill

Between land and sea there is a place where myths are real.
—John Sayles, "The Secret of Roan Inish"

[That place is] a part of my past and in a curiously powerful way a part of my present.
—Theo Richmond, *Konin*

Contents

Acknowledgments

In writing this book I found myself in a fellowship that challenged every faculty I possess. For reading my manuscript or parts of it and helping me to improve it, I credit my teachers and friends Theodore J. Lowi, William H. McNeill, William W. Keller, and Blanche Wiesen Cook. I cannot measure my gratitude for the excellence of their insights. Nupur Chaudhuri, Barbara Penny Kanner, Evelyn Buff Segal, Christopher Herbert, Judith Strong Albert, C. Reynolds Keller, Elizabeth Balanoff, Judy Herman, Margaret Fitzsimmons, Sondra Herman, Jeanne Farr McDonnell, Kim Friedlander, and Elizabeth Van Buskirk provided warmth and a quality of support seldom available. Carole LeFaivre-Rochester encouraged me more than she knows.

I am especially grateful to my sponsoring editor, Marilyn Grobschmidt; patiently and perceptively she worked with me to actualize this book, to enhance the quality of its presentation. To that end my copy editor, Kate Babbitt, contributed generously and knowledgeably. I appreciate as well the discerning comments of the anonymous readers at Indiana University Press.

I am indebted to the San Francisco Institute for Historical Study both for a grant-in-progress and the insightful suggestions of members who listened to some of my chapters.

My husband, William P. Rhetta, has assisted me at every step. There could have been no substitute for Stephen J. Hanna's technical expertise nor for his sophisticated dedication to historical endeavors.

To my associates and friends I offer my deepest gratitude; they played vital roles in helping me clarify and express my thoughts. The shortcomings are mine. May they light a pathway toward brighter "fictions."

Fictions of U.S. History

Prologue

Brantingham: The End of the First Beginning

In the early days of important remembrances when I was 10 or 11 or 12, someone told me some stories.

In summertimes, I would sit at dusk in our flat, gray-green rowboat at the edge of Brantingham Lake in the foothills of the Adirondacks. His face was pale and his hair was dark. He could raise one eyebrow higher than the other. He was tall, the storyteller, and to my mind, he knew every wonderful thing. He kept a personal connection with Julius Caesar. He could translate Caesar's *Commentaries* and almost remember a lot of it without even looking at the book. He knew all about where Caesar had been and what Caesar had done. Once I asked him if he knew about the French Revolution. He replied that he knew everything about the French Revolution, and most of this he related to me.

We called him Frank. Frank told many stories. I shall never forget "The Monkey's Paw" by William W. Jacobs, for my friend told me that story. In the dimming light by the edge of the lake it carried qualities riveting, real, and mysterious; it aroused, as Jacobs himself must have intended, a strange uneasiness.

When autumn came and the storyteller went away to Ithaca to study at the university, he sent me a drawing, a portrait of a blue-eyed Hungarian woman in a beautiful embroidered dress and a remarkable hat, which was, as he told me, a headdress to indicate who she was and where she came from. He wrote wonderful letters to me. I put the letters in a rose-tinted, rectangular tin box with gold tracery around the sides. I stored them in my closet to treasure them. Once he brought me a book that contained a play he wanted me to read: Maeterlink's *Pélleas and Mélisande*. Did I understand it? he asked. Did I realize they were looking for a ring by the river when they had lost it somewhere by the sea?

In our village at vacation times Frank would walk through the snow, up Dayan Street from his house to our front door. By the fire in the living room, I would wait for him, wait to venture farther into the world that seemed to be his; wait, though I didn't know it, for him to show me that I mattered there.

Once, after we had listened awhile to my family's conversations, I asked him if he believed in God. When he slowly shook his head, I asked him "What do you think happens after we die?" His answer, "Nothing," crushed me to the depths of my soul. It was beyond any possibility for me to accept that answer from this young man who knew everything. The next time we met, I told him that I had been thinking. If there was no all-powerful God, perhaps there was one more powerful than we? But that answer was as unacceptable to him as his answer to my first question had been to me.

Many times as I sat on the low child's windowseat in my bedroom I wept and wondered, really about the terrible universe and religion and my friend who didn't believe and could have been right and probably didn't care.

Years passed. On several occasions I was placed in the charge of the Misses Reveley and sent to Tall Pines Summer Camp for girls in Bennington, New Hampshire. Even then I realized my family wanted to send me away from the influence of the tall young man who told the wonderful dangerous stories.

It was too late. He had preempted my mind, and as I understood still later after he graduated, he had taken possession of the whole emotional content of my heart. When I learned he was to marry a girl I had never known, a girl he met at the college in Ithaca, my world fell apart.

But the tall young man left me a precious gift. I believed him, and I believed in his stories. One in particular captured my imagination. A hunter, tiring of his life and of the dull creatures that inhabited his surroundings, departed to search for solace and for inspiration. He journeyed to distant lands, he listened to strange music, he looked for women and for wine. Nothing relieved his anxiety, nothing satisfied his yearnings. Many years he traveled, many places he searched. Despair overcame his soul as he wandered alone and ever away from the delights of his youth. As he followed a trail into the deep forest, he felt himself losing all hope. At that very moment, a soft light directed his gaze upward to behold a bird more beautiful than any creature he had ever seen. He knew that he must possess her, for she was the bird of truth. Leaving all else behind, he followed her, out of the forest and off toward a mountain so steep he knew he could not climb it. He stopped so that he could acquire some rope, a pickaxe, and some tools. And then he began the ascent. The days were long and the nights were wearying. He never faltered. He never saw the bird again, but as he lay dying one white feather floated down to his hand. He died a happy hunter.

Many years later, as I have learned a little about life and love and the quest for knowledge, the fascination of stories rises for me in ever-more-compelling array. Though I do not feel so intense an attraction to the bird of truth as once I did, I know that stories—fictions—matter, that we all make stories, that all of our stories matter, that it is all right to make stories, that stories—and fictions—may lead us beyond the best of our dreams.

Beyond Brantingham

For all of my life a fascination with stories stayed with me. It hovered over my girlhood, it swirled around people I knew, people I imagined. In school times, it eddied and flowed about characters in history books, plays, novels, poems I read, talks with my grandfather, classes with my Aunt Leah (she was, as it happened, my history teacher). In summertimes at Brantingham

I lived for stories Frank would tell. Those stories put as much into my hours as they could hold, delighting my days, filling my days with wonderful discoveries.

The stories troubled my spirit, too, for I loved my Brantingham storyteller. I couldn't dismiss the differences between him and just about everybody else in my family, as well as the people my family knew—around the village, in school, in church, in the Good Manners Club. Despite all that, I longed to be part of the life Frank would lead, a participant in mountains he would climb. In my naiveté, this never became a matter of falling *in* love. It became a deep, spiritual commitment, as much a part of my life as the very living of it.

For years, I could neither separate my feelings and my thoughts nor quite bring them together. But I sensed that stories carry encounters, emotions, traditions, meanings that come to us no other way. Chameleon-like, they become personal, infinitely precious; they also become powerful. We live with them. We turn them into guidepaths by which we fashion activities and form projects. Without putting a word to it, I realized that children develop identities from stories listened to, stories lived with, stories looked at, stories imagined, chosen, never forgotten.

I thought about the magnetic power of stories. Yet I didn't dream I would be sitting here, writing stories, gathering collections of my stories, endowing my stories with the seismic energies of my life as they mingled with lives in historical times, with lives being lived. Nor did I imagine I would be christening my stories my "fictions." As stories merged into patterns, I couldn't have realized how profoundly I had been programmed, programmed in matters vital to my being.

It started in Lowville—the programming, I mean. Lowville, where I began, is an Adirondack village of some 3,500 people. It lies in a sheltered place in the foothills of the Adirondack mountains. We lived in a beautiful soft-red, brick, eighteen-room house on the corner of Dayan and Easton Streets. My sister and I never gave it a thought, but we were protected in every outward aspect of our growing up. Everybody knew us. Indeed, everybody in Lowville knew everybody else. Even the children soon learned everything worth remembering about everybody's family. We walked and skipped and roller-skated about the village. By the time we could do all that, the Good Manners Club was born.

Perhaps I was 8 or 9 when Mary Toussaint's mother conceived of the Good Manners Club. This was a gathering of a few little girls and their mothers. For two or three years or so, we met once a month in each others' homes for supper. We dressed up: pink and white and blue and yellow party dresses, long white stockings, patent-leather shoes with bows, and straps that buttoned across the arches or around the ankles. Hair ribbons, carefully perched.

We came primed with pieces to say. After a three-course supper with flowers and candles on the table and with each girl's mother standing nearby, we took turns announcing a good manner. This could be "As little boats push out to sea, I push my spoon away from me," or "A lady always waits for a gentleman to open the door for her." I remember "It is very rude to interrupt when someone else is speaking, especially your parents," and "You should stand when an older woman enters the room, but you need not stand for a man." "A smile goes farther than a frown." "Thank a gentleman kindly when he carries your books or your packages or pulls out your chair for you." "A lady doesn't chew gum," was another, "Speak when you are spoken to," another, and "A lady never raises her voice" yet another. There were more of the same order. From time to time, as might be expected, many were repeated. We felt proud to roll them forth.

I'm sure we didn't behave in such prescribed fashions at home, but we probably did put on our manners in other places. Before I became a teenager, I well knew what was acceptable. I knew how young ladies should comport themselves.

Years later I slowly realized—still, with a start—that I had been loathe to speak out plainly, that I had gotten the implied messages that men were superior, stronger, in charge, deserving of opportunities; that they were to be reckoned with, managed. Without expressing it, even to myself, I had understood that one wouldn't be able to do this unless she contrived to appear noncompetitive, helpless sometimes, not too smart, and as pretty as she possibly could.

I could see all sorts of flaws in the way I looked. I would need all the help I could get in the important endeavor to appear pleasing; I had acquired several lipsticks and an eyelash curler by the time I was 13. I made a mental note to keep my accomplishments under cover. This had to cause some discomfort, for I was proud of my grades. I loved to read. I loved to play the piano. If I became known for these yearnings, it might alienate my classmates. Yet I had clearly understood the unspoken messages from my father's world! Alas, I had often tailored my behavior to accord with those messages.

A few days after my sixteenth birthday I found myself a first-year student at Wellesley College; there, our housemother Mrs. Davis, a tall, thin lady with faded blond hair and a tight, controlled way of speaking, reinforced the script. Wearing a proper navy knit suit with a white collar and white cuffs, she assembled us in the Fiske House living room. She seated us in folding chairs she had set up in rows. Then she delivered a crisp monologue on how we were to live: Girls should be good housekeepers. Rooms to be kept clean at all times. Special attention should be given the bathroom. Wash out the bathtub each time you used it. Promptly return the books and gym property you would have brought to your room. Put laundry in just the right place, especially damp towels; send most of it home on a certain day each week. It wasn't required, but Mrs. Davis changed her dress for dinner. No food in our rooms, no loud assemblages. Emphasis on entertaining guests, especially male guests. None of them above the first floor ever. They were to be introduced individually to her. Strict rules about leaving and returning—but male students from Harvard and MIT didn't have rules about that. If there were problems, Mrs. Davis would be glad to discuss them in her office. All of this and more, but not one word about what we might learn or do to acquire an education.

Despite my immaturity and lack of discipline I did get a good education that first year at Wellesley, then during three subsequent years at Sarah Lawrence College. I emerged too soon, too young in experience; I promptly married. By the time I reached 22, I was the mother of a strong baby boy; at 36, I was the mother of four children—two more boys and a girl.

But efforts to educate myself didn't cease. Through adventurous years in bringing up children, I took courses at Columbia University, then an M.A. at the University of Toledo. Then a Ph.D. at the University of Chicago. Then a year of advanced study in Paris. I didn't even know the term, but I became a "single parent" just before entering the doctoral program at the University of Chicago. There, in the mid-1960s, you couldn't walk about without encountering the turmoil engulfing universities everywhere. Nevertheless, classes and assignments proceeded fairly smoothly. Fascinating courses, eminent professors, achievers all. And all of them were male.

In the 1960s, women's history, African-American history, and ethnic studies were realms of the future. One day near the time when I finished my coursework, a female protester on campus took my arm and talked to me. She had been working in the admissions office. Did I know there was an index card in the admissions files that read "Do not admit—child-bearing age?" I didn't know about that caveat. Knowing, I couldn't forget it. At that moment, I began to develop a recognition of controls women face, a remembrance of my childhood as well as my difficulties in gaining admission to a first-rate graduate university—on and on.

I suppose that my experiences and my studies have brought me to theories about fictions. They have initiated efforts to describe the propelling centers of my thoughts, which I call the fictions of my histories. Especially, I think of fictions as that complex of attitudes, beliefs, and sensitivities that characterize creative endeavors; they lead to enterprises, be they historic, religious, political, or scientific. They operate personally and they operate socially; they operate academically and they operate culturally.

So I will begin this book with my thoughts about fictions and stories. My disparate tales, gathered over the expanse of a lifetime and from the privileges of a fantastic education, are meant to suggest some inkling of how people function, how they think and act individually, socially, and in academic disciplines. The stories represent some instances of what I conceive to be our general manner of living our lives in vital areas. Then I will tell the first of my own stories, the one about patriarchy.

Many encounters, many events have intervened since I came, so to speak, of a telling age and wanted to share my stories. Each encounter, each event carried an influence, each moved my thoughts toward the fleeting moment in which I write these paragraphs. But thereby hang other stories. Who knows? Other fictions?

1

Fictions and the Missions of History

Our Fictions, Our Missions, Our Selves

Everybody on planet earth leads a life based on fictions. Doctors and lawyers, merchants and thieves, priests and politicians, scientists and artists, housewives and historians—none of them could manage one day without the fictions on which they depend.

A fiction is a myth, yet it is more than a myth. A fiction is an ideology, yet it is more than an ideology. A fiction is a strong, long-held belief, coming to us as aged institutions have crystallized it. Or a fiction can rise from a sudden revelation—yet fictions are more. Fictions can be literary imaginings we treasure in novels, drama, poetry. But fictions are more than all of these.

In striving for knowledge about ourselves and our world, I believe that historical endeavors epitomize *the best* we can do. I also realize that many historians have long known the delicate balance between the histories they write and the verisimilitude of their stories. In my understanding of the term fiction, I would stress that historians can expand knowledge scientifically as well as, shall I say, by inspiration. They can do this just as reliably as anybody else— though in comparison to historians, scientists take a trip more precisely conceived in black and white. But historians are able to deal with hard evidence as accurately as scientists and as finely as novelists, poets, dramatists, and lexicographers. I believe they can do their work with literary dash and style; like those who compile dictionaries, historians can also urge and help forward the evolution of English words.

So what is a fiction? Fiction is one of those loaded words. Given the concept of evolving words to capture the movements, the turns of the times, I see fictions as vigorous, compelling forces. They are sources of living endeavors. They are compelling ideas. They discharge impulses. They can shift. They can metamorphosize. Seen from different perspectives, the same fiction can appear distinctly different. Fictions inhabit lives, societies, and histories. Fictions can lead to missions, though, practically speaking, our missions arise from agencies, for which we are the agents. This is crucial: By becoming agents of our fictions, we bring forth the missions that distinguish everything we think and do.

I do not suggest that all fictions are equal or even similar in stature, purpose, structure or impact on our lives. They differ, partly because from them we become agents; from them we develop missions, creating our missions for different purposes. But our fictions—the powerful, driving ideas that we use to determine loyalties and characterize endeavors and fix the character of societies—become our compasses. We activate them. We commit ourselves to the missions we choose from among those they present. Through our missions, we express our identities, our work, our lives.

Historians are great fabricators of fictions. Scientists invent theirs, too. Activists seize upon fictions that suit their purposes. Priests struggle to bring reality to their fictions, to bring conviction and mystery into accord. Historians make very strong claims that they can be unimpeachable authorities, impartial professionals. Indeed, to some scholars, historians appear almost disconnected from the materials they treat.[1] For other scholars, historians appear to furnish one peripheral dimension of the materials they study with their detached explanations.[2] But in point of fact, key dimensions of the endeavors of historians, particularly their agencies and the missions of their agencies, are often left out.

The problem is that because people believe historians, historians exert a potent influence. They carry heavy responsibilities, for they come upon opportunities to affect the choices new generations pursue. They cannot escape a deep involvement. There is no such thing as objective historical writing, or, for that matter, objective social posturing. Nor is there objective "imaginative" literature or objective science, though in comparison to historians, scientists have it in spades.[3]

For historians and other agents to realize that they are selecting fictions is to legitimize their work. Because they write history from the viewpoint of given fictions, historians as agents have chosen missions. They can preserve salutary features of the past, or they can undermine those features. They—and we—have choices to make. In particular, historians can broaden their contributions by acknowledging which fictions they adopt and which fictions become their missions and by striving to understand fictions of others. Scientists can advance our knowledge, whatever the consequences of their discoveries. Sometimes, unfortunately, they too can display to the past and the world an uninvolved air.

Yet, for all the danger thus incurred, fiction choices and missions remain as necessary for our comfort as for our very survival. Our choices among fictions provide the distinguishing dimensions of our individual and social identities. Fictions become more than shadowy concepts differentiating reality from unreality; as time passes, they become reality. The missions they produce become measures of integrity; they limit or expand our identities. They delineate possibilities for their time and for future generations.

From the beginning, fictions unfold within the frameworks in which we are born. As we develop, they take on definite forms. They become a means of steering behavior. They propel an individual along a life course. They also become forces that drive an entire society's movement in a particular direction. Decisively, they project the scenes for the stories historians tell. They can be used as propaganda, but more broadly, they determine the activities of our lives.

Not that historians have failed to consider these mysteries. In *The Structure of Scientific Revolutions,* Thomas Kuhn introduced the term "paradigm" to summarize his own brilliant insights. Natalie Davis wrote of *Fiction in the Archives* as she considered subjective factors in the explorations historians envision. "I think we can agree with Roland Barthes, Paul Ricoeur, and Lionel Gossman," she wrote, "that shaping choices of language, detail, and order are needed to present an account that seems to both writer and reader true, real, meaningful, and/or explanatory."[4] William H. McNeill looked at "myth-making" as a legitimate and necessary enterprise of historians. More recently, Peter Novick has written of *That Noble Dream,* while Scott Casper has explored how we may go about *Constructing American Lives* in deeper dimensions. Though many historians have ruminated long and insightfully on matters central or peripheral or in some way related to this topic, I like the term fiction. I like it because it carries an inner dynamism: It suggests chance perceptions and energies of movement, change, and relativity as well as the possibilities of choosing within our circumstances. I like the term because it carries overtones signifying creation and development, overtones much muted in terms such as pattern or worldview.

How do we come by these variable forces that gain allegiance from masses and are manipulated by leaders? That can move individual lives in one direction and another? That determine guidelines whole societies follow? That distinctively color the historian's art?

We enter the world on the crest of sets of fictions—established ideas that organize the thoughts and life patterns of those about us. No one avoids such a debut. We know our first fictions as families, homes, neighborhoods, schools, churches, businesses, hospitals, prisons, governments, the customs of our daily lives. These fictions, which at some point become missions, then institutions, represent styles of organizing belief and conduct for manageable living. For little children, they are givens. Individually we begin life enveloped in patterns of fictions these organizations represent. Without them the world is chaos.

But a proliferation of fiction patterns exists. We discover several kinds of families and homes, different peer groups, many neighborhoods, many religions, many professions, many types of businesses, different kinds of government. We understand many dimensions to the ordered institutions we first encounter, to the fictions and the missions they represent, to the stories they embody, to the directions in which they travel. So we become agents. We meet situations, some unanticipated. As they arise, we revise our strategies for dealing with events according to our needs, our beliefs, and the possibilities we can perceive.

As individual persons, we choose whether to continue exactly as we were born, affiliated with and dependent upon the same institutions, the same fictions, the same stories—and missions. Or, as we come to adolescence and young adulthood, we choose whether to alter some patterns, change some fictions, modify some stories, reassess some attitudes, forego some actions, undertake others. We keep some fictions, we mix and combine some, we discard some, we create some. So does every historian. The consequence is that histories are often passed off for objective truth as the historian perpetuates the current fictions and choices of his or her missions.

From time to time, whole societies find themselves out of harmony with the fictions, the stories, the customs on which they have relied. Then they may adopt missions that drive their collective behavior in different directions. This happens when, for whatever reasons, agents in the society are able to set new fictions, new missions in motion. The Utah Mormons of the nineteenth century provide a striking example: Although they originally mandated monogamous marriage, Joseph Smith convinced them that polygamous marriage would produce a superior society.

Historians occupy unique positions. They are agents through whom we reconstruct the past, messengers through whom we guess the meaning of the past in terms of where we are. They become our memories as our memories reach back and push us forward. They mingle their stories into concerns that live with us. More accurately, historians become their memories, for no historian can speak or write of the past without bringing his or her experience, as well as the whole paraphernalia of his or her points of view, to the work. In short, historians cannot escape bringing their own fictions and their chosen missions when they write their stories. It is impossible to measure the impact of fictions and missions historians bring to their stories. But it may be possible to assess the relativities of fictions that inform the stories historians tell.

With time, concerns arise. New requirements alter old assurances so that institutions themselves appear to shift; old guarantees no longer suffice. As they take on different shapes, the fictions by which we have defined our thoughts and from which we have filtered our actions cease to meet our needs. They cease to inform our missions. The opportunity embedded in this situation means that nothing we think or do or say—no belief, no loyalty, no custom, no course of action—need stay inscribed in stone. It means that within the limits of our circumstances, we have choices. This amounts to the most distinctly human characteristic we possess as well as the most precious possibility I can conceive.

So I'm going to tell some stories that illustrate the relativities of fictions, missions, and histories. I do this with full knowledge that my stories arise from my fictions and my missions and that they emerge from the changing psychoscapes I have seen my fictions traverse. My stories recount instances that have come to the center of my thoughts. They reflect the ways I have learned to understand people and the movements of peoples and historians and their fictions; they do not reflect any "objective" reality. My fictions and my missions have become the varied designs and pathways by which I strive to interpret the world, its peoples, and myself, nothing more, nothing less.

My first story concerns the overriding fictions and missions that lie at the roots and grow through every fiber of our society. It describes the origins and the growth of the patriarchal way of organizing society. Then it touches fissures that have developed in our time in that manner of living. By patriarchy I mean the exertion of male control over women and children in families and in social activities; this entails the exclusion of women from sharing control of major institutions that educate children, develop industrial capacities, and manage public policy; the result is the exploitation and often the rejection of women in carrying out projects in all areas.

Why, I used to wonder, have so few memorable women appeared in our stories? Why did historians and myth-makers tell us mainly about "suffragettes," war nurses, perhaps Pocahontas or Martha Washington, perhaps a movie star or two? Why did they fail to tell us about women writers, artists, composers, physicians, scholars, lawmakers, and thinkers? How did it happen that our military-industrial-complex world subscribed so deeply to a style of organization that honored the winning of wars but left out the achievements of women? I will bring forward some tales that feminist scholars are telling us now. I will contrast their fictions and their missions with the fictions on which most stories about our society depended. Much of my first story devolves from the question of the importance of a whole history to our possibilities on earth. How can a civilization reach a high destiny while forgetting the existence of half its people? How can a civilization avoid disasters of titanic proportions when it knows only half its population?

My second story concerns the backgrounds of historians themselves. After the Civil War split our nation, after Confederate exertions ceased in the 1860s, a time of tremendous pain—and tremendous opportunity—ensued. We call that period our Reconstruction. The task at hand was to put together one viable nation. But that could not be accomplished in a vacuum. It could not be accomplished if it was powered by the same fictions, the same missions that led to civil war. The problems would remain unsolved. If we reconstituted the nation exactly as it was, if we failed to deal constructively with old ills, if we failed to honor new fictions and new missions, more troubles would be assured. Whatever we named it, the onus of slavery would remain. In my second story, to which I bring my fictions and my missions, I survey some of the stories historians have told about Reconstruction as the saga of the nation played forth. How could historians have told such different tales about the same events? I look with an eye to the awesome power historians exerted as well as to the different fictions and the different missions they brought to their stories about that drama.

The third story I relate, as always from the viewpoint of my fictions and my missions, for that is all I can do, shows how a religious society jettisoned their fictions. It shows how they accepted new fictions presented to them in midstream, as it were, how they then allowed new missions to alter their lives dramatically. In the beginning, the nineteenth-century religious Mormons gave monogamous marriage their support: "There shall not any man among you have save it be one wife," declared the first Book of Mormon, "and concubines he shall have none."[5] Approval of monogamous behavior emerges again in the Mormon Book of Commandments: "Thou shalt love thy wife with all thy heart, and shalt cleave unto her and none else."[6] Originally, therefore, monogamy was an article of the Mormon faith, a decisive expression of the fictions and the missions on which this religion rested.

But Mormon founder Joseph Smith experienced revelations. As his church expanded, one revelation, a key revelation, made known to Smith the principle that plural marriage for men would yield a more virtuous society.[7] For the next forty-some years, polygamy and its diametrically different set of marriage practices became official church policy. So drastic a change suggests at least a reversal of sustaining fictions and a change of direction in the mission of the group.

The last of my stories has to do with how one woman lived her life as my fictions lead me to see it. I will tell how she altered fictions she inherited and what I take to be the missions she created as her life progressed. Over the twentieth century, Eleanor Roosevelt emerged as a most admired but most controversial figure. Her life displayed changes of directions as she met challenges. It showed an American child beginning life enveloped in customs of the old elite but altering those ideas and creating a mission as she became a powerful, compassionate champion of the distressed and the needy.

Curiously, we also see this metamorphosis reflected in the coverage historians as professionals chose in reporting her activities, beginning with a period when the scope of women's public activities was little noticed. In a widely used college text, the 1966 third edition of Thomas A. Bailey's *The American Pageant*, Eleanor Roosevelt's name does not appear in the index.[8] In a revised 1991 edition by Bailey and David M. Kennedy, however, her name rates one index entry while that of her husband rates thirty-two index entries, many pertaining to matters in which Eleanor Roosevelt deeply involved herself and to outcomes over which she wielded influence. Though in that one reference Bailey and Kennedy remark that "another of Roosevelt's great personal and political assets was his wife, Eleanor," they characterize her briefly as "tall, ungainly and toothy."[9]

In *The United States: American Democracy in World Perspective* by Ray Allen

Billington and others, Eleanor Roosevelt gets one index entry, and in that reference she rates one sentence.[10] Her husband rates twenty-two entries. In John A. Garraty's 1975 text, *The American Nation: A History of the United States since 1865,* Eleanor Roosevelt's influence shows in three entries, while those of her husband come to twenty-nine. Once again, many entries under her husband's name refer to matters in which she played a significant role.[11] In volume III of *American Epoch: A History of the United States since the 1890's* by Arthur S. Link with the collaboration of William B. Catton, Eleanor Roosevelt's name does not appear in the index, although the authors mention "Eleanor Clubs" in a passage titled "Negroes and the Home Front." There is no mention of her role in the United Nations.[12] Taken together, these historians expressed the dominant professional fictions and the missions they created from their times and backgrounds.

Like the missions that suffused Eleanor Roosevelt's life, the reflections historians deemed meaningful have changed directions. The new views show revisions of the earlier fictions and missions. Prominent among historians and biographers who find Eleanor Roosevelt's life significant are Blanche Wiesen Cook, Joseph P. Lash, William Chafe, Lois Scharf, Joan Hoff, Doris Kearns Goodwin, James MacGregor Burns, Allida M. Black, Frank Freidel, J. William T. Youngs, Susan Ware, and Joanna and Robert Zangrando. From essays and whole biographies to survey texts, they have accorded Eleanor Roosevelt's role a prestigious, influential place. The entries under her name in any of these books easily total more than the index entries in the earlier books combined. To bring about such a difference in coverage of one individual's life, the guiding life-missions of that person—as well as the guiding professional missions historians chose—must have undergone striking progressions.

In telling my stories, I intend to illustrate how we change fictions and how we select missions. Scientists, artists, and priests—as well as historians—select their fictions. The rest of us create our fictions. All fabricators of fictions assume formative roles in shaping everyday events. We grasp their tales and add tales of our own. On the basis of these combinations of fictions and missions and the stories for which they provide a structure, we continuously decide what we shall believe and how we shall behave. We form our own missions. This amounts to deciding who we are.

At the level of planning how to put missions into practice, we select styles of operation. Sometimes we choose misrepresentation and "disinformation" in the manner U.S. army liaison officer Oliver North championed. In 1987, North faced a committee of the U.S. Senate to explain our covert operations in Nicaragua. He assured Congress that deceit was "usual," that it was necessary in order to prevail. If, like North, we choose "disinformation," we may look for a framework that other people will accept. Or a framework to hide intentions. Or a framework to confuse opponents. Or perhaps a framework to deceive ourselves. Or we may employ so narrow a focus that we create fictions that obliterate whole portions of the large picture.

If instead we set out to tell stories rising from the most reliable evidence we can find, we can tell the story by narration or we can tie together previously disconnected fictions to create a different story. If we choose the latter strategy, do we understand that the new fiction is vulnerable, subject to disproof? If we choose narration, the story may strike out to describe events or it may descend from stories of others, stories we wish to emphasize for one reason or another.

In creating missions, we decide how to employ our fictions. Is it possible to distinguish honesty from "disinformation"? Can we reach accommodations of comfort in understanding our fragmented, conflicted, influential inheritances? Can we hear and see fictions of others so that we can create whole stories, viable missions? If we remove unbearable scenes, as the Japanese did for five decades in their public school history textbooks, can we understand their magnitude by means of stories we hear?

I began to wonder whether we can recognize the daily presumptions by which we live. I use the words of the political scientist Theodore J. Lowi to ask if "form"—for which I substitute fiction, by which I mean the form or fictions we choose—if "form" is "a method ensuring the fulfillment of purpose"?[13] And can we understand our shifting purposes as missions we create? And stories as ways historians implement their fictions? Rising as they do from unique inheritances and commitments, the stories historians tell thus furnish case studies in the reaches of fictions. They exemplify relativities in human points of view. Einstein said it best: We can take any point as fixed and consider that everything else is in motion relative to it. There is no fixed "center" of the universe.

Seeking clarification, and a way to say what I mean, I looked in dictionaries. The *American Heritage Dictionary* speaks of a fiction as "an imaginary creation or a pretense that does not represent actuality but has been invented." The *Oxford English Dictionary* (OED) first mentions "the action of fashioning or imitating." That dictionary and the *American Heritage Dictionary* give the term fiction a second meaning: Both note that fiction once meant "a lie," a "feigning, counterfeiting, deceit, dissimulation, pretense"; the OED notes that that meaning—deliberate deceit—is obsolete. That meaning pigeonholed the making of fictions in the sense of invention as a dishonorable activity. The new *Shorter Oxford English Dictionary* suggests "a thing feigned or imaginatively invented." Emphasis in the definition of the word fiction has been shifting with the compass of knowledge about ourselves and our world.

Sometimes Latin origins yield clues: The term fiction descended from the Latin *fictio*, to fashion or make, and from *fictus*, past participle of *fingere*, to touch, to form, or to mold; it survived through old French *feindre* to *fiction* and, through middle English, to *ficcioun*. Always it carried the connotation to form or to mold; more important, it suggested creation. Since Roman times it has ceased to imply deceit. So where do we stand? For us, fiction becomes a promising term. It consists of inheritances, creations, possibilities.

Eleanor Roosevelt delighted in fiction, by which she meant "imaginative" storytelling; she believed an author "can reveal what he has learned through observation and experience of the inner working of the souls of men . . . without hurting anyone and without humiliating himself."[14] She apparently viewed imaginative literature as a device for delivering messages so that they could be seen and heard. To avoid hurting people and to avoid humiliation certainly can contribute to communication. But taking fiction and the forming of missions to describe the seeking of understanding exclusively through imaginative literature neglects exciting possibilities: Scientific advance, political literacy, the long historical understanding and the demands of everyday living are quests as alluring as those of "imaginative" literature.

The dictionaries do, however, give us a clue toward amending the stripped-down dictionary concepts: In law, fiction means "feigned statements of facts which the Courts authorize in order to bring cases within their jurisdiction." With this understanding, fictions can stand as frameworks that define or explore any situation; when they become missions, they can operate as guides to living and learning.

In their travels across times and nations, words reflect expanding ideas. Perhaps each of us can become an authorizing court. Perhaps this use of the term fiction can be brought to bear on the search for knowledge in science and in histories as well as in "imaginative" literature and in daily living. It seems that the best efforts of scientists, historians, and theologians use "feigned" statements, counterfactual statements—theses—they do not know to be correct in order to bring problems within their scope. It may also be that the fictions and missions scientists and historians use parallel the fictions and missions people use to conduct their lives.

Intellectual history records a dazzling array of insights—the guesses of Albert Einstein, the guesses of Stephen Hawking, and the guesses of Roger Penrose or the guesses of Isaac Newton before Einstein's. I think of the guesses of Karl Marx and Arthur Schlesinger, Jr. Brilliant they were. But none of their insights, none of their fictions or their resulting missions rendered final verities. All became markers along uncharted paths, paths scientists and historians might have failed to discover had they never tried their fictions, had they never selected specific modes to explore their fictions, had they never formed missions. Sometimes in science, as in history, being wrong leads more directly to the truth than being right.

The concept of fact looms in discerning what a fiction can be; I wanted to put the thoughts from one historian's piece, "What Are Historical Facts?," into my realization of the possibilities of fictions.[15] Carl Becker saw that facts are slippery. Search as we may, we can never find all the facts about an occurrence or a movement; we can never fix the boundaries of events to come up with facts so solid that we can be sure where and when an event or a movement starts or stops. We can never be sure that the next discoveries will not alter the evidence. If we could find all the facts, as historians Leopold von Ranke and his successor Johann Gustav Droysen hoped we could, they would tell us nothing. The facts would only pile higher and higher because we would not have created a fiction.

Becker respected historical evidence; he probably distinguished between facts and evidence. From this, I am guessing that he would have approved of a new understanding of a fiction. Like the philosopher-historian Karl Popper, Becker realized that we can and do and must guess meanings of events, then test our guesses in light of evidence. We must create and test fictions. Popper stressed that our guesses ought to rise from significant issues. "History has no meaning," Popper thought, "but we can give it meaning." We can ask questions rising from the adventures of our lives. We can create or adopt fictions and try them to learn the meaning of evidence we select to explain events. This is precisely what historians do when they write about the past. This is what people do as they go about their lives. Some simply accept fictions of others as they look for missions, sometimes from indifference or habit. Some create fictions—and missions—daringly.

In the springtime of the year 1985, historian William H. McNeill wrote that "intellectual breakthroughs happen when someone pushes hard against older limits and starts talking nonsense." Nonsense? In *Mythistory and Other Essays,* McNeill reflected upon the ways by which we learn about our past and the ways by which historians influence our understanding of it. His title, he said, was "a usage that was not very widely welcomed" in the historical profession: *Mythistory.* Yet by combining the myth idea with the idea that myth-making "is indeed what we do as historians" and is what we *legitimately* do as historians, McNeill opened vistas through which to see ourselves and our world more clearly.[16]

A decade later, French art historian Bernadette Fort suggested that historians create fictions so that their work becomes meaningful. In an essay commemorating the bicentennial of the French Revolution, she asked "What could be less fictional than the 'Hard Facts' of the Declaration of the Rights of Man, the execution of Louis XVI, the march of the Parisian women to Versailles, the excesses of the Terror?" Yet, she suggested, we could never conceive one of these "hard facts" except through a "prism of fiction."[17]

To grasp the significance of any movement, to reconstruct any movement, to understand its origins, to write or act in the light of knowledge about it, historians, Fort suggested, perform acts of creation, "poetic" acts. They compose fictions. Starting from these fictions, they develop missions; they tell their tales from dimensions they see or dimensions they want other people to see. It would follow that the ways they tell their stories, as well as the emphases with which they endow their stories, often become established belief about what happened and why it happened. Thus, the term fictions can evoke the most exploitative aspects of the mind or it can express the most explorative, creative insights of the spirit. Or it can simply reflect the voice of the teller, as it does in the forming of missions. It can determine events of daily living. It can influence the course an individual or a society travels.

Similarly, and less than a decade after McNeill's essay, William Cronon spoke of stories. In an ingenious comparison of the different impacts of two stories historians told about "the long drought that struck the Great Plains during the 1930s," Cronon displayed the power of fictions and stories. One historian wrote that "nature made a mess and human beings cleaned it up." The survivors achieved "a triumph of individual and community spirit." But as another historian's tale had it, "The story of the Dust Bowl is less about the failures of nature than about the failures of human beings to accommodate themselves to nature." Tragedies happened because of "willful human misunderstandings" and consequent social collapse.[18]

Laying aside the questions of where either of these stories came from and what were the missions involved, it is plain that ecosystem management depends upon which belief, which story, which history, which fiction, which resulting policy dominates. For example, what we decide about the fires and floods in Yellowstone Park could decimate that park or could preserve its beauty for generations. What politicians conclude about clear-cutting our redwood forests could bear upon the quality of the air we breathe. Society's peril or society's comfort hang in the balance of prevailing fictions, of *prevailing stories.* Our choices of fictions, of stories, of missions as they implement fictions, provide the cement that holds us together individually and as communities. We carry out our narratives according to those choices and the style we have adopted: either deliberate misrepresentation or conveying the story according to evidence and according to choices of narration, imitation, or innovation.

In effect, William Cronon's stories connect with Bernadette Fort's fictions; both relate to William McNeill's myths. McNeill appreciates historians' reliance on "scientific history," however they conceive it; he recognizes the achievements of "scientific" historians. But he stresses the "constricting limits" such a reliance imposes, for science and histories can only advance by means of the most imagined, the most creative of fictions and the most deliberate plans for realizing them. While Fort highlights the fictions historians sometimes knowingly and sometimes unknowingly create, it follows from Cronon's suggestions that individuals and peoples act by means of whatever stories, whatever missions carry out their choices.

The theme that readings of happenings—what has happened and what may happen—our fictions—are decided again and again by who we are, where we come from, what is going on with us, how we view the world and how we decide to act—that theme hangs in the air. It hovers over *The Woman Warrior* and *China Men,* the novels of Maxine Hong Kingston. It inhabits our everyday lives. Eleanor Roosevelt noticed this when she said in the 1930s that "everyone writes from his own point of view." Long ago in Puritan New England, Cotton Mather noticed this in 1693 when he described the "witchcraft delusion" while trying to justify the Salem trials: "We know not," he wrote, "at least I know not, how far the delusions of Satan [which refers to the fictions at issue] may be interwoven into some circumstances of the confessions."[19]

The same theme sounds in the words historian Lawrence W. Levine wrote in 1993. Levine referred to "the prism through which [historians] chose to look at the past." Levine suggested it could profit us to understand that personal plans—missions—condition the interpretations historians present.[20] Historian Michael Kammen wrote movingly of disastrous effects when the public demands *the* truth—*its* fictions and *its* missions—by pressing historians. "How should the 'last act' of World War II be recalled?" Kammen asks. "As a celebration of the valor of American military personnel who risked their lives in the name of freedom. . . . Or should the use of atomic weapons on large urban sites and civilians be presented in terms of a moral calamity?"[21] Which fiction, he meant, which storyline, which mission ought our society to believe? How ought we to carry out the missions we select? How are we to allow for the relativities of histories?

I would add that historians' personal positions, expressed by fictions and missions they select and by methods they choose, influence which characters inhabit their scenes and which are forgotten. Personal positions—their fiction-choices and their missions—decide which events become established versions of the past in its continuation in the present and which events and persons are consigned to oblivion. A poignant example: In direct opposition to the evidence most people find painfully convincing, and for motives entirely obscure to the Allied armies that came upon Auschwitz in 1945, some neo-Nazis insist that the Holocaust never occurred.[22]

Together historians speak eloquently of tangled connections among novelists, historians, scientists, histories, and societies. Together they reveal the fiction-stories that produce protest, the created myths that sustain movements, the fiction-stories that support transmissions of customs, the fiction-stories that historians, scientists, theologians, and activists invent, live, and project, each in a chosen fashion. I have called such choices fictions and missions because they are contrived, agented, current, and not necessarily permanent in the lives and the work of their makers.

To push the insights of scholars, we may ask how myths, fiction-stories, and missions differ from social ideologies. Social ideologies are ideas exemplified in groups or movements by characterizing attitudes and by unfolding events. They are fixed by social adoption. At such a time an ideology can become a dominant fiction. Then it becomes a more inclusive concept, a mission. For example, in the mid-1900s, Russians widely believed that class polarization was implicit in capitalist economies, that this would lead to violent revolution, and that Marxian communism, exempt from this cancer, would deliver a classless society and the good life for all. Here, the term social ideology leaves out the concept of agency. It leaves unaccounted-for the question of how Russians came by this belief. What persons and what situations brought them to it? When we also ask how these ideas were implemented, the ideology becomes a fiction-story and a mission.

Fictions and missions designate energies injected into myths and ideologies; they bring about social movements as well as personal loyalties and personal decisions. By fiction-stories I refer not only to social ideologies but also to the agency that interprets these attitudes and events. This means the historian's agency in writing in the vein that he or she chooses. It means the agency of any scientific or religious or political participant in steering events. Without this agency, the myths, the social ideologies, metamorphosize or expire. The terms fiction and mission capture the agencies that provide pressures to fuel happenings, to set up postures. Thus they designate energies injected into myths or ideologies that bring about social movements as well as personal loyalties and personal decisions.

Agency summarizes the differences among ideologies, myths, fictions, and missions. Fictions create ideologies that can be driven by agencies. Powerful fiction-stories arise from troubled social, political, intellectual, and scientific climates. Depending on the purpose of the originator, they arise to heal, to explain, to energize, to control, to denigrate. They arise to meet the many needs human beings feel. Fiction-stories are planned, mesmerizing visions which become historical, political, religious, scientific, and military ventures; depending on how they are agented, they become governing pressures which operate upon individual and social conduct. They play leading roles in our lives.

The making of fictions and missions so becomes a pulsating, working principle, a necessary, significant act of mixing knowledge, motives, insights, hopes, beliefs, talents, and skills. It becomes an act of finding the useful and excluding the futile, of seeking the honest and avoiding the deceptive. Fiction becomes a concept the dictionaries only suggest and missions a concept expanded through our selves.

The value of these terms is that they portray frailties as well as strengths. A look at a fiction tells us which stories carry danger, which stories enhance possibilities, and which may become missions. It helps us realize with Nancy Mairs, author of *Voice Lessons,* that "the past, that ramshackle structure, is a fabrication . . . [that] I make it up as I go along."[23] And it helps us know with writer Graham Swift that "man [or woman] is the story-telling animal. . . . He has to go on telling stories. He has to keep on making them up. As long as there's a story, it's all right."[24] Swift may have been thinking that if the secrets of the universe elude comprehension, still it's possible to live and to learn as long as we keep trying to compose and to implement fictions and missions that make sense.

The best stories turn out to be stories about all of us. The questions resolve themselves. Who uses fictions? We do, all of us, all of the time. Journalists do. Scientists do. Artists do. Novelists do. Politicians and preachers do. And, of course, historians can no more escape using their fictions than the rest of us can. Who needs fictions? Everybody needs fictions—and missions—for any approach toward civilized living. Having selected fiction-stories, everybody operates according to his or her designs. Everybody carries out missions.

Accordingly, this book represents an inquiry into relations among fictions and missions and their origins and their products—histories, scientific discoveries, novels, poetry, political ventures, religious undertakings. Such an inquiry need not reduce our strivings to a single interpretation of how we do things. Histories and scientific studies can be seen through many lenses. The balances between thinking and living and our connections with our past and each other often yield ambiguous, sometimes contrasting, even paradoxical stories. Our efforts are flawed only when we leave no room for creating and implementing fictions.

So some of my stories follow. They are case portraits to illustrate what I have said. They represent only my fictions and my missions, because that is all they can represent. I hope you will view my stories as modest attempts to search the reaches and depths of my fictions and my missions.

_____2

The Grandest Fiction

A Pathology of Patriarchy

Speaking of grandeur, fictions, and patriarchy together may seem incongruous. Grandeur means looming large and carrying high importance, while here fictions refer to imperatives—rules—governing societies. Patriarchy means that men dominate women and children in families as in every aspect of wider social and political systems. As to guiding ideas, my fictions suggest that patriarchal control has long, but not forever, been institutionalized. They confirm that patriarchal institutions linger in politics, religions, universities, businesses, and museums. Yet in reflecting on the deep, rolling sounds of the early twenty-first century as well as those of the late twentieth century, sounds intimating that patriarchy is eroding, my fictions hint that we may experience explosions of firestorms in the century ahead. We are reckoning with two factors: technological advance and women's involvements. Both are producing fissures in established institutions. More profoundly, both figure to alter the designs which hold these institutions in place.

The situation calls for a pathology of patriarchy and a revision of the guiding principles supporting it, perhaps even for a building of new principles. Perceiving directions in which the patriarchal system travels carries an urgency to improve the well-being of the stressed societies in which we live. But many men and women have looked differently at the patriarchal setup. Let us consider the origin of their views and let us consider mine and how I came to them.[1]

As to guiding principles, we have seen that they come in many shapes and structures. We have seen that some can be trivial, some can be potent. Some are insubstantial, some are based on evidence. Some pass from sight, some endure. We have seen that they come to us as we have formulated them in the past. We have discovered that we can expand, shrink, or confront the expectations, the perceptions that come to us. We can create them. We can obliterate them. We have seen that such designs power the world.

Patriarchy furnishes the single most outstanding example of fictions that have dominated civilizations. How can such influences determine ways we set up societies? How do they dictate ways a society functions? How do they arise and where will they take us? Aside from interpreting one aspect in one setting at one historical time, my guesses suggest two ways to consider patriarchal civilizations and the ideas which control them.[2] Project this long-dominant set of gender notions toward the future, as Margaret Atwood has done. In her novel

The Handmaid's Tale, Atwood guessed the circumstances to which patriarchal customs might lead us.[3] Or look back at its distant, tangled origins, as Gerda Lerner has done in her history *The Creation of Patriarchy.*[4] Lerner brought into play what we may know about its origins as she fixed her theories about its endurance. Perhaps a combination of these approaches can illumine our situation. Are there categories of responses to patriarchy that foreshadow disaster or transformation?

We have inherited ready-made notions about principles from the moment of birth. Thus, all of us in the west, in the Middle East, in Asia, in Europe, in Eurasia, in North America, in South America, and in much of Africa have begun our lives enveloped in gender customs that a patriarchal world has mandated. The systems have been carefully nurtured.[5] In no area could ready-made customs have proved hardier than in this area of relations between the sexes. Yet even here, time and technologies have wrought changes fundamental to our everyday lives. In the last two centuries they have exposed portentous fault lines. But let us first explore the origins of the most pervasive system of social organization on earth.

The cultivation of the earth for food began in Neolithic times about 10,000 B.C.[6] Before that, Paleolithic and Mesolithic peoples roamed or gathered food where they found themselves.[7] Writing began to appear about 6,500 years after cultivation of the earth became known, or about 3,500 years B.C.

Fragments of information about gender arrangements from times before people could write and before cultivation drifted into view. Geological backgrounds, fossils, stone tools, polished tools, caves, burial places, artifacts—all suggest people's circumstances. Some artistic or perhaps religious expressions have survived; for eons they have played roles in lives that people have lived. Despite modern technologies, we can still look at a few remote societies that have survived with little change. Stelae, shrines, containers, sun clocks, pottery, remnants of language, legends, surviving lunar and solar rituals, remains of ancient structures and great temples—these sources have cradled stories about our Paleolithic, Mesolithic, and Neolithic forbearers.

Oftener than we might hope we can surmise how people lived in the worlds they faced; we can glean inklings about what mattered to them. We can learn about stages that characterized their journeys from primitive kin connections toward established societies.[8] Much information is tenuous, ambivalent, theoretical. It depends on theories created by anthropologists and historians. But a substantial portion tells persuasive tales. In this respect, our knowledge differs little from the most reliable knowledge in other fields.

From the beginning, as at the end, interpretations of information depend on questions and convictions the storyteller brings—that is, on constructs in the mind of the writer. We shall see in Chapter 3 how historians act as agents and how histories rise from values the historian determines.

From questions I find significant, it appears that from about 10,000 B.C. to about 3500 B.C.—almost to the present moment—dominance of one sex over the other passed through ancestral lines that increasingly supported male supremacy in every aspect of human activity.

Probably that situation prevailed here and there well before 10,000 B.C. But other models did appear; we know that different gender fictions influenced the character of early societies and that social living was always dynamic, never static; that some arrangements lingered, some dwindled, some vanished. Taking the year 3500 B.C. to mark the early use of writing and about another thousand years to mark the beginnings of western civilizations, it seems that a patriarchal ordering of activities was already functioning and was escalating by 2500 B.C. At 3,500 years before the birth of Christ, it had probably already become deeply embedded in social customs.[9] Implicit in the most overreaching of these gender arrangements are the beliefs that the male part of humanity is more valuable than the female part and that only male persons possess capabilities fit to determine the character of societies.

Why did this happen? How did it come about that the sexes seemed to hold different values and that one half of humanity could dictate the social, economic, educational, and political possibilities of the other half? That despite aberrations and gender ambivalences, a patriarchal order prevailed?[10] We have noticed in Chapter 1 that we inherit some customs and some collections of opinions at birth. We shall see in Chapter 3 that historians play crucial roles in sustaining customs and the views that support them. Recent clues lead us to think, however, that some very ancient societies lived with gender views at variance with those of patriarchal dominance. Though never strictly opposite to patriarchy in character, it is clear that some early peoples did express gender principles through matrilineal, if not matriarchal, modes. And some developed matrifocal societies in which the roles of mothers in kinship systems became central features of the society, even though women did not dominate it.[11]

Let us imagine a time out of mind, a time before anyone kept records, a time many millenniums before the birth of Christ. This amounts to looking back at least 700,000 years—probably more. Through those eons people lived as best they could, as we do. Like ourselves, they must have created and cherished fictions, some of which they must have expressed through symbols, metaphors, myths, and stories. Through such channels people as agents attempted to instill order into their lives, to find meaning, to hold together and remember the wisdoms they learned.

They developed cults and built religions to explain their presence on earth, to satisfy hopes and dreams, to minister to sorrows, to put themselves in touch with one another and with the mysteries of the universe. Then, as now, religions gave substance to worldviews people developed as they went about daily tasks. Often they conceived religions to see universal mysteries in the context of their own lives. My fictions suggest that it is not strange that religions incorporated the origins, imagery, fears, and longings of groups from which they arose.

At the same time, ancient tribes worked out arrangements for day-to-day living. We cannot be sure of likely scenarios. But allowing for distinctive arrangements in many dissimilar areas, we can make a few educated guesses. For example, legends about Amazon women have been around for millenniums. When and where did these fabled women live? How could anyone conceive of powerful, beautiful women who ran matters according to their inclinations and who excelled at the warlike skills of triumphant men?

Tales abound in ancient myths. One, an old tale, tells of Atalanta, a beautiful maiden who "loved adventure as much as the most dauntless hero, and who could out-shoot and outrun and out-wrestle the men of one of the two great ages of heroism." Though Atalanta prevailed in many a contest, the less athletic Malanion was able to seduce her by diverting her attention with apples of pure gold, "beautiful as those that grew in the garden of the Hesperides."[12] Did Atalanta really exist?

Philosopher-historian Abby Wettan Kleinbaum guesses that "strong, competent, brave, fierce, lovely—and desirable" Amazon women such as Atalanta never existed at all, never exercised great powers, never developed fictions; but since they came to inglorious defeat in most of the stories, she believes they peopled "a dream that men created, images of a superlative female that men constructed to flatter themselves."[13] Amazon images did arise again and again. Kleinbaum notes that Herodotus, the Father of History, could begin one of his stories in the fifth century B.C. with an offhand reference to the war between the Greeks and the Amazons and that he must have felt secure in the knowledge that his readers would know about this long enmity. To pinpoint *which* of the ancient wars he had in mind, Herodotus mentioned that the events took place after the Greek victory "at the River Thermodon," in Asia Minor, legendary site of Themiscyra, the Amazon capital.[14] Did these superwomen represent a deep, male fantasy for partners like themselves as part of their fictions?

It does appear, however, that in Mesolithic periods, powers were sometimes shared to a greater and lesser extent between men and real women. Although men finally came to exercise authority, women in Mesolithic periods sometimes wielded powers. This does not necessarily mean that women shared in planning scenarios. Neither does it necessarily mean that women catered to male demands, though instances of both sometimes appear. Some societies did establish lines of matrilineal descent; a man's family affiliation became that of his wife and that of all her relatives. It is possible that in Paleolithic times, women in some areas dominated social living.

For instance, perhaps for more than 10,000 years in the Basque country, an area of old Europe spanning either side of the Pyrenees mountains of south-western France and northwestern Spain, a woman's role as *etxeko-andrea,* or mistress of the house, carried basic authority. According to Roslyn M. Frank and an interdisciplinary research group that included sociologists, linguists, archeologists, historians, and anthropologists, living arrangements and community arrangements were based on the institution of the household; Basque women as heads of households made decisions in the ordinary life of the society. They were keepers and guardians of the family. "If a husband was lazy," Frank wrote, "or if he was a drunkard, a gambler or simply a poor administrator . . . a wife could declare him incompetent and replace him with a more able individual."

In ancient times, Basque women served as religious and political representatives of the family. They held local and valley-wide assemblies in the open air, usually around an oak tree, the sacred symbol of the Basque people. The women sat in circles of stones, each circle designated for a particular household. There they served as official spokespersons, dispensing judgments and forming policies. In later times, they moved their meetings to the doors of the parish church or to the graveyard adjoining the church. Later still, the female heads met in the village plaza where stone seats were placed in a circle around a great oak tree.[15]

Such a functioning of home and community might have suited smaller agrarian units and even town developments. Classicist Joan Markley Todd and sociologist Joseph Cono discuss another concept. They suggest that the family in some of its manifestations may have served as a training institution for women as well as for men and that such circumstances may have persisted for men and for advantaged women into more complex societies. They suggest that shifting concepts of gender roles and fluid relations in merging affairs of family and state—*polis*—likely characterized many ancient situations.

At the time when the Greek historian Xenophon wrote of the influence of women in affairs of state, for example, we see evidence of significant and equal exchanges between Greek philosophers and privileged women. Xenophon reports conversations which Todd and Cono believe mirrored genuine gender partnerships. They point out that Xenophon expected women "like the men in his books, to be interested in and capable of learning." Xenophon depicted women who had opportunities to make decisions: "Panthea, the beautiful woman of Susa, Theodote, the lively lady who spars with Socrates, and the young wife of Ischomachus who is establishing a household"—a princess, an intellectual, and the wife of a well-to-do landowner.

Xenophon saw these women as equals to men; he did not see them as inferior or superior. Todd and Cono note the recurring role of such women "in the *polis,* a concept [like the concept of patriarchy itself] often incorrectly limited to political considerations." Although the conduct of public affairs certainly was limited to powerful men and perhaps to advantaged women, Xenophon's men—and women—were expected to practice the virtues of "authority, friendship and partnership."[16]

Again, it appears that in some early Native American nations women wielded powers of state seldom realized. A few such arrangements have survived long enough for us to look at them. Though many times women exercised authority in consultation with men, historian Gregory Schaaf has discovered documents showing that Queen Coitcheleh of the lost Shawnee nation may still in the year A.D. 1776 have been "the most powerful woman leader in America." The women of this tribe chose Semachquaan, brother of Coitcheleh, as head war chief. At the same time, they retained the veto power to stop the tribe from going to war when they felt such an action unwise. They also kept the right to go into battle; occasionally the women chose one of themselves as head war chief.

At the very moment when frontiersman Daniel Boone and squatters of his band decided to settle in the middle of the Shawnee hunting grounds and just as delegates to the Continental Congress were debating the question of American independence, Coitcheleh and her tribal council were deliberating on how and whether they could put an end to the vicious battles their situation occasioned.[17] In the fashion of her predecessors, this Indian queen negotiated with George Morgan, Washington's first Indian commissioner of the United States, to try to find a peaceful solution.

Further research reveals similar patterns in ancient societies, some of them Native American.[18] At other times and places, there also seem to have been arrangements in which, to whatever extent, men and women shared the conduct of affairs. In most of the communities that have survived, however, women gradually lost authority or used it under increasing male supervision.[19]

Since for long periods no one could write or read and no one kept regular records, do we know anything substantial about the lives of ancient peoples beyond such scraps of information? Some believe that stories of a wondrous garden of Eden and of comparable "paradises" in ancient lands represent actual situations. Anthropologist Elizabeth Judd, for example, believes that myths and stories of the "Golden Age" reveal truths about how people lived in particular eras.[20] Details with which the myths abound, she says, are specific enough to confirm their reference to ancient styles of living. She notes that information relating to climates, metals, economic practices, and social customs provides particulars difficult to dismiss as altogether imagined. These details, she writes, "emphasize gathering as an economic form, as well as an absence of social stratification, of warfare, and of gender distinctions and rape." She believes that in earliest times "the killing of animals was outlawed and vegetarianism prevailed."[21] In this model, nobody dominated anybody else. No fictions dictated the dominance of either gender.

To strengthen these views, she cites the ancient writer Hesiod. Poets and theologians—Pindar, Horace, Homer, Virgil, the anonymous scribe of the book of Genesis—have hearkened to his voice, for Hesiod drew on myths that were already venerable. Hesiod composed the passages in his *Works and Days* around 700 B.C.; in our framework, he would have been looking back several millenniums. Hesiod confirms the shadows stories cast. Of prehistoric peoples and the circumstances of their lives, he wrote that "the fruitful earth unforced bore them fruit abundantly and without stint. They dwelt in ease and peace upon their lands with many good things, rich in flocks and loved by the blessed gods." Hesiod also ventured a thought about how they lived: "They made merry with feasting beyond the reach of all evils."[22]

This fortunate state, which predated biblical times and recorded history, Judd observes, prevailed well before the invention of writing in about 3500 B.C. and before cultivation in about 10,000 B.C. A few hundred years later than Hesiod, the Roman poet Ovid also looked toward our misty origins in his *Metamorphoses* as he supported Hesiod's and Judd's inclinations. "The earth itself, without compulsion, untouched by the hoe, unfurrowed by any share, produced all things spontaneously," Ovid wrote, "and men were content with foods that grew without cultivation."[23] Rising as they do from immemorial fictions, such conjectures have drifted through the centuries.

People, Judd thinks, once lived simply and easily on the pleasant lands where they found themselves without recourse to wars or the killing of animals. We can gather that if indeed the myths reflect circumstances of some pastoral times—and a little later—men did not always dominate women and women did not dominate men. Where valleys and plains existed, where rivers flowed into the seas, where weather permitted, where no one worried about private property, this must indeed have been at least a temporary possibility.[24]

Yet common sense tells us that while some may have inhabited idyllic climates where survival was easy, most ancient peoples must have known privation and peril at times earlier than or as early as those of the Eden legends and the paradise stories. Some encountered harsh climates. Some lived their short lives as nomads, roaming plains and crossing mountains as seasons mandated, hunting forests and steppes for food. Often they experienced disease. Often they must have gone hungry. For these ancient pre-biblical peoples, life was precarious. The labor that permitted survival in severe climates must have proved exhausting and hazardous for women and for men. Classicist W. K. C. Guthrie concluded that the life of our early human ancestors was not "idyllically happy, but rather that it was uncomfortable and wretched."[25] Often enough, and in diverse areas, whole clans perished.

Land within range belonged to no one, or rather to everyone. If there were times when the earth yielded plenty, there were times when it did not. Most of the time for most people, staying alive demanded ceaseless effort. Sharing knowledge, burdens, and prizes became life necessities. The scarcity of resources led to conflicts. It also led to clinging to others of one's kin connections as people produced extended families, as they learned to live together, as they parlayed their advantages into "archaic" tribal states. Everyone's physical and mental strengths provided assets; the energies of women and children proved as irreplaceable as those of men. Sometimes they were deemed more valuable. So my fictions suggest.

Assuming that biological knowledge must once have been slight, that the mysteries of childbearing were once believed beyond comprehension, it is even possible that woman's ability to bear children was deemed of greatest value. In their thinking, in the forming of their fictions, ancient tribal people linked this power to divine mysteries of the universe.[26]

How can we infer this? There is strong evidence that to gather some thinkable concept of the universe—of the vast skies, the sun, the seas, the stars, the storms, the wonders of birth and death—and then to incorporate the realities of their own hazardous, often helpless positions, people invented symbols. What inventions they were! Men and women designated signs, drawings, small artifacts to stand for the myriad of connections formed in their minds, much as we designate red, white, and blue flags to stand for the United States of America. Referring to the power of religious symbols, historian Mary Elizabeth Perry wrote of a statue, a figure of a small black Madonna that carried meaning for European peoples for more than eight centuries; in Montserrat in northern Spain, she wrote, the statue demonstrates still "the remarkable power of religious symbols which persists even as their meanings change."[27]

Like ourselves, the earliest peoples must have stood in awe of natural phenomena they could neither comprehend nor control. They must have stood in awe of woman's power of giving birth, linking that power with their longing for life everlasting and with the reality of death.[28] They may have dreamed of rebirth, of reincarnations. We have seen in the cases of Basque women, women of early Indian nations, and privileged women of ancient Greece and ancient China that such hopes and beliefs must have translated into a guiding principle that allowed women to figure importantly in policymaking and sometimes to control activities.

People solicited divine assistance in surviving famines, as they still do. They prayed for mercy and they prayed to prevail over other tribes. Often conceiving of gods and goddesses in the image of angry humans, people attempted to appease them. They sought protection, offered sacrifices, though scholars disagree on the circumstances under which these practices began. Ancient peoples elevated their own behaviors to universal levels by inventing metaphors and parlaying what they perceived in their daily lives to godlike proportions.

Solemnizing and institutionalizing their imaginings into guiding fictions, they added festival rituals and rites for the dead. They created religions in such a way that their gods and goddesses behaved as they behaved—with one difference: Their gods and goddesses possessed powers no human being could attain. Although some scholars seek further supporting evidence, or different terminologies, my ideas suggest that these were the first grandiose fictions.

Religions became ways of linking human beings to that which they did not understand, that which they celebrated and feared, and that which they therefore worshipped, that is, with the divine. Everyone knew the power of elemental forces. Everyone wanted to operate in harmony with that power. We know that out of experiences and needs, early peoples invented, revered, and worshipped female goddesses. They were the most powerful of figures. They created and controlled humankind. They ruled the universe.

The evidence is abundant. We shall see that older societies deferred to female goddesses, that they were often perceived as the embodiment of awesome powers lying beyond any human range of perception. They were known by different names in different lands—Kubab or Ishtar in Babylonia, Nut in Egypt, Ninhursag or Inanna in Sumer, Nugur and Kuan Yin in China. Myths, stories, and rituals, many originating in the fourth millennium B.C. and persisting for thousands of years, featured the mother-goddess as the source of life and power, a measure of divine authority.[29]

Paintings on walls of caves express respect for nature's animals as well as fearful encounters with them.[30] It has been suggested that some ancient peoples believed women lived close to nature, especially to children and animals, and that these paintings expressed that connection with divine forces. Historian Sherry B. Ortner has noticed, however, that distinctions between closeness to nature and a lack of involvement with culture as contributors have often been used to overlook women's cultural accomplishments. It seems likely that women may themselves have painted some of the ancient murals.[31] As time passed, the figures appeared and reappeared as designs on pottery, as motifs in weavings, as thematic stories from fragments of old walls.

It can scarcely surprise us that stone-carved figures of goddesses abound in lands where ancient peoples roamed or hunted or gathered food thousands of years ago. Archeologists have conducted digs over all of eastern Europe, from Russian Siberia to the Balkans, from Viennese countrysides to those of France. Everywhere they have turned up figurines, female statues that frequently depict pregnant women.[32] Though subject to other interpretations, the stylized statues most likely arise from fictions female divinities represented. Often small enough to hold in one's hand, the little faceless figures display exaggerated breasts, abdomens, and hips, signs of respect for woman's fertility and her close relationship with the divine.[33] Later, splendid temples honoring female goddesses elaborated these small testaments to the origin and the power of early fictions.

The mother-goddess, a concept of a supreme being, whatever the name she was given, became the central figure in the most important Paleolithic and

Mesolithic systems of belief. She overlooked the world. She epitomized the ascendancy of female powers. But expressions of purpose, belief, and guiding fictions tended to transmogrify as centuries slid by; though her influence lingered, her symbolic power over societies declined. We may find it difficult to recognize her shadow in the goddess figures of later ages.

Sometimes her image merged with others as religions developed. Athena, the most powerful patron goddess of the city of Athens, appears in later manifestations as the daughter of Zeus alone. It was then believed that she sprang full grown, in full armor, from the head of this father, and that no mother-goddess bore her. In the *Iliad* stories, Athena seems a fierce and merciless warrior-goddess, but in earlier myths it appears that she represents the arts and the wisdom of civilization, that she protects the city. She was said to have invented the bridle, so first taming horses for the benefit of people.

Caesar Augustus became emperor of the vast Roman dominions in approximately 8 B.C. At that time, the date of August 13th marked the festival of the goddess Diana, who had been known and revered in her various incarnations as Queen of the Fields or as Queen of Heaven, Earth, and Hell. Augustus changed this festival to commemorate his birthday; it then became the Feast of the Assumption of the Virgin Mary to honor her death and ascension to heaven.[34]

How did men feel about bestowing status on women and, in earlier times, according them respect and influence? How did they feel about the little goddess figures that must have played a part in daily living?[35] The rich supply of the figures suggests that everyone felt their relevance to conditions of living, at least in eras before written history. In ages past, men as well as women probably worshipped female goddesses and accepted the imaginings they expressed. To this day in rural districts of modern China, men customarily follow religious rituals to express respect for graphic portrayals of female genital organs, although, as Professor Qu Yajun points out, "They do not know why they are following these customs."[36]

As recorded times merged into later eras, even as different belief systems began to emerge, women connected by marriage or kinship ties to strong men still received appointments to temples. There they dedicated their lives to serve the mother-goddess, and there they could accept and distribute favors and patronage. As temples dominated societies, privileged women wielded commensurate authority. They wielded it, however, at the pleasure of the dominant men to whom they were attached. Into later ages, societies accorded some prominent women ochre—or purple—burial honors, signs of eminence and respect. In the fifth century B.C., the Greeks were moved to dedicate the most exquisite of their temples to Athena, long the kind and gentle patron goddess of the fabled Athens. In words given to Athena herself (1029–1025 B.C.), we hear of the women she represented:

Flower of all the land of Theseus,
Let them issue now, grave companies,
Maidens, wives, elder women, in processional.
In the investiture of purple stained robes, dignify them.[37]

Fragments of such gender relations persisted into modern societies. We shall see in Chapter 4 that as Mormon followers of Joseph Smith reverted to Old Testament customs, women such as Joseph's first wife Emma could achieve positions of influence.

But in the earlier struggle to stay alive, it had to become customary for ordinary women and men to share the tasks required for survival. In describing stages of early social evolution, sociologist Friedrich Engels saw the first divisions of work as "purely primitive, between the sexes only." His concept was that men fought wars, hunted and fished, procured "raw materials," and were major providers of food. He thought that women looked after the house, prepared food, made clothing, cooked, wove cloth, and sewed as needed and that each sex exercised authority in these appropriate spheres.[38]

"Not so," said historian Ann J. Lane. "Women were jointly involved in food production, not just by processing that which the men brought home."[39] Though Engels connected distinct stages of development in primitive societies from savagery to barbarism to civilization with gender roles, and though he saw at all levels the urgency of dividing work, Lane observed that he never fully understood the bearing and nurturing of children as the demanding factors they were. Nor did he ever accurately assess the roles of women in procuring food. But Engels did understand the importance of steady supplies of it; he did understand the close connection of gender roles with the economic character of social living.

Yet no less than in our time, shifting power arrangements between men and women reflected shifting technologies, some of which empowered women and some of which enhanced the control of men.[40] In the past, many kinds of arrangements could have taken place; it is conceivable that women at times might have played powerful roles and that their treatment of men at times might have been inconsiderate and cruel. Whatever may or may not have occurred, changes happened gradually, unevenly, often covertly, sometimes violently. We have seen that remnants of some beliefs—some fictions—surfaced in new arrangements. But changes happened.

As ability to cope with environments increased, as societies grew more complex, more profound shifts in authority patterns and in fictions supporting them took place. We can suppose that tribal states developed out of wrenching conflicts among tribes over food supplies and over desirable territories. Still, in commercializing societies, there could have been no building blocks more basic than those which the gender arrangements between men and women supplied, even though new technologies altered those relationships and even though different interpretations gave substance to new relationships. What shifts supported the changes?

It became increasingly important to designate control of the complex labors required for groups to survive and then to prevail. Some labor assignments began with bartering among tribes. But before the primitive commerce thus enabled, men learned to rule over women's domestic and sexual availability within their own tribes.

According to historian Gerda Lerner, this was how human slavery first happened.[41] In learning to "exchange women," men could more easily accomplish what they wanted to do. They dominated, then enslaved women—those of their families or kin groups, those of their households, then those of other tribes. In some lands they required women to wear veils. In China, they bound the feet of women to keep them situated or to enhance sexual charms. Usually men preempted the training of boy children; sometimes they sold girl children, forced them into prostitution, or arranged to murder them in infancy. In southwest Ethiopia, the Nuer people forced young girls to insert disks the size of dinner plates into their bottom lips so that they could scarcely speak or eat. Some tribes forced women to wear heavy iron collars about their necks.[42] Had the collars been removed, the muscles of the neck would have been too weak to support the woman's head. In some African situations, genital mutilation of girl children damaged women irreparably. In India, child marriage secured the very young girl child to her husband's family for all of her life; *sati* was the practice by which a widow was expected to cremate herself on her husband's funeral pyre.[43]

In later times, and with the collusion of religious establishments, men "cloistered" women—segregated them, took them out of ordinary life—placed them in religious enclaves or "enclosed" them at home. Historian Penelope D. Johnson has noted a tradition transmitted to Europe from Asia Minor and the Holy Land in the early part of the fifth century A.D. In this monastic framework, the church adopted guidelines riddled with fear of and contempt for the appetites of the body and, more particularly, fear of the sexuality of women. "In contrast to men," Johnson wrote, "women were suspect as the very essence of bodiliness, while men were seen as the epitome of the spirit and the mind."[44] Churchmen and other male leaders refused women access to information, education, and opportunities. They arranged tight controls. They instituted extremely severe penalties for transgression. In many places, permissible physical punishments, even death, became—and still are—routine.

Men learned that they could invent sustaining beliefs, persuade women to accept them, build religious and social systems, and trumpet them far and wide, particularly by indoctrinating children. It became possible to enslave anybody—members of minority groups, captured peoples, non-elite men.

Once the idea of inducing or forcing others to do work or simply to do one's will came about, it was possible to turn that idea into a custom, then into a conviction, then into the most durable of fiction-institutions. This could be done by physical force and it could be done by psychological coercion. Or both. All too often, and sometimes still, this meant violence, rape, murder, and war. Such practices could be sustained only by establishing principles sanctioning these methods.

In ancient times, female goddesses, especially the mother-goddess, achieved stature as the highest expression of the group's belief in women's powers. In ancient agricultural societies (and in pre-agricultural societies), the mother-goddess stood as the supreme expression of birth and death, of wisdoms learned, of the unity of human experience with divine mysteries. She stood for giving life and for receiving her children in death. She stood for cultivating the fruits of the earth. She stood for beauty, for art, and for love as expressions of religious culture. She symbolized the most important fictional principles. Before she was merged with other deities or transformed into male or quasi-male figures, the mother-goddess appeared to have seldom stood for aggression, for tribal conflict, for violence, or for war. Yet images shifted. The Chinese goddess Kuan Yin began her role in Chinese fictions as a benign and omniscient female mother-goddess. As time passed, she took on a "male" character, then finally retained both aspects.[45]

After trade between tribes and then tribal wars became common, men no longer looked on women as earthly connections with the divine mother-goddess; they began to see women as commercial assets. They began to see women's role not merely as that of giving birth, and so assuring a tribe's continuance, but as facilitating trade arrangements, thus aiding the establishment of federations of "archaic" tribal states. Then—and, sadly, still—warriors could kill men of conquered groups and they could rape and enslave women and children of such tribes, kill them, or take them prisoner. The more women a tribe could retain, the more secure it felt. One man could acquire many wives; witness how the Mormon theocracy of the nineteenth century retrieved this idea or how polygamy functions still in theocracies around the world. Or men could treat the idea of human slavery as a given; as we look at the Mormon theocracy in Chapter 4, we shall see that even in later times, many could come to believe that unthinkable ideas were virtuous.

Fathers could sell or bargain or marry away their daughters, and husbands could acquire wives and slaves as bargaining chips. Once they captured females and enslaved them, men could sell their slaves or trade or give them to aspiring rivals. They could and did barter wives, female relatives, children, and slaves for sufficient consideration; they institutionalized these practices. Usually they did so with little concern for the wishes of those involved.

Thus women came to be regarded as objects, as chattel; they were seen as expendable. As the story of the lovely Helen of Troy illustrates, women became valuable prizes. To use a term from the anthropologist Claude Lévi-Strauss, women in many places became "reified"; that is, they were looked upon as things, as commodities rather than as human beings.

What changes in gender fictions had to occur to legitimize aggressive male behavior and the establishment of patriarchy? Why have so many human beings accepted unquestioningly the devastation from global wars, unregulated technologies, and frantic preparation for mutual destruction that patriarchy has produced? These are significant questions. A reader of the twenty-first century cannot but realize, as we shall see in Chapter 3, that just as historians of the Reconstruction period after the American Civil War omitted the accomplishments of African Americans, so also many historians through time have left women out of the human experience.

Some explanations for these significant omissions involve economic survival, some involve the different biological makeup of male and female hormones, some involve power plays, some involve male psychological reactions to female ascendancy, some involve the emergence of private property, some involve female complicity, some involve industrial revolutions of increasing complexity. Eminent anthropologists and historians have suggested whatever explanations seemed most apt in constructing their particular interpretations. My fictions suggest that as technologies advanced, as agriculture became dependable, gender relations and supporting fictions metamorphosized and tensions between the genders escalated.

To make the changes seem reasonable, to secure compliance, to provide unimpeachable authority, societies revised religious structures. Some shifts were subtle, veiled; some were gradual; and some were blatant. In this evolution, male gods, and later one male god, displaced female deities and became transcendent figures. In a sporadic progression, the new religious fictions asserted that man, God's chosen bearer of the seed of life, should dominate all worlds by virtue of his mission to initiate life and by virtue of his superior strength and intelligence. In the new alignments, woman gradually became an adjunct. She had to be seen as a less necessary, inferior being.

As time passed, prominent male teachers and religious leaders mulled over these notions. After a long ambivalence, Aristotle the Greek, the pupil of Plato,[46] crystallized the supporting opinion that women are damaged, biologically unfinished human beings and therefore inferior, unfit for higher tasks.[47] He defined girl children as "infertile males" and women as "mutilated" beings.[48] Naturally, then, they ought to play roles subordinate to those of men. Naturally, the ideal family would be that guided by the father alone, the patriarchal family. Historian Maryanne Cline Horowitz notes that Aristotle's observations determined the "scientific" background of his biological and political studies, but she points out that his *historical* importance is that "in the medieval and early modern periods of Western civilization Aristotelian generalizations were set down and perpetuated as universal and natural truth" [italics added].[49] This provides a preeminent example of the observation that people believe authorities.

The Bible provides numerous examples of the ways that women were assigned less value than men. Leviticus asserted in the Old Testament that women should be paid less than men for the same work: "If your valuation is of a male from 20 years old to 60 years old, then your valuation shall be 50 shekels of silver, according to the shekel of the sanctuary. If it is a female, then your valuation shall be 30 shekels."[50] In the New Testament, Saint Paul concerned himself with the unity of the church. In I Corinthians, he stated that "the head of the woman is the man."[51] In a later passage, he amplified this: "Nor was man created for the woman," he stated, "but woman for the man."[52] In writing to his co-worker Timothy, Paul specified the work that women could do to become eligible for membership in his church: They could bring up children, lodge strangers, wash the saints' feet and relieve the afflicted.[53] He also specified what women could not do: "I suffer a woman not to teach," he wrote. Nor could women preach, "engage in the life of the forum" or even speak in his church. "Let them learn in silence, with all subjection" he added.[54]

Saint Peter emphasized Paul's words, endeavoring to render Paul's ideas palatable: "Likewise, you wives," Peter wrote, "be submissive to your own husbands." "The incorruptible ornament of a gentle and quiet spirit [woman's spirit], which is very precious in the sight of God," may win errant husbands to the word.[55] Saint Peter, too, approved the quiet, thoughtless consent of women who were workers for his enterprises. They could not speak in his church.

Despite his brilliant explorations of the subconscious mind, Sigmund Freud bought Aristotle's rationalizations. He thought that women are biologically handicapped, that as human beings they are incomplete men, that they suffer from penis envy. Therefore they are slated for neurotic, nearly sub-human lives. What reversals of the one-time reverence for women's powers of giving life, of enhancing life!

Coming as these pronouncements did from generations of respected teachers and churchmen, such underpinnings were constantly woven into the texture of social beliefs and of societies themselves. There were also generations of lesser writers. Some of the smaller minds amused themselves and the public by comparing woman's intelligence to that of animals. In the late 1700s, such sensationalists as the English critic Samuel Johnson put forth remarks about women's intelligence. It is, he said, "like a dog walking on its hind legs. It is not done well; but you are surprised to find it done at all."

In alliance with new religions, scholarly findings showed women to be lesser persons in every aspect of human endeavor. Those who needed to feel superior took advantage of this climate of opinion. In some societies women were shunned during menstrual periods. Everywhere, they were denied the education that made careers and afforded power. They were prevented from direct access to God. They lost their ancient connection with the divine. What women had accomplished was downgraded, forgotten. Their value in living life was vastly lessened.

In tandem with these reversals, the earliest codes of law institutionalized woman's sexual and political subordination. The law codes of Hammurabi in about 1750 B.C., Blackstone's *Commentaries* in about A.D. 1760, Napoleon's Codes in the early 1800s A.D., and American adaptations of English property and child-custody statutes in the eighteenth, nineteenth, and twentieth centuries A.D. all subjected women to the legal control of men. They became dependent, legally powerless. They became underlings. Even in the United States, they could not gain the suffrage until 1920.

Why did women let this happen? The most amazing part of the story is that the majority of women condoned it. Although there are and always have been stellar exceptions, many women went along with altered, distinctly denigrating ideas about themselves.[56] The most extreme examples of women's cooperation can be found in the Chinese practice of foot-binding and in the African practice of female genital mutilation. Programmed themselves, grown women carried out these disgraceful practices. Often the results of changed arrangements were sugar-coated with the assurance that women, though weaker and less intelligent, are finer and purer than men, but since they are less intelligent they must accept male dictates.[57]

Despite the price, some women may have thought this reasoning presented an easier way to meet the challenges of life. Others probably found the demands of bearing, rearing, and often supporting many children too great a burden to carry alone. The most likely explanation may be that most women never realized what was happening to their humanity and that they simply acquiesced in the prevailing ideas men created to hold them in their place. Some women, however, knew themselves to be exempt from belittling consequences because of connections with powerful men. Others steeled themselves to perform exactly as men intended, to become surrogate males so as to place themselves among the privileged.

It is clear that no "symbolic" or "meaning" system could survive without the consent of the majority of the people. I would suggest that men—and women—came to believe the systems supporting male hegemony and that they translated these systems into directives that determined the nature of activities and the character of societies. On a large scale, it became acceptable—indeed prestigious—to go to war, to annihilate enemies, to enslave victims, to force obedience, to destroy those who disagreed. It became acceptable to foster technologies with slight regard to consequences. There was always the same condition: Men needed the consent of women. They developed assurances that aggression is legitimate and desirable. They even shored up this idea by incorporating it into religions: "An eye for an eye, a tooth for a tooth"; "Vengeance is mine, saith the Lord."

Practically speaking, what steps would make it possible to secure the consent of women to such a degrading agenda? The most effective technique was to deprive women of education, particularly of a knowledge of their history.[58] This meant nothing less than taking away their rightful role in the story of humanity.

It meant telling women repeatedly that they were lesser human beings. It meant leaving their achievements out of the human record, out of the history books, out of public consciousness, even out of private folk knowledge. We shall see in Chapter 3 that many eminent historians ignored all evidence of African-American achievement, so that generations of Negro Americans themselves possessed no knowledge of it. If women did not know that they could sing, act, write, speak, work, invent, and think as well as men, that they had always possessed these abilities, they might lose the confidence to try. If they were never shown that women had painted, composed wonderful music, taken important decisions, performed physical feats, and written memorable stories, they might never believe such adventures possible for them. If they were told that they were lesser persons possessing less intelligence than men, they would accept the onerous tasks that hold society together as exclusively their responsibilities. There were always some men who did not agree. But no part of the human story demonstrates more convincingly the power of fictions by which we consent to live. No part of that story demonstrates more poignantly the necessity of knowing our histories.

Why didn't women enslave men? One possible answer is that guiding systems sanctioned radically different behavior in early ancient worlds, and most women did not readily approve the use of force to destroy people, their relationships, their children, their men, or their environments. Another possibility is that once programmed, women accepted the going designs. Yet on the whole, it seems fair to suppose that action programs reflected choices. Here too, there were exceptions; some women would not fit into this picture. It has also been suggested, and it may reflect realities, that woman's close connection with the human infant taught her to care, to love, and to value the arts of life, that civilization began with her love.[59] Men realized that for the most part they could rely on women to nurture and remain with their children. Therefore, from ancient times, captured women of other tribes would stay with their captors if they had been impregnated or if their children had been taken prisoner.

I would propose that full-blown symbolic and meaning systems did indeed operate in ancient ages, as they operate now; that, when triggered by agents, they became powerful fictions that sanctioned behavior for women and for men in all worlds. This is another way of saying that guiding principles consist of meaning systems that human beings activate according to their values. They are, and always were, necessary to institute and to stylize behavior. Once activated, such beliefs and the values they carry are and always were crucial to maintaining behavior patterns. But however formidable they may become, they are not forever fixed in times or places.

According to my fictions, the particular guiding ideas that underlie human slavery arose on the back of male adventure, gender-oriented competition, new commercial technologies, and far-flung quests for control. They entailed a denigration of the entire female sex and, with that, the entire human condition. Male entrepreneurs became agents activating necessary beliefs. Realizing that human slavery could only be countenanced when enough people of both sexes believed it virtuous, men created exclusive idea-connections with sanctions of the divine. On American plantations, white preachers read to Negro congregations that "God made the master and God made the slave." That idea was to function as a final, untouchable dictum.

For either men or women to lower the status of the other sex so far as to rationalize human slavery, people had to reconceptualize gender beliefs and both sexes had to acquiesce in the changes. Thus, with the rise of states and civilizations over time, the mother-goddess figure faded while lesser goddesses disappeared. If the once-prestigious mother-goddess and other goddesses were not obliterated in the making of new guidelines, they lapsed into dependent or insignificant positions. Male gods of many names—Zeus, Ares, Jupiter, Neptune, Mars, Mercury, Thor, Jehovah—gained precedence.

As peoples approached Old Testament times, one male god became supreme. The most tragic aspect of this change was the attack on the character of women. In the best-known Old Testament story, woman was shown in the person of Eve as a distinctly immoral being who lured man toward destruction, toil, and sin. The blame for everything that followed could thus be focused on her. Her transgression was that she longed for knowledge and that she tempted Adam to desire it.

In the wake of so powerful a female and sin fiction, it had to be decreed that only men could talk directly to the only god, a male god. Woman lost her prestige and her long connection with the vast elements of the universe. Different gender notions thus acquired status. Although in the western world this single legend encapsulated many changes, they occurred in jagged fashion. They happened over centuries, irregularly, in different places and often in tandem with power alignments. Such shifts are always possible; indeed, they are probable unless, contrary to all indications, we assume our situations to be frozen in eternity.

This is how my fictions put the likeliest story of our shared past—at least, for civilizations of the west: Woman was once believed to be a virtuous human being. She did not deserve a fall. Nevertheless men of influence, power, and education so reversed the ideas guiding societies that woman came to occupy a vastly lowered status. Others have told stories different from those to which I have listened, if not in the outcome for woman, then in their appraisal of her character. Most other stories say woman did deserve a fall. Most highlight her decadence.

In an essay she calls "The Myth of Matriarchy: Why Men Rule in Primitive Society," Joan Bamberger describes the beginnings of male power in the customary fictions of South American Indian societies: Among the Yamana-Yaghan people the *kina* is an actual structure—a lodge—at the same time that it is a particular ceremony. The purpose is to remind women of their ancient duplicity. Once, according to this well-respected story, women held superior power. They issued orders to men, who followed obediently. Men did all the work in the *kina;* they cared for the children, tended the fires, cleaned the skins. They did this because the women had invented a crafty stratagem: They had fooled men into believing that women were "great spirits." Stepping out of the *kina,* the women had donned masks, painted their bodies, and come forth with yells, howls, and roars: "Simulating the spirits, [the women] beat the earth with dried skins so that it shook." Then the women hid in their own huts, managing to fool the men into submission so that they would thenceforth obey orders.

But one day the sun-man, a hunter whose job was to supply the women-spirits with game, chanced to spy girls as they were washing paint from their bodies and practicing the agitated disturbances that terrified the men. He told on the fraudulent women. A great battle ensued, and ever afterward, a social order reversing the power structure has justly prevailed.[60] In this recitation we see clear justification for male dominance: The Yamana-Yaghan women had proved themselves forever treacherous and untrustworthy.

So it went for women in widespread areas of the South American continent. In the northern Amazon area of Brazil, several versions of a Jurupari story prevail among Tukanoan-speaking Indians. All the varieties turn on woman's perfidious nature, and all of them are accepted by men and by women. The structure of the story is that Jurupari, a hero and respected lawgiver, was the son of a virgin girl child impregnated by the juice of a forbidden fruit. Jurupari became the headman in a tribe of women whose men had died from an epidemic sickness. He taught the women never to intrude in male affairs, never to participate in sacred male rites, never to attempt to play the sacred musical instruments. Any woman who transgressed these dictates must die. If any man revealed the sacred laws to a woman or showed her the sacred instruments, he must kill himself or be killed by the tribe.

Eventually the women discovered the instruments and learned about the laws and the male rituals. When Jurupari's father, the Sun, sent him on a quest to find the perfect woman, he stipulated that "she must be patient, know how to keep a secret, and not be curious." Sadly, Jurupari realized that he would not find such a woman, for "if a woman is patient, she does not keep secrets; if she keeps secrets she is not patient; and all of them are curious, wishing to know everything and to experience everything." In this story, promises of death cannot deter woman's reckless treachery. She would even deceive the Sun.[61] A far cry from the legend of the early mother-goddess and her close and nurturing relationship with nature!

From these stories and many like them, Bamberger concluded that "the final version of woman that emerges from these myths is that she represents chaos and misrule through trickery and unbridled sexuality." Bamberger saw that as long as women choose to accept the fictions of such a myth, they will remain prisoners to its tenets.

So on the basis of the evidence I can find, my fictions suggest that a social evolution of immense complexity is underway. For some periods in some areas, women predominated in influence. But gradually, then precipitately, men superseded women, then became themselves the dominators. Both sexes, probably to greater and lesser degrees, tailored gender fictions to support their supremacy. It seems possible that over long eons, each sex forgot some needs and contributions of the other sex. I think that the enduring foundations of this evolution are the gender-related interactions between the sexes as they affect the survival of human kind. At this time, many fissures appear in the structure of the patriarchal fiction. To survive, we have begun to demolish it and to create a new fiction-structure.

I do not find women innocent of the results; the upheavals necessitated the downgrading of women's own self-images, which women allowed. In denigrating women's influences, however, men have brought the world they share with women close to total disaster. The remedy, if there can be a remedy, is to balance the roles of the sexes so that gender functions equitably. In looking about, in accounting for a long evolution, in reflecting on the wonders of human intelligence and human emotions, my fictions lead me to feel hopeful that, however painfully, a mutual recognition of our situation and a shared participation in the future may come to pass. My glass is half full.

A Category of Fissures in the Patriarchal System

What signs suggest impending change? Over the past two centuries we have seen in this country a rising tendency among women to express their humanity. Their activities are producing clefts in the structure of patriarchy itself, and therefore clefts in the guiding principles, the fictions, that uphold it. No system so firmly implanted in social custom, so robustly supported by such formidable fictions can easily be transformed. Yet women are demonstrating a determination to participate fully in the human adventure and to create a

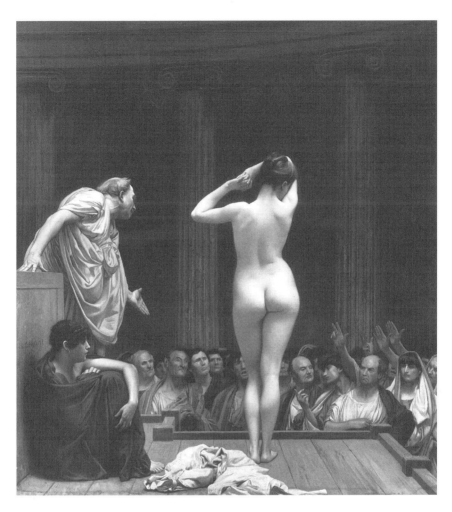

A Roman Slave Market by Jean-Léon Gérôme. From ancient times to the present, women have been exploited without regard for their humanity. This painting depicts the brutality of selling women for commercial gain. Courtesy The Walters Art Museum, Baltimore.

shared set of guiding ideas. They have first created a pathology of patriarchy, then moved to a multiple-pronged attack on the leading imperatives that support it. If we view the American situation as an advanced demonstration of the erosion of the idea of patriarchy, let us look at the particular countervailing trends women's activities support. Let us construct categories to show what women are doing.

Out of a pantheon of thoughtful American women, I will call attention to an early few. Many of them are becoming known, rating biographies, making their way into history texts. I must omit more than I can cite, not only in this country but in the world and through the ages. But I will select American women whose pioneer lives span the nineteenth and twentieth centuries and who are among the first to represent distinct categories of responses to fictions supporting patriarchy. Their successors in the twenty-first century are intensifying and expanding their insights. Taken together, the concentration of these women in this country in these times is creating and developing a pathology of patriarchy. It could be cooking up a social earthquake. For the structure of society this foreshadows profound alteration—perhaps just in time.

Politically inclined, Elizabeth Cady Stanton learned about women's issues before she and her husband became known as abolitionists. As a child, Elizabeth heard her father, Judge Cady, explain to a despairing widow that she would be penniless and that the small farm the widow had bought with her own earnings would now belong to her reckless son—that there was nothing a widow could do about it.[62]

Stanton remained interested in civil rights issues such as that of the widow for the rest of her life. With a group of Quaker women in 1848, she became a major organizer of the once infamous, now respected Seneca Falls Convention. She offered a revision of the Declaration of Independence, calling the revision a Declaration of Sentiments. Sixty-eight women and thirty-one men signed the document. It followed the design of the 1776 Declaration of Independence exactly. The most telling part of the effort was to be found in the first sentence of the second paragraph: "We hold these truths to be self-evident, that all men and women are created equal."[63]

Stanton founded women's organizations; pushed for more equitable divorce, property, child custody, and wage laws; and later in her life toured the country to give lectures on women's rights. Perhaps the most significant part of her life endeavor was also a revision—this time, a revision of the Bible. She completed this work in her eighties. Her version was meaningful because it reordered the expression of fictions underlying biblical stories so that they neither ignored nor denigrated women; it brought the wrath of religious and patriarchal communities upon her and even alienated her longtime friend and colleague, Susan B. Anthony. We remember Stanton as an organizer and as a person who supplied a basis for an American women's rights movement. Her work underpins many different, purposeful signals of distress with the patriarchal systems of the nineteenth and twentieth centuries.[64]

In all other matters, Susan Anthony had indeed been Stanton's trusted friend and confidante. Over fifty years the two worked together, sharing insights, commitments, even household tasks. At age 28, Anthony came to women's rights organizations from a teaching career. Although she did not attend the Seneca Falls Assembly in 1848, she heard about it, traveled to Seneca Falls, and thereafter threw herself into securing the vote for women with a memorable single-mindedness: "Failure," she said, "is impossible." For attempting to vote in Rochester, New York, she was arrested and taken into custody. Neither Stanton nor Anthony lived to cast a legal ballot, but Anthony's dedication to the justice of votes for women and her brilliant organizing talents brought about the passage of the Nineteenth Amendment to the Constitution of the United States. Denying women the right to vote had been a foundation-stone of nineteenth- and twentieth-century patriarchy.[65]

We see another line of assault upon the patriarchal system in Amelia Bloomer's explorations. As assistant postmaster in Seneca Falls and as a temperance supporter and publisher of *The Lily,* a small temperance newspaper in Seneca Falls, Amelia Bloomer felt uncomfortable in the fashionable, constricting corsets, laces, and great skirts women were expected to wear. She wrote an editorial defending a costume worn by another woman, Elizabeth Miller. It featured loose full pantaloons and a short overskirt. After Amelia Bloomer wore the costume herself, it became known by her name. Subsequently other women's rights leaders took to "bloomers." Ridicule grew so intense, however, that they had to retreat to the old, restrictive, uncomfortable garments. But Elizabeth Miller and Amelia Bloomer had opened a fault line in patriarchal authority. What women can wear turns out to matter in the public perception of who they are and what they can do.

Sojourner Truth was born as the slave Isabella. She participated in an abolitionist movement that grew in tandem with an awareness of women's rights. Many women, including the Grimké sisters, Sarah and Angelina, and Quaker Lucretia Coffin Mott were among the first to shatter the tradition of public silence long required of women. Sojourner Truth traveled through the eastern United States. She began by preaching the word of God, but after learning of the abolitionist movement and women's rights, she became a speaker in those causes. Altogether uneducated, Truth displayed a native intellectual power and a memorable linguistic brilliance. Speaking of the hard physical work she had performed in her life, she is often quoted as saying "And ain't I a woman?" Whether these were her words or simply an expression of her sentiments, they have echoed over the decades. The conviction of these women who dared to speak to audiences opened another crack in the patriarchal overhang.[66]

Another women's rights activist also became a lecturer, an eloquent speaker for women's rights—and for the abolition of slavery as well. Lucy Stone graduated from Oberlin College just ten years after it opened its doors to women students. In 1855, she married another ardent abolitionist, Henry Browne Blackwell—but strictly upon the condition that she retain her maiden name. The two made a famous public appearance in which both specifically rejected the domination of husband over wife and in which both refused to live by "couverture," the legal control of the husband over the wife.[67] Since that time, women have learned that naming themselves is important. They have learned to think of themselves as persons rather than simply as daughters, sisters, wives, and mothers. Stone's decision to keep her name said to the world that she was an independent, separate human being who possessed distinct rights and duties, a concept at variance with the laws of the land.[68] It also laid the foundation for naming abuses from which women suffered, abuses such as arrogant dictation, sexual harassment, wife-beating, rape, and date rape. By her gesture of publicly retaining her own personhood, Stone challenged a concept at the heart of patriarchal tradition—that man and woman are one, and that one is man.

This concept had been explored by an earlier literary philosopher, a woman profoundly influential in every subsequent feminist endeavor. Margaret Fuller's influence grew not only through her long association with the transcendentalists of Concord—with Ralph Waldo Emerson, Henry David Thoreau, and Bronson Alcott—but with her editorship of their famous journal, *The Dial.* Historian Judith Strong Albert tells us that Fuller set forth "a concept we take for granted in the nineteen nineties because she asserted it in the eighteen forties"—that is, the idea that women must think and act for themselves.[69] Margaret Fuller was a brilliant, complex, disciplined, driven woman. She experienced all of the prohibitions patriarchy could impose on a woman of genius. She strove to bring to a public persona the talents and insights with which she was richly endowed. In her *Conversations* with a circle of gifted women she set in motion ideas that vibrate still.[70] Margaret Fuller and her circle actually undertook an examination and an analysis of the fictions that hold patriarchy in place.

Lecturer and author Charlotte Perkins Gilman wrote one book that has been translated into seven languages. Her title, *Women and Economics,* treated a single matter—but a basic theme. Gilman set forth the revolutionary concept that has produced profound changes in many social situations, in industrial systems, and in guidelines that empower as well. She believed that in order to become full human persons, women need to become economically independent. The idea goes to the heart of patriarchal power in the modern world, as it did in times too ancient to recall; it has produced a rift in tenets vital to patriarchal control. It has been strengthened by women who became lawyers, doctors, professionals of many callings, despite the opprobrium they encountered. Women who become economically independent, who control their own earnings, cannot be easily dominated.[71]

Perhaps the scandalous Victoria Woodhull presented the challenge that was taken most seriously. She first came to prominence as a clairvoyant and charismatic leader. Capitalizing on the "spiritual" powers believed to emanate from her father's traveling medicine show as well as on the rather widespread Spiritualist movement of the times, Woodhull became a spiritual and financial advisor to the railroad entrepreneur Commodore Cornelius Vanderbilt. She also became the first woman to address a joint session of Congress to promote woman suffrage.

But most notoriously, she insisted that women should have complete sexual equality with men. In the Victorian climate of her time, she let her view be known that "free love" might be as desirable for women as for men: "*All* which is good and commendable, now existing, would *continue* to exist if all marriage laws were repealed tomorrow," she wrote in *Claflin's Weekly* in 1873. In one of her speeches she said that "people may be married by *law* . . . and they may also be married by *love,* and lack all sanction of law. Law cannot compel two to love. . . . This is a matter that concerns *these two* and *no* other living soul has *any human* right to say aye, yes or no." Woodhull actually entered the lists as a candidate for the presidency of the United States. One of the factors contributing to her downfall was that her past career as a prostitute became known. But Victoria Woodhull did go to the foundations of the patriarchal system by denying any male right to control woman's body, her sexual behavior, or her standing in the law of the land.[72] Coupled with the "naming" insights of Lucy Stone, this stance eventually lead to the renaming and reappraisal of many oppressive practices.[73]

Antoinette Brown Blackwell was another women who was fortunate enough to be admitted to Oberlin College in 1843. She earned a bachelor's degree in 1847. To the dismay of the college, she then applied to study theology. She finished the requirements for the second degree, but even for Oberlin, that particular second degree proved too much. The college never permitted her to receive it. Determined to pursue her chosen career, she was ordained in 1853 as minister of the First Congregational Church of Butler and Savannah in Wayne County, New York. By whatever circuitous route, Blackwell became the first ordained woman minister of a recognized religious denomination in the United States. Blackwell had trod upon the most sensitive fault line yet, the masculine hold over organized religion.

Perhaps it would not be too much to credit Oberlin College for complicity with the women's movements of recent centuries. That college early admitted women to the halls of higher education; today it wears this honor proudly. Among Oberlin graduates, Anna Julia Cooper distinguished herself by a very effective lifelong dedication to the education of women and black people. She fought a long and bruising battle against those who belittled her efforts to preserve college entrance courses in a Negro preparatory school in Washington, D.C.; there she taught classics and mathematics, and there she became principal. Later she instituted one of the first community colleges, holding many sessions in her own home. For thirty years, Freylingshuysen University offered standard college courses to employed adult students of both sexes; it was structured for those who needed to work as they attended classes.[74]

In 1925, Cooper published *A Voice from the South by a Black Woman of the*

South; this book stresses women's concerns as it shows their operation in her own life. It is a plea for women's access to higher education. At the age of 66, and at the price of great struggle, Cooper earned her own doctoral degree from the Sorbonne in Paris. Her dissertation in French, "Slavery and the French Revolutionists," was published there, though not in her native land.[75] Her emphasis on educational opportunities for those who could profit from them touched yet another sensitive nerve in the hierarchy of patriarchal prohibitions. She thought it not surprising that "woman may seem a nonentity so far as . . . concerns the solution of great national or even racial perplexities."[76] Once women gained equal access to higher education, Cooper believed, they would solve their own concerns. They would contribute richly to solving concerns of the nation.

Through all of this time women had been unable to participate directly in the political process. It is miraculous that they accomplished the social improvements they did achieve. In the settlement house movement of the nineteenth century, Jane Addams set a pattern. As a middle-class, educated woman, Addams found all avenues closed to her; she found her life empty, devoid of purpose. She learned, however, something about the desperate situation of immigrants pouring into this country in the late 1800s. She learned of sweltering tenements, city slums, neglected refuse, undernourished children, despairing young women and young men—all the evils besetting newcomers to crowded American cities. With Ellen Gates Starr, and her own money, she acquired a home in the heart of the tenement district in Chicago. There, at Hull House, she opened a center dedicated to improving opportunities for immigrants. There she provided courses tailored to this purpose, as well as instruction in practical means of getting along. As time went by she added many advanced courses and many opportunities.[77]

This became an undertaking of huge proportions, for the need was greater than any two women could have met. Soon the settlement house movement became a foremost expression of "Republican Motherhood," an ideology dedicated to the improvement of society and involving many women and many women's organizations.[78] Other women devoted their lives to settlement house work, among them Florence Kelley and Rowena Jelliffe.[79]

Though women could not vote or hold political office at this time, they took a personal and effective interest in child labor, the conditions of mill girls and of those working in city sweatshops, public health issues, temperance, recreation, wage scales, and any number of ills attendant upon the burgeoning industrial life of the nation. Jane Addams—and Florence Kelley—ventured innovatively and successfully into political arenas, for they found that political cadres controlled many of the conditions affecting those who needed help. The scope of their activities and the connections they made came to nothing less than formal and practical participation in weaving the social-political fabric of their time; by implication, it profoundly questioned the fictions supporting patriarchy. Politicians soon found it necessary to account for their actions to these women—and many more.

We see that these eleven women—and many of their colleagues in the nineteenth and twentieth centuries—posed far-reaching challenges to the patriarchal system under which women and men have lived for the last several millenniums. In these eleven categories—woman's equal right to organize, to speak and be heard, to vote, to clothe herself, to retain a name of her choosing while naming abuses and denying couverture, to enter intellectual scenarios as an equal player, to become economically independent, to possess jurisdiction over her own body on a basis of sexual equality, to enter religious enclaves on an equal footing, to receive an education equal to that of men, and to join in every detail of the local and national social-political polity—women made significant strides. Women carried out these ideals in many areas by the books they wrote and in the actions they took. Profoundly, each in her fashion, women confronted the established fictions that supported the patriarchal system. Women continue to do so.

So established and broad a system as that which has institutionalized relations and customs between the sexes for millenniums cannot easily be replaced or even modified. Buttressed by age-old ideologies, doggedly preserved by eminent male and female figures, patriarchy remains a formidable structure. Yet as the twenty-first century unfolds, the efforts of these eleven women—and many successors—presage powerful challenges. We see reasons to hope—for women and for men. Through channels these women proposed, and others, we may yet recast the fictions that prove as vital to the quality of our lives as to our survival.

—3
The Scramble After the Civil War

Stories for Grown-ups

We have so many beliefs we know are not true.
—John Steinbeck

Is it surprising that historians purvey fictions? That they cannot tell us about our past without bringing in their convictions? That they are creatures of time and place and happenstance—and choice—as are we all? That historians occupy positions of enormous consequence because their beliefs guide our deeds? That historians themselves experience hopes and fears about how far their stories travel?

Let's think about their legacies. The sequel to the Civil War—the Re-Construction of the nation—dramatically influenced American life from the middle days of the nineteenth century to the early days of the twenty-first century.

Historians have told stories about it. Indeed, Reconstruction became a historical space of deposit for our national racial flotsam and jetsam from as far back as 1619 when the first slave ship arrived in Jamestown. Reconstruction also became a launching pier for the Civil Rights movement that lay ahead.[1] The events of 130-plus years ago and stories about those events still carry power to influence our attitudes. Someone has said that Reconstruction opens a window overlooking all of American history. It is a window reflecting attitudes and convictions behind the stories historians tell.

Let's consider how particular historians of Reconstruction figure in our thoughts. How did they come to play the prominent roles they play? How could historians have told different tales about the same occurrences of that troubled time? Putting the nation together a second time amounted to a formative experience for all Americans. What could the manner of telling stories about it have meant for the nation?

No less weighty an issue than the role African Americans would play in the life of the nation was on the line. No less weighty an issue than whether any state government could supercede the national government was still on the line. For that matter, the civil rights of all Americans were on the line. We had repressed these issues as well as knowledge of consequences of stories about them. But old issues surfaced, menacing hopes. When they did not surface, they endangered the republic, as Abraham Lincoln movingly perceived: "We are engaged," he said, "in a great Civil War testing whether this nation or any nation so conceived and so dedicated can long endure."[2] In explaining the aftermath, historians introduced fictions that foreshadowed a worrisome sleep. Those same fictions still foreshadow an American nightmare: the demise of the democratic dream.

As historians portrayed Reconstruction, they disagreed as ardently as participants at the Battle of Gettysburg. When they told stories, they saw events and movements according to their own climates of opinion. They carried tensions from their different experiences, tensions that were traditional, class-specific, often racially oriented, sometimes vicarious. They carried their guiding principles with them as they worked. Their histories revealed ways in which they chose their principles. They purveyed their convictions.

Since the beginnings of constitutional government in 1787, politicians had tried to resolve dilemmas that beset the new nation.[3] Could legal slavery exist? Could it even be recognized? Could states wield powers? And which powers? Or was the federal government supreme? These questions roused passions. For the majority of Americans, neither the efforts of politicians to forbid petitions and outlaw discussions in the early 1800s nor the series of compromises from the 1830s to the Civil War of the 1860s nor the decisions of the Supreme Court nor the Civil War itself laid those tensions to rest.[4] Each historian who told stories about these issues purveyed particular beliefs with all the logical and emotional force that could be mustered.

For historians, the questions were and are: Can anyone write about the past without experiencing a share in it? Can anyone write about issues affecting all Americans without injecting personal experience? The act of writing a history carries responsibilities well beyond the satisfactions of expressing oneself. It carries a long-term potential to influence others. It offers promise. It cradles danger. One historian aptly titled his survey of Reconstruction stories "The Dark and Bloody Ground of Reconstruction Historiography."[5] Never have historians more ominously differed about which persons, which events, which acts, which omissions mattered, which could be discounted. In no area of historical writing can we discern more clearly the personal convictions of writers as well as their ways of implementing their views. In no area do dilemmas as well as potentialities of historians more poignantly appear.

How can disagreements of historians threaten the national life? How do potentialities of historians offer solutions? I suggest that a fine distinction exists between political resolutions of issues and viable solutions of problems. I suggest that the dilemmas politicians encounter grow more intense for historians. As surely as anyone else, a historian is a historical participant. Historians share all the daily concerns and general decisions of living. They also share responsibilities that arise from public awareness of persisting problems; as historians, they provide knowledge of governments, wars, movements, and societies—knowledge as they see it, knowledge that influences succeeding generations.

Oftener than not, we base our actions on this received wisdom, and therefore on beliefs of those who give it to us.

When it came to Reconstruction, historians proved themselves stellar actors. Political compromises failed to settle differences. As issues and problems stretched toward the future, historians as well as politicians needed to discover solutions that could not necessarily be found in compromise. As the first historians of Reconstruction wrote, disjunctions between the ideals of the Declaration of Independence and the realities of the legacy of slavery prevailed. Recognition of those disjunctions mandated dealing with them; only then would they cease to threaten the republic. To shunt them aside prolonged uneasiness and apprehension. It ensured that anxieties would not go away. Worse than that, it meant that anxieties would find political and social expression. Yet most politicians felt they had no choice but compromise. And many historians felt they should not compromise.

Perhaps some historians believed the best they could do would be to realize their own stakes in relating the story as *their* fictions dictated. Perhaps some realized that the alternative to acknowledging positions and to examining their importance, as well as one's manner of telling them, is to take no stand, to deny moral choice, to see oneself and one's histories as predetermined and disconnected from humanity. Yet despite the strongest intentions, every historian has rendezvoused with climates of opinion; based on background or evidence or both, every historian has formed convictions.

For each position a historian employs to tell a story, he or she must choose a modus operandi. I believe a historian's positions provide stepping-stones toward understanding—if and when they are acknowledged. But some historians dismissed their own involvements. Some believed a historian is justified in offering a particular belief as the only possible belief, offering his or her manner of expressing that belief as unassailable. Some took the view that a historian is able to write objectively. Those historians never realized that they cherished a stake in how the nation ought to be reconstructed, that each in his or her fashion singled out evidence to support the views expressed. They didn't realize that willingly or unwillingly, no one escaped the entanglements of his or her situation.

What happened as the Civil War ended, as politicians struggled to put the nation together again? Who won? Who took charge? Who perpetrated outrages? Who performed commendably? In the saga of the republic, which outcomes proved worth attaining? Which produced further calamities? What stories should future generations know? Which interpretations seemed to indemnify writers who adopted the prevailing consensus? These questions rose anew because historians brought different projects, differently implemented, to their stories.

The tellers of stories didn't agree about how long it took to put the union together again or when it was accomplished or who ought to have done that job. They didn't agree about what should have been the terms for coming together. They disagreed because they were dealing not with "old, forgotten far-off things and battles long ago," as Wordsworth put it, they were dealing with deeply rooted, present anxieties in which they felt themselves involved.

Therefore when they considered the restructuring of the union, the Civil War, its precursors, and its sequels pulsated in their thoughts. The result: Depending on where historians found themselves, we got skewed pictures. One-sided as those pictures were, they affected the lives of students, of readers, of generations. Since it was possible to find some evidence for almost anything, and since a writer's particular convictions dominated the scene, parts of the picture became at times obscured, at times distorted, at times burdened beyond belief. Seldom if ever did whole pictures appear. In projecting their fictions, numbers of historians found it difficult to deal with evidence they perceived faintly, if they perceived it at all, evidence that would challenge their fictions and their manners of relating them.

Viewing historians according to projects that dominated their thought rather than chronologically, we see that a first series of historians believed Reconstruction took a long time after the close of hostilities in 1865. As they saw events, it may have taken the twelve years from 1865 to 1877, or it may have taken the thirty-five or so years to the 1900s. Probably the resolutions these historians favored did take that long. Often involved in the post–Civil War industrial surge, these historians envisioned reestablishment of pre–Civil War styles of operation rather than the institution of changes Congress required.

A second group of historians, many of whom had been schooled in "objective" German scholarship, preferred "consensus" practice; that is, whatever is well established by might or majority is preferable and should become the will of the nation. North and South, Civil War or no Civil War, they saw consensus as the authority that should precipitate itself into popular support. These historians too desired pre–Civil War styles of operation. Both groups believed that Reconstruction ought to mean undoing the "upstart" congressional requirements that briefly operated. In the interests of North and South, they believed an enduring Reconstruction of the nation should mean a solid return to old controls rather than readjustment. They believed they could show by objective evidence that old ways and old methods had proved the road to wisdom. They thought that returning to arrangements akin to old controls took longer than the first two years when Congress did attempt to enforce its laws. In that assessment they were right.

By the 1890s, when historians started to publish stories, and well before that time, politicians and historians of both orientations wanted—and were pleased to see by the 1890s—less change than the Congress of 1866–1868 envisioned in the Thirteenth, Fourteenth, and Fifteenth Amendments, which set the requirements for states to be readmitted to the Union. It seemed reasonable to show only utter chaos when changes did happen.

A third group of historians were displaced southerners; still smarting from their losses, they too desired the pre–Civil War conditions they thought favorable to future enterprises. These circumstances formed their beliefs. Thus historians from three points of origin largely agreed in their interpretations of the aftermath of the war.

But a fourth and growing group of historians from both sections felt that any attempt to adjust priorities lasted for only a brief period, at the longest the two years prior to 1868. They believed that the new conditions Congress laid down at that time, including good-faith enforcement of the Thirteenth, Fourteenth, and Fifteenth Amendments, were absolutely necessary to the future of the nation. They believed that chances for democratic advancement vanished with the ingenious southern defiance of Congress and the resurgence of old struggles, old controls. These beliefs dominated their thoughts.

Many were influenced by progressive turns in state and national politics; exposures of unrestrained industrial development spawned new constituencies in political arenas. Racial concerns influenced the thinking of others. Historians who began to write from the 1920s and through the twentieth century constitute a heterogeneous group. Generally their work appeared at later dates, so that its impact has been delayed. The rough groupings I outline are subject, of course, to overlapping, and plenty of that occurred. A few of the fourth grouping wrote earlier; some from the first three groupings wrote at later dates.

Historians from the first three points of origin believed that male Negro suffrage became so disastrous that it should have been eliminated by whatever means; one historian described black legislators as "blatant, dishonest, insolent megalomaniacs."[6] Another often-quoted historian pictured Negro participation in southern governments as a "long dark night"; his description roused enthusiastic echoes in both sections of the nation.

Others—mostly from the fourth grouping—believed that male Negro suffrage strengthened civil life, that democratic ideals could prevail in the New World, and that Negro suffrage could finally begin to absolve the nation from the practice and the guilt of slavery. At odds with the earlier historians, they showed that Negroes acquitted themselves with believable success during the two years after 1866 when they did participate in some state governments. Still others, bringing their most pressing fictions, believed that the new suffrage amendments should at least have included white women, north and south.[7]

Some from the first three groups thought that from the Civil War to the new century, the activities of the Ku Klux Klan escalated to sustained levels of unspeakable terror only because Congress turned government over to illiterates and criminals. Others, mostly from the fourth group, believed the Klan grew from a long, distinctly southern vigilante tradition, that slavery carried a built-in necessity for violence. They found that after the 1860s the Klan no longer represented even pious attempts to maintain order; instead, it descended to unbridled barbarism.[8]

Some of the historians in the third group believed that every newcomer seeking to take part in postwar southern society came for greedy, dishonorable reasons; they thought that any southerner who cooperated with Congress had turned traitor. Others, again from the fourth group, were to see "carpetbagger" and "scalawag" elements as a hope for the future. Some members of the third group resented attempts to educate Negroes. Others of the fourth group believed that the endeavors of northern teachers and black leaders represented the most commendable of undertakings.[9]

Competing fictions, some long established, supported such clashes of opinion. Indeed, struggles that peaked during the Civil War and surfaced at Reconstruction were centuries old: Englishman Sir John Hawkins, a cousin of Sir Francis Drake, inaugurated the slave trade to the Americas in the 1560s. From the Caribbean, the trade spread to the English colonies.

For some time, however, the status of Africans who wound up in Virginia was ambiguous. Would the early laws of the Virginia colony see Africans as indentured servants who, like indentured servants from England, might go their way in seven years? For a time, Virginia law did see Africans in that position. Or were they to become field laborers, indispensable forever? Historian Herbert Klein found that after 1640, "the colored population of Virginia began to be increasingly divided between servants and slaves"; in 1662, the first legislation ordering perpetual Negro servitude appeared. Though uncertainties in laws and in the fictions that supported them thus yielded to the need for labor, or in some places lapsed when labor wasn't needed, differences in points of view lingered. Interminably, the differences persisted. They played into fictions of historians.[10]

The shaping of the Declaration of Independence in 1776 and the framing of the Constitution in 1787 grew out of adversarial attitudes—and finally out of dominating beliefs among participants and then among historians. While these documents signaled living ideals, as well as stability and privileges for some, others wondered why the Continental Congress deleted the nineteenth "grievance" Jefferson listed in the Declaration, the "grievance" accusing England of fostering the slave trade. What lively fictions prevented framers of the Constitution from mentioning the word "slavery?" Partly because of this, Theodore Lowi, an astute twentieth-century observer, wrote of the new government as an incomplete conquest.[11]

Differences among politicians and then among historians over census counts, regulation of trade, taxes, and voting appeared after the Revolutionary War and reappeared after the Civil War. Disputes at the framing of the Constitution in 1787 required an elaborate "Great Compromise" in order to frame any Constitution at all. Disagreements at the close of the Civil War played out as southern states, each in its fashion, found ways to maintain the old order, to control the voting places, and to defy the authority of Congress. Victors and vanquished and those who wrote about them brought old quarrels, old emotions, old fictions as they gingerly approached old problems in new frameworks.[12] Which fictions and which projects mandated the stances of the participants and the stances of the historians? Which did they suppress? Well through the twentieth century, historians told tales based on different views, each in a chosen fashion.

So the first historians of Reconstruction told stories grounded in inherited dilemmas as well as in projects that were current for them. As historians wrote their histories, they included those participants they deemed significant and used the methods they had chosen to convey their preferences. Preferences influenced where they would look for evidence, which occurrences they would select, which occurrences they would ignore, and which weights they would assign to evidence they did select. Predictably, a few chose to disengage their thoughts from those of other historians. The more wrenching the conflicts, the more earnestly historians propelled their particular projects as well as their chosen styles of implementing them.

The stories that made their way into print profoundly influenced political decisions and public policies about schooling, religion, and housing. As cities grew, would schools, north and south, be segregated? Would neighborhoods? Would police and fire and sanitation departments? Would libraries, public accommodations, professional licensing policies, land policies, labor arrangements, real estate sales, and job opportunities function according to race and class? Where did they intersect? If it turned out that exclusion had been the case all along, north and south, should it continue to prevail in social situations? Should it prevail in government agencies, including the armed forces?[13] Should it prevail in legislative bodies? Should it determine qualifications for voting? What would be conditions of public education? What marriage protocols would states sanction? Could arrangements continue almost as they had functioned in slavery days? Or was this a matter of the rights of the states versus those of the federal government? Which fictions would dominate the work of historians as they related these important decisions?

Who was going to obey the laws of the states and who would comply with those of the federal government? Who would knowingly ignore the laws? Should new generations continue to seek compromises? The striking reality is that projects that powered stories historians told and projects that reflected views historians held determined stands next generations would take on all these questions. The considerations historians used influenced how people were going to respond to unsettled and recurring challenges. Historians wrote as agents. No era of historical writing more tellingly displays the influence historians and their fictions exerted. No era is more faithfully duplicated in histories of later dates. No era, alas, more convincingly portrays the losses for society when historians bypass one another's stories and, more significant, when historians bypass responsibilities that came to them because they chose to be historians.

So we may ponder: Exactly which arrangements of the post–Civil War years did historians project upon succeeding generations and their societies? Which historians are choosing and creating scenarios that are unlike the early frames and so are relating different stories, richer stories, projecting different frameworks, influencing public inclinations differently?

So much has been written by so many that it is impossible to follow their paths. I will try, however, to select a few Reconstruction historians, the circumstances of whose lives are available and whose work can be seen to represent fictions that cast broad shadows. Remembering that, in the words of historian Lawrence W. Levine, "history today is written, as it has always been written, by human beings who are part of their own societies and cultures,"[14] readers will understand that I can only write from the point of view of my own fictions and that I must leave out many more historians than I can study. Otherwise this chapter in a book about fictions could become a long book. Realizing with C. Vann Woodward that "a full-dress bibliography in Southern history has never been attempted,"[15] I will, with appropriate fear and trembling, choose a few historians of Reconstruction to illustrate how fictions form and to represent how fictions become identifying features of political and social voyages we undertake. I will make these choices with deep regret that I cannot include many who are writing today, many whose work displays an excellence, many whose contributions I cherish and whose research remains lastingly important.

Historians and Competing Commitments

James Ford Rhodes was among the first historians to tell a story of Reconstruction. Rhodes was born in 1848 in Sudbury, Vermont, as his father began a climb to industrial success. James was 13 when the Civil War began, 17 when hostilities ceased. His mother, a devout Connecticut Episcopalian, instilled strict religious precepts into her son. All the while, his father's company prospered in coal and iron production—undertakings basic to the driving industrial energy of the time. Without coal and iron, without such operations as that of the Rhodes family, there could have been no transcontinental railroad by 1869, perhaps no far-flung American industrial revolution by 1900. So consuming were the demands of this enterprise that at 17 James entered his father's firm rather than move toward a college education.

At 17, however, James did realize other inclinations. As the war ended in 1865–1866, he began to take courses as a special student at the University of the

City of New York. Sporadically thereafter, he read H. T. Buckle and *The Nation*, took metaphysics at the University of Chicago, and traveled to Paris and Berlin, ostensibly to study metallurgy. He attended lectures on Montesquieu in Paris, however (although he did attend lectures on metallurgy in Berlin). Next, he toured iron and steel mills in Germany and in Great Britain.

Upon his return his father sent him to survey coal and iron deposits in North Carolina, Georgia, and Tennessee. There he encountered others interested in developing the resources of those areas—others dubbed "carpetbaggers" by disgruntled local residents. Rhodes himself might have been thought eligible for this pejorative category had he remained in that area pursuing his father's business. He did write monthly circulars describing the condition of the pig-iron trade. But he had no reason to care about further increasing the family wealth. Because his family's prosperity gave him freedom to travel, to take courses here and there, to investigate other possibilities, he came to consider money a convenience rather than a life goal. Twenty years after beginning a career at Rhodes & Company, he retired. He was 37, well versed in industrial practices, well subsidized.[16]

Rhodes wrote his stories about Reconstruction in the 1890s, thirty-some years after the events took place. During his early years, he had witnessed close at hand the unrestricted industrial expansion of nineteenth-century America. He had seen these developments from the point of view of a successful entrepreneurial family. Six years after his retirement from Rhodes & Company, he began the publication of a series on the history of the United States, starting with the Compromise of 1850. According to reviewers, the first volumes were carefully researched. He was considered one of the first historians to view the South and its potentialities sympathetically, if somewhat condescendingly. But it has been suggested that by the time he came to the volumes dealing with Reconstruction, he based his work on evidence less attentively obtained.

In the last two of his books, Rhodes pictured many an evil outcome of the congressional Reconstruction effort. In his largely political view, the lawmakers never achieved an acceptable arrangement of relations within states or between the old Confederate states and the federal government. These mighty misfortunes occurred because the northern Congress forced male Negro suffrage upon the South, thus handling this sensitive matter callously. While Rhodes found all of the Reconstruction acts of Congress deplorable, he found male Negro suffrage the most drastic, the "worst provision."

Rhodes lived north of slavery. The fictions he brought to his work must have grown from his early experience in his father's business, from a day-to-day familiarity with the style of nineteenth-century industrial practice. He must have brought convictions that unfettered industrial enterprise ought to determine the future of the union and that harmonious relations between the North and the new South would provide the most desirable climate. He must have believed that such good relations would depend upon rapprochement with old enemies and would especially include management of labor, education, and political opportunities by elites.

The modus operandi of industrial development at the time Rhodes wrote his histories harmonized with that of the old plantation economy: It was patriarchal, wide ranging, preemptive, rampant, distinctly undemocratic. The party line for those bringing these convictions was that any state could disagree with federal authority and could find ways to modify compliance with federal law, that Negroes would always be inferior in intelligence and civilization, and that the slave traders and the colonists actually elevated Negroes by bringing them out of Africa. Whatever their sufferings, Negroes were better off than when they lived on that tribal continent. Though now legally free, Negroes were socially and economically childlike. They needed guidance, just as children need guidance.

Industrial welfare was the wave of the future; metallurgy in particular would rely on orderly mining and manufacturing programs and on dependable labor supplies. Salvation could be achieved by returning control to the elite heirs of the old South, by working with them, and by accepting guidance from them in dealing with their Negro population. These intentions underwrote the customs of the old South and much of its preferred labor policy for the new South. It is easy to imagine that Rhodes would have been supported by intellectual descendants of John C. Calhoun, George Fitzhugh, Alexander Stephens, and Ulrich B. Phillips, spokesmen of the old South, and that he would have supported them as well.

Rhodes did furnish an influential story. In the late 1890s, his fictions resonated with fictions in favor in the South and in the North: In the North, industrialists were looking to invest their new capital in the South. They saw rich opportunities. They needed raw materials. They needed cheap, menial labor, both black and white. It was advantageous to believe that Negroes were inferior beings. Rhodes's fictions also resonated with those of the elite old South; there bitter memories flourished. Displaced southerners, whose preferred fictions had not prevailed, longed to return to the comfort and dominance of slavery days. Rhodes implied that much of that setup would not be a bad idea. Though important to scholars and to certain segments of the population, Rhodes's Reconstruction volumes never attained a wide popular currency.[17]

But his books sounded notes that harmonized with those of a succeeding group of historians. At Columbia University, William Archibald Dunning established a most influential seminar, a seminar that casts a shadow still.

Born in Plainfield, New Jersey, about a decade after Rhodes, Dunning came from a background similar in some respects to that of Rhodes. Before the advent of automobiles, Dunning's father, John Dunning, was a successful manufacturer of carriages. Though profiting from the initial postwar industrial surge, the senior Dunning suffered serious financial losses from the Panic of 1873. Known to be an amateur painter and art critic, John Dunning also harbored a respect for intellectual endeavors. He knew and felt the intellectual climates of his time; he thought that peoples descended from Anglo Saxons represented a type superior to all others, that Social Darwinism—survival of the fittest—was a natural imperative, and that therefore expansionism and imperialism were expectable, desirable outcomes in political arrangements. He shared the pervasive anti-Negro feelings of his day. He accorded no credence to achievements of the former slaves or the black freedmen.

From this background, the young William began as a news reporter in New York City. He soon left that calling to go to Dartmouth College, from which he was expelled for "a reprisal raid on certain sophomores." This experience seems to have sobered him. William Dunning became a serious student at Columbia; he took his B.A., his M.A., and his Ph.D. from that university. There he came under the influence of John W. Burgess, a devoted student of German scholarship. Like Rhodes, Dunning next went to Germany, where he studied at the University of Berlin. Upon his return he became a lecturer, an instructor, and eventually a full professor at Columbia.

In Berlin, Dunning had come in close contact with the methods of Leopold von Ranke. Like his teacher John W. Burgess, he came to a firm belief that von Ranke had developed uniquely reliable procedures for approaching evidence. Deeply committed to scholarly endeavors, Dunning established a seminar at Columbia patterned after the prestigious von Ranke model. Dunning had come to believe with von Ranke that the ideal should be "to remain detached in interest and objective in method." He believed it possible to write free of influences, to select sources without bias, to review evidence impartially, and to report almost without interpretation or involvement; he believed that eventually one could find all of the evidence, that one could subtract oneself and one's background from the choices one made, and that a historian need only allow the evidence to tell the story. These conclusions Dunning superimposed upon the intellectual fictions of the time, fictions he learned from his father, notions that powered the ideology of "Manifest Destiny."

In 1898, Dunning published his essays on Reconstruction; in that book he projected a line of belief that long persisted: "Few episodes of recorded history more urgently invite thorough analysis," he wrote, "than the struggle through which the southern whites, subjugated by adversaries of their own race, thwarted the scheme which threatened permanent subjection to another race."[18] The belief that a long domination by the Negro race had loomed in the immediate future became a starting point for Dunning's work, as it did for that of his colleagues and his famous students. It came to play widely in the fears of the public.[19] For fifty years, these views dominated high school and college textbooks and teaching; they permeated most of the historical literature of that time.

Several scholars—John W. Burgess, Walter Fleming, Woodrow Wilson—elaborated the views of Rhodes and Dunning. The particular fictions of these historians laid the foundations for generally understood beliefs about what happened after the war as well as why it happened. In subtle and obvious ways, but often using loosely defined terms, they all deplored "carpetbaggers" and "scalawags" and "Negro rule" in the southern states. Yet even as they wrote, a few scholars, journalists, and historians of different backgrounds began to look questioningly at Dunning's works and those of his students and colleagues. Despite such early questionings, it is nearly impossible to overestimate the prestige the Dunning seminars reached or the influence on public policies and private customs his particular fictions generated.[20] They dominated high school and college textbooks; for more than fifty years, the standard belief among young Americans was based upon the views and fictions of William Archibald Dunning.

Dunning students thought that Negro intelligence was inferior to that of whites, that during the "long dark night" of Reconstruction, graft was more common and corruption more grievous than at any time in memory. They thought this happened because the old elite was excluded from political power and because Negroes were included in that power structure during Reconstruction and because of the activities of those whites whom they dubbed "carpetbaggers" (undesirable newcomers) and "scalawags" (treasonous southern whites who supported the Union and congressional Reconstruction). They believed the nation could only be restored by returning to an approximation of the old order. They looked with favor on the efforts of the southern states to reestablish legal white supremacy. Rhodes and Dunning represented the first and second groups of historians—those oriented in industrial perspectives of the last years of the nineteenth century and those trained in Europe to emulate the model seminars of Leopold von Ranke.

Representing the third group of early historians, Walter L. Fleming held haunting memories of the old South. Once his family occupied a prominent position in Brundage, Alabama. But Fleming's father, a southern planter, suffered severely from the ravages of war. The family lost buildings, land, and slaves; they sustained great distress from engagements of the struggle. As a boy, Fleming knew the pain of defeat and the psychological burdens of his family's misfortunes.

At 22, Fleming began to teach history, English, and mathematics and to serve as a librarian in his home state of Alabama. He became an officer of the 3rd Alabama Infantry as well as a quartermaster in a field hospital during the war with Spain. In that brief engagement, he served as a member of the 4th Army

Corps. After that war, he decided to go north to Columbia University to study history. He became a member of a Dunning seminar. While completing his training, he lectured at Columbia in 1902 and 1903. But soon he returned to the South to teach history at West Virginia University from 1903 to 1907. He received his Ph.D. from Columbia along the way in 1904; from 1907 to 1929 he progressed from teaching at the State University of Virginia to becoming dean and director of its graduate studies programs.

In 1905, his historical writings began to appear. The subjects arose from southern history, particularly the Civil War and Reconstruction. He edited a history of the Ku Klux Klan; he compiled documents of the Reconstruction period; he edited a 12-volume series, *The South in the Building of the Nation*; and he offered monographs on *Reconstruction of the Southern States*; *Civil War and Reconstruction in Alabama*; *William Tecumseh Sherman as College President*; and *The Freedmen's Savings Bank*. In 1927, he became editor of the *Mississippi Valley Historical Review*. His influence spread, not only through his editorship of this esteemed journal but also through the seminars he sponsored as a graduate dean. His work was frequently quoted in other books. His fellow historians believed that he furnished the evidence to substantiate a "long dark night" of Negro domination. Though congressional Reconstruction lasted no more than two years anywhere, a belief in a "long dark night" was embedded in his fictions; this was the party line Fleming's students went forth to proselytize.

John W. Burgess was born in middle Tennessee, near the Alabama border. His grandfather was a New Englander who moved to Baltimore; his father crossed the mountains to Tennessee with his mother, a daughter of a Virginia-born physician. While his father cannot be said to have been among the planter elite of the old South, he did become a successful farmer and he did own slaves. When John was a very small child, the family witnessed the bitterest kind of clan and family-against-family strife in Tennessee. The young John learned to abhor such a way of life; he never forgot this early commitment. Like the Reconstruction president Andrew Johnson, also of Tennessee, both father and son became American nationalists who remained loyal to the Union during the war.[21]

For their son John, Burgess's parents procured a private tutor and then sent him to Cumberland University. In 1862, as a Union army advanced, that university closed its doors; tormented by local Confederates, the young Burgess fled to join Union forces. Though he became a second lieutenant, he was mustered out for health reasons in 1864 before the end of the war. He always kept in the back of his mind a strong desire to substitute "the conservative methods of peace for the destructive effects of war."

After the war, Burgess resumed his education at Amherst College. There he added to his beliefs something from the philosophy of the German scholar Georg Wilhelm Friedrich Hegel, with whose works he had become familiar in

Germany. Hegel asserted that inexorable laws of historical destiny exist. A basic outcome of these laws is the principle that the state is the product of all history, that the state is "the march of God through the world." This conclusion deeply impressed John Burgess, who was already a nationalist in his own country; though he was a southerner, he never approved the secession of the southern states.

Burgess decided to specialize in history, in political science, and then in law.[22] A bout with typhoid fever meant that he would be too late for registration at the law school. He did, however, find a law clerkship in Springfield, Massachusetts. He soon returned to the academic scene, this time in Göttingen, Germany, then in Leipzig, then in Berlin. He studied directly under Johann Gustav Droysen, an heir and successor to the views of Leopold von Ranke. According to his biographer, Burgess "was inspired to establish in the United States the opportunities for advanced study and research he had found [in Germany]." When he returned to the United States, Burgess brought the whole apparatus of German scholarship with him. He also brought a burning desire to establish a school to train American students for public service. While this desire grew from an undoubted integrity of purpose, the fallout from his beliefs led to convictions modern scholars question. Burgess came to believe there can be no "natural rights" of an independent nature: "There never was and there never can be any liberty upon this earth and among human beings outside of state organization," he wrote. "Mankind does not begin with liberty. Mankind acquires liberty through civilization." As mankind developed he saw some expansion of the area of liberty; guaranteed property was the key: "Property became a human right of the highest order."

How did these views translate into his particular beliefs and his books on reuniting the states? In promoting "the re-establishment of a real national brotherhood between the North and the South," Burgess called upon northerners to acknowledge that "the Reconstruction [meaning the two years of congressional Reconstruction] had been an error as well as a failure." The Radical Republicans in Congress, he said, failed to realize "that there are vast differences in political capacity between the races, and that it is the white man's mission, his duty and his right, to hold the reins of political power in his own hands for the civilization of the world and the welfare of mankind."

Because a whole decade passed without this recognition, Burgess wrote, "the dark night of domination by the negro and adventurer had rested upon the unhappy section [the South], until it had been reduced to the very abomination of desolation." He thought that "Teutonic races produced the great state builders of history." They had a duty "to carry the blessings of their superior civilization to lesser breeds." "I do not think that Asia and Africa can ever receive political organization in any other way." He wrote that under certain circumstances, the Teutonic element "should not even permit participation of the other elements in political power."[23] Burgess formed his fictions from early experiences and early loyalties and he added the belief that we can "objectively" note and record everything. It is easy to see that this important opinion-maker wanted no different construction of the nation than that which led to Civil War.

Woodrow Wilson, a southern historian of a similar professional stripe, was born in Staunton, Virginia, in the year 1856; he could be found among those writers who favored the Dunning fictions. Wilson was the son of a Presbyterian minister and, on his mother's side, the grandson of a Scottish Presbyterian minister. As Wilson was growing up, his father moved from one church to another; he lived in Virginia, Georgia, South Carolina, and North Carolina. Themes that formed his fictions and then played out in his life as far as and during his presidency of the United States are traceable to the intense piety of his family in combination with certain strong southern affiliations of his surroundings. Almost uniquely, the Wilson fictions demonstrate connections between historians of Reconstruction and politicians. The situations of both Woodrow Wilson and James Ford Rhodes also testify to thriving fictional alliances between religions and politics in the North and in the South.

After college in North Carolina, Wilson studied law at the University of Virginia; then he opened a law practice in Atlanta, Georgia. But he returned to graduate school at Johns Hopkins University in Baltimore, Maryland, to study history with Herbert Baxter Adams.[24]

Wilson believed, with justification, that it was a "difficult and hazardous matter to reinstate the states." But in line with Dunning historians, Wilson also believed that southern governments had been "given into the hands of the negroes," who "were but children still." He thought that "unscrupulous men,— 'carpetbaggers' . . . came out of the North to use the negroes as tools for their own selfish ends; and succeeded, to the utmost fulfillment of their dreams. . . . The negroes were exalted, the states were misgoverned and looted in their name."[25] Negroes, Wilson continued, were "excited by a freedom they did not understand, exalted by false hopes; bewildered and without leaders, and yet insolent and aggressive, sick of work, covetous of pleasure—a host of dusky children untimely put out of school. They were a danger to themselves as well as to those whom they had once served and now feared and suspected."[26] Though he wrote this essay in 1901, Wilson carried the same fictions, those which underlay his histories, to the presidency in 1912: He still believed that Negroes were children. He refused to hear the views of prominent Negro leaders. He permitted a thoroughgoing segregation in the nation's capital.

Some thirty years after the Civil War, J. G. Randall, another early historian, published *The Civil War and Reconstruction*. This book became a standard text. North and south, twentieth-century students read Randall's story and believed it to be the one and only, *the* "true" story, the complete story of the Re-

Woodrow Wilson as a young historian, 1902. *Courtesy Princeton University Library, Public Policy Papers, Department of Rare Books and Special Collections.*

construction of the nation; it became *the* story told and told again. Though in 1961 David Donald revised the book, and though Donald did introduce evidence of little interest to Randall, the book essentially reinforced the fictions of Rhodes and the Dunning School and it told a story similar to Randall's original story.

James Garfield Randall came from mid-America. He was born at Indianapolis, Indiana, in 1881, just about a decade before the first histories of Reconstruction began to appear. His father Horace Randall, a businessman, sent his son to public schools in that city. Very early the young James exhibited a strong artistic talent and a fascination with Abraham Lincoln. Both stayed with him. In his youth he rendered many drawings of Lincoln, and he once gave a speech at church on Lincoln's career. An important facet of Randall's life work was to be his reevaluation of Lincoln and the Lincoln legends. But by the time he received his A.B. degree from Butler College in 1903 and his advanced degrees from the University of Chicago in 1911, he had probably studied the

Reconstruction works of Rhodes and the Dunning School. By that time they were becoming well known to college students.

Randall's major concerns differed from those of most of the Dunning historians, however. For Randall, the crucial decisions emerged from large structural and constitutional issues rather than from economic or social or business or cultural concerns. He also cherished a belief that wars cannot be considered inevitable. He believed in extensive research; never trite, picayune, or credulous, Randall nevertheless placed faith in the promise of "objective" research. He allowed historians to escape the difficult stands: "A cautious historian," he wrote, "may well choose to record the event, not indeed without interpretation, but without committing himself to a particular formula of determinism or indeed to any hypothesis." Through his lifetime Randall adhered meticulously to a confidence that "objective" findings can be obtained without reflecting the historian's bias.

Though economic outcomes were less than his main concern, he did present a sophisticated picture of forces at work in the nation's economy. He wrote of great industries, the oil and steel combinations, the railroads, their plans for expansion, their hopes for "developing" the South. He dwelt on utter disruption in parts of the South where armies had tramped. He quoted a Louisiana citizen who remembered that with the "Devil of Slavery" in the land, there existed "a picture of fully cultivated fields, neatly whitewashed cabins for the hands, and sugar houses of the best construction, making the whole scene a paradise to the eyes.'" But without the "Devil of Slavery," "sugar houses had been destroyed, fences burned, weeds and brush were taking possession, and not a plantation was in decent order."

In the wake of Sherman's march, South Carolina "looked for many miles like a broad black streak of ruin and desolation: the fences all gone; lonesome smoke stacks, surrounded by dark heaps of ashes and cinders, marking the spots where human habitations had stood."[27] Undoubtedly his words described the scene. But in this nostalgic account, Randall took no notice that other areas—New Orleans, Memphis, Montgomery, large areas of Texas, Arkansas, Louisiana, and Florida—had felt little damage. In determining his own fictional stance, Randall omitted large portions of the picture as he emphasized evidence that supported his positions.

"Elections in the South became a byword and a travesty," Randall wrote. He cited W. L. Fleming's *Documentary History of Reconstruction* to affirm that "ignorant blacks by the thousands cast ballots without knowing even the names of men for whom they were voting."[28] Randall argued that the South was subjected to "the misguided action of these irresponsible creatures directed by white bosses." He believed, usually on Walter Fleming's authority, that "carpetbag" and Negro government were responsible for leaving the state "a wretched heritage of defaulted obligations." He wrote that Radical Republican state machines "plunged the Southern commonwealths into an abyss of mis-government."[29] "Delicate women," he lamented, "were reported selling provisions needed for their hungry children, in order to pay taxes."

Nearly seventy-five years after the last battle of the war, and thirty-five years after the heyday of the Dunning seminars, Randall's book thus renewed fictions that had guided those seminars. Before he conceived his book, Randall believed that the early years of congressional Reconstruction—1866 to 1868—were an ultimate calamity for civilization and society. With the Dunning-type historians, he buttressed these beliefs with constitutional and legal arguments, tending to allot less importance to economic and social concerns. This was the foundation on which he built his works; he sought and found evidence to support them. Because of the fictions to which he felt bound, Randall selected that evidence over all other possibilities.

We can read in Randall's book a recital of instances—honestly researched—that do suggest fraud and misuse of funds during the first two years after the war. But Randall's book is more conspicuous for evidence it omits. We find no evidence that would mitigate or contradict his original expectations. There is no suggestion that "carpetbaggers," some of whom were black, came south with capital to establish legitimate enterprises, no instances to show that corruption was rife before and after the period he designates as the bleak period of Negro rule. Randall says nothing of the construction of necessary roads, bridges, and buildings. We find no evidence differentiating states according to local patterns.

We find no evidence to suggest that during Reconstruction, legislators, officers of the Freedmen's Bureau, schoolteachers, and Negroes themselves sought to bring justice to the South and its people; we find no evidence to suggest that they attempted to elevate human rights. Randall makes no acknowledgment of their charitable attitude toward participation of former Confederates after the Civil War.[30] Later historians, who began with different fictions, would find that information. Randall did state at one point that he sympathized with President Andrew Johnson rather than with the "Radical Republicans." Randall noted in his work on Orville Hickerson Browning that by the time he worked on his book on Reconstruction, he had come to "a sense of revolution, of social unrest and of threatening anarchy." For someone who believed, as Randall did, that salvation can be achieved through rigid constitutional controls, such a condition of anarchy would loom as the ultimate horror.

Randall believed the fiction that Negro militias were among the worst trials forced upon the South; although this fiction conveyed a perception still psychologically valid for many southerners, it ignored logistics. Most troops, white and black, were withdrawn from southern soil very soon after the last battles of the war. But, quoting Fleming, Randall stressed that groups of Negro troops became "murderous mobs." They displayed a "defiance born of the belief 'that crimes committed . . . as a mob . . . [would] not subject them to . . . punishment.'" Randall related that one detachment "dashed into an Arkansas town and galloped about, cursing, threatening, raiding a grocery store and breaking into a jail."[31]

Even as students at far corners of the nation were studying *The Civil War and Reconstruction,* an Indiana-born journalist reinforced Randall's views. Born in 1878 in Whitestown, Indiana, Claude G. Bowers never went to college. Instead he went to Indianapolis, where at 17 he launched a journalistic career grounded in the Democratic Party; all his life, he felt particularly partial to old-line white southern Democrats. They were misunderstood as "unreconstructed" holdouts; they were instead heroic, virtuous guardians of the best of national values, prevented by "power-hungry, rapacious, vengeful leaders of the Republican Party" from restoring order to their ruined homeland.[32]

Bowers thought of his most famous book, *The Tragic Era: The Revolution after Lincoln,* as a history. It could more accurately be described as a novel, for it contained many errors of evidence, by then conspicuous, in detailing events of the Reconstruction. It became a very popular novel. Bowers never received training in historical techniques, although had he received training, the fictions from which his work emanated might scarcely have changed. His sources for this book and others were limited to documents supplied by the Daughters of the Confederacy. He did study scores of their intimate family letters and diaries, some written by young girls. He believed that these materials threw "a white light on the actual living and thinking of the people." He thought that "reading these, I really lived as a contemporary through those tragic days." His biographer wrote that "*The Tragic Era* lets readers experience problems and feelings of outraged helplessness and homelessness of inhabitants of the postbellum South."

But it is clear that this source did not include the feelings or dire circumstances of most people, especially poor white people and black people, of the South. Because of his books and articles, Bowers became a favorite son of the Democratic Party, oriented as it was toward the views of southern Democrats. Throughout his political-journalistic career he championed living and dead heroes of the solid southern Democratic Party. In them, he discovered no contradictions, no flaws. Over the course of his lifetime, he experienced little modification or change in the fictions he brought to his work as a 17-year-old in Indiana. To the end of his days, he celebrated—flamboyantly, imaginatively, melodramatically—those particular old-line southern Democrats on whom he built his career. Because of its pretension and its wide influence, and even though he wrote later than historians of the Dunning School, we can place Bowers's *The Tragic Era* among stories from the first three groupings of historians; he became an enthusiastic latter-day champion in the popular press of many of their ideas.

Yet before Bowers and even as the first historians of Dunning-like persuasion were producing their books, another perspective arose. It was powered by a different set of fictions. The black historian William Edgar Burghardt DuBois was certainly one of the first to take a sweepingly different view of events of the middle 1860s. How did the DuBois interpretations arise and materialize?

DuBois was born in the little town of Great Barrington, Massachusetts, on February 23, 1868. According to his own memories, his family stayed pretty much among themselves and their relatives. Yet as a black child and as a young person, he seems to have known the protection of the residents of Great Barrington—perhaps because of his outstanding scholarly aptitude, perhaps because of his poetic nature. He always led his class; he was the youngest member and the only non-white member. He delivered the high school commencement address. He wrote beautifully—so beautifully that church people of Great Barrington procured him a scholarship at Fisk University in Nashville, Tennessee.

DuBois entered Fisk as a sophomore in the fall of 1885. For the young man, this proved a dramatic awakening; it was the first time he had lived among people of darker complexions, people like himself. "Suddenly," he wrote, "I am in a Negro world where all the people, except the teachers (and the teachers, too, in thought and action) belong to this colored world, and the world was almost complete. We acted and thought as people belonging to this group and I got the idea that my work was in that group."

Never till then had DuBois realized the meaning of living, as he had lived, in a segregated world; never had he known the wonder of Negro spirituals; never had he felt he lived among people as beautiful as the students and teachers he knew at Fisk. From the first he became one of them, one of their leaders.[33] He had relished the classes that were conducted according to New England traditions and taught for the most part by white teachers. But he loved best the new experience of being with his black people. In the summertime he taught in back-country black schools in Tennessee.

Because of his New England background, DuBois could say "I had always thought as a boy that I was going to Harvard." Yet when he did find himself at Harvard in 1890, first to complete his bachelor's degree and then as a graduate student, he noted that "I never felt myself to be a Harvard man as I had felt myself a Fisk man." He avoided seeking contact with white students. "If they wanted to know me," he wrote, "the effort would have to be on their part."[34] He received his bachelor's degree from Harvard, with distinction, in 1890. He was one of six commencement speakers in a graduating class of 281 students.

One way and another DuBois spent two graduate years at Harvard on fellowships. He received a master's degree in the fall of 1892, then departed for a year in Germany. "That was a time," he wrote, "when every American who wanted to get a real position in a University had to go to Germany to get his degree." He wrote that in Germany "I had a tremendous new experience. For the first time in my life, I was just a human being and not a particular kind of human being."[35] For DuBois, this experience proved yet another dimension. But because he had only enough money for two semesters at the German university, he couldn't meet qualifications for the degree he had earned. It was conferred some seventy years later when the University of Berlin reviewed his records.

In 1901, DuBois published *The Souls of Black Folk,* a preview of fictions that would characterize his life. This book set forth opposite views to those that were becoming an academic and political party line. In unforgettable language DuBois affirmed that Negroes are in no way inferiors, that their rights are human rights, that their rights are the rights of citizens, that they are protected by the Constitution. This book became his manifesto. It set the fictions he would champion in a long career. This early, DuBois realized that "the question of slavery was the real cause" of the Civil War as it was of the painful struggles of the Reconstruction, that the question of slavery was inextricably bound with questions of constitutional structure.

His first history, his dissertation, was titled "The Suppression of the African Slave-Trade to the United States of America, 1638–1870." Subsequently, DuBois produced some twenty volumes and many articles and editorials. His *Black Reconstruction* displayed a meticulous scholarship. It told stories about the sequel to the Civil War, stories taken from a careful collection of neglected evidence and an entirely different orientation. It blazed a trail many white and black historians followed.

In a discussion, DuBois quoted *Reconstruction and the Constitution* by John W. Burgess, one of the historians affiliated with the Dunning seminars: "It was a great wrong," Burgess had said, "to put the white race of the South under the domination of the Negro race. A black skin means membership in a race of men which has never of itself succeeded in subjecting passion to reason; has never, therefore, created any civilization of any kind."

DuBois believed and showed that the Negro race never dominated the white race during the two years of congressional Reconstruction. He believed that the whole body of information "concerning what Negroes actually did . . . is masked in such a cloud of charges, exaggeration and biased testimony . . . that most students . . . have simply repeated . . . all the current legends of black buffoons in legislature, golden spittoons for field hands, bribery and extravagance on an unheard-of scale."

Because of the way he perceived his origins, that is, his experience in living in three dimensions—among white people, then among black people, then among people where color was not an apparent consideration—and because of his moral conclusions, DuBois constructed different fictions. He looked at records differently. His research began with records theretofore ignored; for

DuBois, that research affirmed his suspicions. DuBois saw that the Burgess view—and the stories arising from it—conveyed woefully incomplete and therefore skewed pictures. Until that time, historians had bypassed most of the evidence DuBois produced.

Up to the time of the Burgess book, DuBois wrote, we had seen only histories written "for purposes of propaganda." This was to say that the premises—the fictions—on which the books had been written were inadvisedly taken. Although DuBois finally turned toward Marxism, and although that view underpinned his own conclusions, he began a study of legislative procedures in South Carolina and he documented extensively his belief that "there was not a single reform movement, a single step toward protest, a single experiment for betterment in which Negroes were not found in varying numbers."

He did note corruption in the state at the time of the brief but effective Negro participation in South Carolina, but he also noted greater corruption before and after that time; he did this while pointing out that "the responsibility of Negroes for the government of South Carolina in Reconstruction was necessarily limited." Negroes did, he said, help choose officials and they did furnish a large number of the legislators. That didn't change the power structure. It remained in the hands of whites, who were "Northerners who had come South as officers or officials or to invest money, or to appeal to native Southerners, both aristocrats and poor whites, who had undertaken to guide the Negro vote." Despite the towering influence of Dunning-type historians, despite the Marxist trend in his own thoughts, the DuBois book brought a strong voice to directions of Reconstruction histories.[36]

For the rest of his long, productive life, DuBois championed the beliefs that crystallized during his student days and during his young manhood. Though he believed that the nation never accepted fictions he thought desirable and just, his work sparked a cataclysm of investigation and the surfacing of interpretations unthinkable in the climate that earlier prevailed.

DuBois grew increasingly militant. He deplored the relegation of Negroes to lesser opportunities. For many years, he taught and wrote; he edited *The Crisis,* a black newspaper that gained a wide currency as it defended his demands for opportunities for African Americans. He expanded his views: "The problem of the twentieth century," DuBois had written, "is the problem of the color line—the relation of the darker to the lighter races of men in Asia and Africa, in America and the islands of the sea."[37] Though the fictions that powered his work failed to gain wide acceptance in white circles, they indelibly influenced thinking and planning in black communities. In the end, it became impossible to neglect international dimensions DuBois first pointed out.

It is easy to understand how DuBois developed the fictions and the stands for which, after his lifetime, he is more honored than when he lived. Here was a brilliant thinker from New England, a seemingly fearless black intellectual driven to expose the cruelties of racial oppression in his native America. We are perhaps less capable of easily understanding how C. Vann Woodward, another native Southerner, a white man, adopted fictions that support, contain, and broaden much of the work DuBois and others have started.

Living with and in and through the oldest, most established tenets of the South itself, C. Vann Woodward knew his historical-literary terrain. He was born in 1908 in Vanndale, Arkansas, to a father from Tennessee and a mother descended from an English family of early North Carolina settlers. He grew up in Morrilton, Arkansas. There his father became superintendent of public schools; there he experienced southern living, the achievements as well as the racial customs, the taboos, the excesses of the Ku Klux Klan. There from his Methodist parents he learned of the existence of southern liberals and of their proud traditions.

Through his college years at Henderson-Brown and then at Emory, Woodward also learned the wisdom of a galaxy of writers, the stars of the southern literary renaissance. He read widely in works of William Faulkner and Katherine Ann Porter. He knew the views of the southern agrarians represented in their manifesto: "I'll take my stand." He spent time in the company of Robert Penn Warren and Eudora Welty, reading their works. Years later he wrote with a bittersweet feeling of loss about "the Southern literary awakening that had lighted the national skies in the [1880s]."[38] He seems to have absorbed views of the modern individual—not as a helpless, estranged human but as a vigorous, thinking, feeling person likely to influence and be influenced by surroundings yet able to choose a course. It is not surprising that, in words of biographer Elizabeth Muhlenfeld, Woodward came to see his "beloved" South as "a fertile microcosm of the human experience."[39]

Nor is it surprising that Woodward's positions came to reflect interconnected, interwoven complexities that would not yield to simple interpretation. The "twilight zone that lies between living memory and written history is one of the favorite breeding places of mythology," he wrote in the preface to the first edition of his legendary *Strange Career of Jim Crow*. In this book, Woodward explored intricacies of white supremacy laws as they had never been explored.

As he grew up, Woodward observed the ominous, selfish, and wicked aspects of human nature, and his parents saw to it that he met and could observe some of the southern liberals they knew. These included his uncle Comer M. Woodward, a professor of sociology; his neighbor, Rupert B. Vance, also a sociologist; and another neighbor, Howard W. Odum, a professor at the University of North Carolina. Woodward himself taught English and traveled to France, Germany, and Russia. There he perceived that Russian scholars saw the turbulent state of race relations as a central theme of the American experience. On his return, he taught English again in Atlanta. There he made many friends, among them prominent black members of the Atlanta community. He came to know Will W. Alexander, Glenn Rainey, and Angelo Herndon.

With the onset of the Great Depression, he lost his teaching job. As the Depression lengthened in the 1930s, he worked briefly on a farm survey for the Works Progress Administration. Here he began his pivotal biography of an agrarian rebel, Tom Watson. From this experience, Woodward came to the study of history as a life career. In taking his advanced degrees, he studied with Howard K. Beale, famed author of *The Critical Year.* He came to know writers Gertrude Stein and Paul Green. He met publisher William T. Couch.

After that he went to teach at the University of Florida in Gainesville. There his own fictions began to display definite form. There important interpretations of southern history emerged. He came to understand that the present never duplicates the past but that respecting lessons of the past can yield dividends. Woodward saw and documented that the key to understanding South and North after the Civil War could be found in their collaboration, not in tussles between plantation life and industrial expansion. He saw a whole nation confronted with struggles within a society deeply in agreement about the pursuit of industrial goals. He saw that the rise of a "redeemer" elite in the old South proceeded from views and fictions that were harmonious with those of industrial tycoons of the not-so-new North. In *Reunion and Reaction: The Compromise of 1877 and the Era of Reconstruction* as well as in *Origins of the New South, 1877–1914,* he retrieved and related in minute detail the neglected events of this merging philosophy.

The fictions he brought to his works expressed a tragic understanding of human life, of the fatal minor and major weaknesses all human beings inherit. Living and working as he did in the South, it was almost inevitable that this historian would come to a lifelong involvement with relations between the races, in daily contacts and in writing.

A most arresting feature of Woodward's histories is the honesty with which his beliefs allow him to portray contradictions that permeated the lives of his subjects. He neither ignores nor denies those contradictions. In the South, he finds style, impressive organization, political expertise, concern for justice, intellectual excellence. At the same time, he finds a lust for power, cruelty, greed, betrayal, and exploitation of the less powerful, black and white. While his own concern for fairness, for civil rights, for justice in relations between the races emerges in all the fictions on which his work is founded, it does not prevent his dealing with treachery and moral stagnation wherever he finds it. "Capitalism," he thought, "makes brothers of us all."

With these perspectives, Woodward looked at whole societies and studied how they influenced and were influenced by those who lived in them. These perspectives formed the fictions Woodward brought to his histories. They exemplified a many-faceted approach to writing histories, an awareness of complexities in fictions of white and black southerners as well as in those of northerners.

John Hope Franklin lived with racial discrimination almost from the moment of his birth on January 2, 1915. Some of his ancestors were Indians; his grandfather was a freed slave. In the little black town of Rentiesville, Oklahoma, his father, Buck Colbert Franklin, was the first African-American lawyer in the area then known as Oklahoma Territory. Franklin's father had also served as a justice of the peace and as postmaster, and he had operated a farm. His dominant concern seems to have been building a community that would reward its inhabitants. Once Buck Colbert Franklin traveled with his client to Shreveport, Louisiana, for a trial. When the case was called, the young lawyer stood. "Why are you standing?" asked the judge. On being told that he was representing his client, the judge ordered the young lawyer to leave the courtroom. "No nigger will represent anyone in my court!" he proclaimed.[40]

For many reasons, among them religious strife and resentment of talents, it became impossible for African Americans to make a decent living in Rentiesville. Franklin's parents decided to focus their hopes on the nearby city of Tulsa. Their hopes soon clouded over. On her way with her young children to shop in the nearby county seat at Chacota, John Hope's mother, a teacher, flagged the train for the 6-mile journey. As it happened, the family got on a coach designated for whites only. When the conductor ordered the family to move, Mollie Franklin refused. They were put off the train and obliged to walk back through the woods to Rentiesville. John Hope told his mother he felt sorry. You have nothing to be sorry about, she replied, unless you feel sorry for those who did this. It had become clear that small black towns and small black schools were never going to provide an antidote to racial wrongs. But Tulsa still seemed a magnetic city.

When John Hope was a young boy in 1921, a black man had accidentally stepped on a white woman's toe in an elevator. There were rumors of harassment. The incident escalated into charges of sexual assault; it precipitated three days of fighting, bombing, and torching of property. Fearful of competition from blacks in north Tulsa, whites went on a rampage. They destroyed buildings, killed 100 black people, and even went so far as to drop dynamite from a plane. In John Hope Franklin's words, "it became tragically clear that the destruction was for nothing." The "offender" was tried and acquitted—although not before the whole miserable affair had caused a summer of rioting.

That incident and the riots which followed were scarcely unique. It turned out that the first episodes became only one chapter in a summer of riots and burnings. A fire destroyed the Franklin home. It took years to rebuild it. John Hope's father and his law associates opened their office in a tent.[41]

As an adolescent and as a young man, Franklin frequently felt the stings of racial discrimination. He was only allowed to attend the Booker T. Washington high school for black students. Languages were not taught in that school, which offered largely vocational courses. His parents encouraged him in his studies. But they refused to go to the opera in Tulsa because of segregation. Although he did go to the opera, John Hope lived with doubts about his own participation in segregated events.

He expected to use Fisk University as a launching pad for a career in law. But he changed his mind when he became fascinated with American history in the class of Theodore Currier, a young white professor. This dedicated teacher assured John Hope that a lack of money was not going to prevent his going to graduate school. On his own credit, Currier borrowed the $500 needed for tuition at Harvard University. John Hope never lived in Harvard dormitories. Even so, he encountered racial prejudice. He had learned to expect it. But he did not expect to encounter the virulent anti-Semitism he saw for the first time. Despite this deplorable state of affairs, he completed his doctorate in 1941.[42]

It would have been impossible for a young Negro boy who witnessed the events of John Hope's childhood and whose family found themselves at the center of racial turmoil to avoid an enormous sense of injury and a conviction that racial concerns are central to American life. In the latter belief, John Hope stood in eminent company. From the beginning, American statesmen shared this realization, though they shared none of the humiliations it caused.

Without doubt, the circumstances of Franklin's early life played powerfully into fictions he adopted for writing his histories. Nor did circumstances change. When he volunteered for service in the United States Navy in 1942, bringing every office skill and his new Ph.D., he was refused with the remark that everything was "O.K." but he was "the wrong color."[43] While traveling across the United States at the age of 38, he and his family found it impossible to rent a motel room for the night. A woman in Michigan bluntly stated that she didn't "take blacks."[44] The family had to cross the border to Canada.

Franklin became the author or editor of twenty books and more than 100 articles. His *From Slavery to Freedom: A History of African Americans* traces the story of African Americans. It has gone through seven editions and has become a classic text, a text that by the end of the twentieth century exerted a wide and powerful influence over students of American history. Though other scholars had written about the Negro in this country, Franklin gave black people and white people their intertwined story in a way that enabled them to hear it. In the preface to the first edition, he enunciated his awareness not only of his own background—his own circumstances—but of the relation of the Negro to "'historical forces' that are all pervasive and that cut through the most rigid barriers of race and caste."[45]

Nor did early experiences or more recent assessments recede from John Hope Franklin's horizons when it came to focusing his own interpretations

John Hope Franklin

and to writing his histories. These considerations figured in when it came to writing the books he most wanted to do, *The Militant South* and *Reconstruction after the Civil War,* and his favorite, a biography of the first American black historian, *George Washington Williams.*

"The way I look at problems is to try to see if the past teaches us anything," he said in a 1997 interview.[46] Though customarily he took strong stands in matters of public concern, Franklin refrained from writing or speaking in an adversarial mode. He preferred to find and present the available evidence.

This philosophy formed the core of fictions Franklin constructed and brought to his work. It is difficult to understand from Franklin's early experience how he avoided the bitterness and sustained militancy evident in the DuBois fictions. Yet his books reach more readers than those of all the Dunning historians put together; his books have become the expression of his choices, unveiling as they do his testament not only to his own people but also to the life of the nation.

He was asked to chair President Clinton's commission to set an agenda for racial priorities in the twenty-first century. "I hope it will turn the corner for this nation once and for all with respect to the question of race," he said of his appointment. He didn't expect to come out with a perfect agenda; not long before the presidential appointment, he had echoed for the twenty-first century the famous DuBois insight that "the problem of the twentieth century is the problem of the color line."[47] But Franklin hoped that "we can look back and say this was the deciding moment, this was the watershed."[48] Commenting on his projects, and on the commission and its mission, Franklin noted that "world attention has been focused on the issue of race as never before. . . . This very scrutiny has had a most salutary effect."[49]

His compatriot Kenneth Stampp also earned his doctorate in 1941. Born in 1912 in Milwaukee, Wisconsin, in the heart of mid-America, Stampp got his education during the devastating 1930s, the years of the Great Depression. He began his professional life as the nation began its economic recovery.

But many influences that were to contribute heavily to this historian's fictions had left their mark. It is said that as a boy, Kenneth knew his mind, that he informed his young associates in the fifth grade that he intended to become a history teacher. Surely it would have been unusual to grow up in the 1930s in that part of the world without knowing the pains and the deprivations that come with deep economic depression. But he attended the University of Wisconsin, where he received his bachelor's degree in 1935. He took a minor in economics, and he gave serious consideration to a legal career. His biographer John G. Sproat has suggested that he was strongly influenced both by the socialist-pacifist elements of his home community and the then-current economic determinism of historian Charles A. Beard. As a young man, Stampp probably considered himself a New Deal liberal.

But an association with another scholar seems to have contributed decisively to Stampp's intellectual development. William Best Hesseltine made Stampp aware of the importance of the history of the South. Stampp took his doctorate under Hesseltine's direction, then began his teaching career at the University of Maryland in 1942. There he met historians Richard Hofstadter and Frank Freidel and economist C. Wright Mills. With this distinguished galaxy Stampp shared his first teaching and writing years, the years when the fictions that would influence his work crystallized.

In 1946, he moved to the University of California in Berkeley as an assistant professor. In his first book, Kenneth Stampp noted that he had passed too slightly over the "racist political rhetoric" of the North, especially that of the "Peace Democrats." He questioned his own former points of view: He wondered if "even the best methodology will ever transcend our limitations of vision and produce definitive historical works."[50]

To his understanding of the theme of economic issues, Stampp added problems of racism as a major concern; these concerns mingled in constructing his fictions. He focused at once on the reasons civil war had become inevitable. In *And the War Came: The North and the Secession Crisis,* he saw that as long as southern owners persisted in their chattel slavery and northern politicians persisted in their special interests, there could have been no way to avoid collision.

Stampp confronted the views of Ulrich B. Phillips, John C. Calhoun, and George Fitzhugh that legal slavery could ever have been benevolent. He argued that at best there was pragmatic accommodation on most plantations and that just beneath the surface lay great social tension. As he progressed in his career, Stampp included dimensions of ever greater historical complexity. He treated issues of civil rights and questions of race relations in advance of the struggles over these issues on his own campus at Berkeley during the 1960s. These issues proved decisive in the formation of beliefs Stampp brought to his most mature contributions.

Sensitively, Stampp realized that each historian is a product of the times and the influences that sweep over historians and others alike. He seems to have been amused when someone labeled him a "neo-abolitionist." "To understand fully the perceptions of each historian on these highly subjective questions," he wrote, "one must understand the historian himself." He believed that in any generalization, we impose our own perceptions on evidence that at best can be only "fragmentary." Stampp never denied that his own books reflected discernible biases. He probably would have enjoyed the witticism that "I am an open man, open to all good prejudices."

According to Kenneth Stampp, there could have been no one "slave personality." Slave personalities were "complex matters." He took particular umbrage with a work called *Time on the Cross* by Robert Fogel and Stanley Engerman. By attempting to reduce the existence of black people to mathematical statistics, these authors, he thought, took away the whole human complexity of slave life before and after the war. Cliometrics, the social mathematics in which some writers placed their faith, ignored "the untidy world of reality."

Stampp realized that the whole reality of the Reconstruction period must be retrieved, that public perception of that troublesome time had become woefully simplistic. He offered his *The Era of Reconstruction* more as a revision and a correction and a summation than as a work that looked to the future. Yet for Stampp there were no stark extremes. No one ever came off as entirely virtuous or entirely evil. There was, however, a mystique which must be dispelled: The South did not remain physically or psychically incapacitated. Its institutions were not defiled, nor was its land permanently occupied and decimated. Nor did uncivilized, ignorant Negroes seek unspeakable revenge. Nor was it true that descendants of plantation owners drove out the northern invaders—

carpetbaggers—in a gallant rescue operation, thus "redeeming" the southern states.

In both *The Peculiar Institution: Slavery in the Ante-bellum South* and *The Road to Appomattox*, Stampp showed that many in the South had long cherished doubts about the morality of human slavery. Summarizing his understanding of the enormous complexity of individuals and the histories they create as well as his understanding of the Civil War and of the Reconstruction period, Stampp wrote, "If it was worth four years of war to save the union, it was worth a few years of radical reconstruction to give the American Negro the ultimate promise of equal civil and political rights."[51] From these books and these statements, Kenneth Stampp's fictions appear: We now see a white historian offering fictions exactly opposite to those of earlier historians whose fictions had informed the beliefs of much of the nation.

Since Kenneth Stampp, C. Vann Woodward, John Hope Franklin, and W. E. B. DuBois wrote their histories to disavow, indeed to discredit, much of the former common understanding of Reconstruction, many historians have brought their fictions and their training to bear upon that seminal era. It isn't possible to name them all or to examine their many backgrounds. No doubt some are as complex as the histories they have conceived. I feel no question, however, that they have also brought strong commitments—well-developed personal fictions—to their studies and their stories.

Some have brought innovative techniques as well as new sensitivities. Certain trends are discernible in the work of Joel Williamson, Willie Lee Rose, Winthrop Jordan, Ann Firor Scott, Herbert Gutman, Eugene Genovese, James McPherson, Lawrence Levine, John Blassingame, and Leon Litwack. In the stories these historians tell, we see a deep concern for details of Negro attitudes, contributions, and needs and a deep concern to understand the interactions of black and white communities. We also see a deeper understanding of white attitudes. Other historians offer in-depth observations of geographic differences in areas heretofore neglected and biographical studies of figures who have been little appreciated.

With these few considerations from the abundant outpourings of historians of the second structuring of the United States, the Reconstruction, I hope to have raised a possibility: The fictions historians bring to the stories they tell about our past definitively influence their work and our convictions. Those stories influence our acts, sometimes unto many generations. No writer or reader can afford to ignore this probability. As a priority, historians may, as some have demonstrated, come to realize not only where they come from but also where they are taking their nation and the peoples of the world.

——4
From Mormon Polygamy to
American Monogamy
Shifting Fictions in the Life of a Society

In nineteenth-century Utah, fiction-stories about women's and men's roles within the patriarchal system became central, especially in the shift among Mormons from polygamy to monogamy. The fiction-stories were planned, institutionalized, and socially developed. What fictions, what stories from what agencies opened doors to such profound changes—from original monogamy to official polygamy then back to monogamy? How and in what circumstances did the changes occur? What part did theocratic organization take in determining the reach of the supporting fictions and the extent of the dislocations? Did state and religion merge or did they separate as fiction-loyalties shifted? Which catalysts played decisive roles in activating particular stories? Which individuals bestrode which forces? What were the origins, what were the complexities, what were the unexpected repercussions?

Forces from without and within the Mormon power structure combined to produce fictions that empowered the shift from American monogamy to Mormon polygamy then back to American monogamy. The external force was democracy; it provided space for ideas and space for styles of living that led to polygamy. Yet the fiction of monogamy was entrenched in the laws and polity of democracy. In a jagged evolutionary sweep, it unfolded a vision of women's and children's needs. The internal forces were psychic commitments of a quality leading to spiritual discomforts; among such discomforts, many Mormon women felt a need for warm, mutually nourishing, dependable interactions. Many felt a yearning to believe that the religious assurances of their church merited trust.

Finally, with polygamy, the dominating fictions increased economic hardships for women and for children. Both forces precipitated dissatisfaction with certain fundamental tenets of the new Mormon theocracy. Taken together, these forces—external democratic developments and internal spiritual and economic discomforts—reveal the reach of fictions of the Mormon theocracy. Taken together, these forces illuminate the complexity of motivations as well as the origins of fictions. They illustrate the advent of agencies. The forty years during which polygamy was the official policy of the Mormons highlight the influence of the shifting marriage customs over every detail of life in this society.

In this case, marriage customs also demonstrate that gender stands, as it has always stood, at the center of social construction. Gender is the mediator of social comfort, and it supplies the fountainhead for an ultimate political power. Writing to the *Deseret News* in 1885, a Mormon "Old Timer" put that matter precisely: Polygamy, he wrote, "is the very keystone of our faith, and is so closely interwoven into everything that pertains to our religion, that to tear it asunder and cast it away would involve the entire structure."[1]

The "Old Timer's" summary could have characterized the polygamous belief systems in theocracies of other societies, ancient and modern, in disparate areas of the world. It could have expressed philosophies that support all patriarchal systems. Fictions of an intentional, agented kind shaped such systems, just as such systems entrenched themselves by shaping the fictions. Yet how could Mormon polygamy have happened in the mid-1800s in democratic America, constructed as it was on the fictions necessary to monogamous practice? Did the appearance of polygamy express a recurrence of a centuries-long, Old World custom that legitimized plural marriages for men? Did it license male irresponsibility? As the latest of several attempts to institute polygamy in the western world, did it threaten democratic development?[2]

At its beginning in the 1830s, Mormon theology relied on two ideas: the authenticity of revelations and the rectitude of a return to ancient beliefs and ancient customs. At that time, the time of the Second Great Awakening, a return to certain long-honored religious and cultural ideas frequently surfaced among sectarians.[3] Many communitarians also shared the discontents and the millennial beliefs of the Mormons.

But in Mormonism, this return became entrenched after the 1830s by asserting the divinity of continuous, even if conflicting, revelations and by reinstitutionalizing Old Testament customs. So powerful is the yearning to find salvation from the alien immensity of the universe, so intense is the desire to achieve everlasting life among loved ones, that then, as now, as from time immemorial, many hungered for stability and any credible assurance of physical and spiritual comfort.

To those who felt distraught by the pressures of daily life and by the swirling confusions of the new democracy, the world of the early 1800s appeared to be a sea of social ferment. People responded to the lure of the West. Populations shifted. Many Americans found themselves living in environments so unyielding as to invite religious tranquilizers; environments so meager, so uncertain, so contentious as to nourish religious catalysts. A folklore offering mystic solutions for every deprivation arose on farms and in villages. From the hills of Vermont to western New York, in western sections of the southern states and westward toward Ohio, Illinois, and Missouri, revivals, magical spells, rituals, peep stones,[4] rabbits' feet, witch-hazel rods for divining, and the like characterized the climate of many communities.

The conflicted, emotion-laden world of this America became a cauldron of religious fervors. Echoing the Puritan preachers of Massachusetts Bay in their contests with dissenters Ann Hutchinson and Roger Williams, echoing in variable timbres Elias Smith in Vermont, John Samuel Thompson in Palmyra, New York, and many others, the evangelist Charles G. Finney wrote *Memoirs*.[5] By 1876, he noted widespread conversions from his preaching even as he deplored the transient nature of the conversions.[6] Figures such as Jemima Wilkinson, William Miller, and John Humphrey Noyes preached, attempted miracles, planned communities, and prepared for the millennium when Jesus would come again and Bible communism would prevail among their followers. In New York City, the prophet Matthias proclaimed that he had come to redeem the world. In southern Ohio, the self-styled "Leatherwood God" Dylkes announced his own divinity and stirred his congregation to loud declarations of devotion.[7]

There were tempests of Jacksonian democracy that involved the settled East and the evolving West; there were demands for a democracy of the "common man." There were economic depressions.[8] In the wake of unsettled monetary policies, many families experienced financial woes and geographic relocations.[9] Yet despite widespread religious turmoil, despite relocations, despite the searching for magical solutions, the rationalist Enlightenment dream of the eighteenth-century philosophers lingered. That dream expressed a longing for order, for spiritual and social security in life on earth. It rendered listeners vulnerable to promises, especially promises that projected programs and offered salvation.

In such a climate, around the year 1820, Joseph Smith, a robust, ambitious, rather shrewd, uncommonly gifted farm youth, descended from a mountain near the family land. This boy had been born to Joseph and Lucy Mack Smith in 1805 in Sharon, Vermont. Unable to make ends meet, the Smith family had moved from New England to the heart of the "burned-over" district of western New York.[10] Because speculators held "western" lands at that time, the Smiths paid a high price for their uncleared farm; they were compelled to carry a crippling mortgage.

They settled in Palmyra, New York. Many local inhabitants believed that thousands of years before the 1820s, their area had seen a massacre of titanic proportions and that the great mounds of their area marked burial places of a dimly remembered people. Obediah Dogberry, editor of the *Palmyra Register,* reported that visitors as credible as New York governor DeWitt Clinton reflected on the probable origins of such a people.[11] Since vestiges of long-deserted, ancient strongholds stood along the edges of rivers and since remarkably beautiful artifacts turned up from time to time, speculators wondered about the superior quality of the forgotten civilization. No one living near Palmyra could have escaped hearing the stories and the speculations.

In an apparently artless biography, Joseph's mother Lucy Mack Smith recalled that as a teenager her son loved to tell stories about such long-ago struggles. On occasional evenings, she wrote, "He would give us some of the most amusing recitals that could be imagined. He would describe the ancient inhabitants of this continent, their dress, mode of traveling, and the animals upon which they rode; their cities, their buildings, with every particular; their mode of warfare; and also their religious worship. This he would do with so much ease, seemingly, as if he had spent his whole life with them."[12] In western New York, out of a life of migration and poverty, digging and drudgery, out of the scriptural searchings of his hard-pressed family, out of his own fantasy, the young Joseph perceived the spell his stories could spin. He also perceived the power religious assurances exert over a people.

Joseph was energetic, earthy, lightly educated but immensely talented and imaginative; Joseph's personality thus developed from an uncertain present as well as from deep mystical and religious groundings. Yet some who watched him grow up remembered him as an easy-going, engaging boy, well known for the embroidered tales he told. Daniel Hendrix, a nearby farmer, remembered that Joe had been "the most ragged, lazy fellow in the place and that is saying a good deal. . . . I can see him now . . . with his torn and patched trousers held to his form by a pair of suspenders made out of sheeting, with his calico shirt as dirty and black as the earth and his uncombed hair sticking through the holes in his battered hat . . . yet Joe had a jovial, easy, don't care way about him that made him a lot of warm friends. . . . I never saw so ignorant a man as Joe was to have such a fertile imagination. He never could tell a common occurrence in his daily life without embellishing the story with his imagination."[13] As he became a little older, Joseph Smith gained confidence that he could indeed use his charisma to influence those about him.

Realizing the desperation of the farmers in the hills, realizing their susceptibility to tales of buried gold, he became a treasure-seeker and soon found employment as a "gold-digger," a "diviner"; he spent much time in the mountains. At about 14 he began to experience visions of a mystical nature. He learned from a vision of two personages that he took to be the Father and the Son that existing churches were all wrong. In one of his later descriptions of this event, Joseph wrote,

> While fervently engaged in supplication my mind was taken away from the objects with which I was surrounded, and I was enwrapped in a heavenly vision and saw two glorious personages who exactly resembled each other in features, and likeness, surrounded with a brilliant light which eclipsed the sun at noon day. They told me that all religious denominations were believing in incorrect doctrines, and that none of them was acknowledged of God as his church and kingdom. And I was expressly commanded to "go not after them" at the same

The Young Joseph Smith. *Courtesy Utah State Historical Society.*

time receiving a promise that the fullness of the gospel should at some time be made known unto me.[14]

In another foray into the mountains, Joseph discovered a seerstone that possessed magical powers for finding water wells and for making known the locations of desired objects.[15] Joseph's tales of such visions and such artifacts impressed listeners; up until then, he had lived by grubbing on the land for credulous farmers who would pay him small amounts or by digging in the mountains on his own for buried treasures. Perhaps Joseph once believed that magical powers were invested in particular artifacts. As his life progressed, many early beliefs faded, however, while his preoccupation with immediate desires and metaphysical concepts increased. Still, some of his artifacts and his visions seem to have become centers of the fiction-structure of his personality.

Like a number of others at this time in this climate, Smith also experienced revelations, and soon, evangelistic revelations.[16] He felt the people's need for a prophet to tell them God's plans for the American people. Smith came to believe that he was such a prophet, that he was chosen by God. Visions and revelations from God grew more central to his development. At a later time in his life, he gave an account of another occasion when he had been "caught away" into a vision:

> The heavens were opened upon us, and I beheld the celestial kingdom of God, and the glory thereof, whether in the body or out I cannot tell. I saw the transcendent beauty of the gate through which the heirs of that kingdom will enter, which was like unto circling flames of fire; also the blazing throne of God, whereon was seated the Father and the Son. I saw the beautiful streets of that kingdom, which had the appearance of being paved with gold. . . . [I] marveled how it was that [Adam and Abraham] had obtained an inheritance in that kingdom, seeing that [they] had departed this life before the Lord had set his hand to gather Israel the second time.[17]

According to some accounts, Joseph experienced on one of his ventures into the mountains the most compelling of his visions: A voice directed him to carry from the mountain plates he had found hidden in the ground by the use of his peep stone. An angel appeared in a flood of white light to caution him to wait until he should prove worthy and then to guard the plates for God's purposes. The plates have become known as the engraved golden tablets on which were inscribed, in characters indecipherable to all but the prophet, the messages from God.[18]

In the months ahead, Smith dictated the meanings of these messages by using magic stones, sometimes called "seer" stones, or spectacles, called the Urim and Thummim.[19] His words were then recorded by Oliver Cowdery, a scribe seated on the other side of a curtained recess, or by Martin Harris, a farmer and would-be publisher, or by Smith's wife Emma.[20] For hours at a time, Smith "translated" the messages of the tablets, sitting "with his face buried in his hat wherein he had placed the seerstones."[21] Although he allowed his family members to lift the container in which he kept the plates, they never saw them; Joseph warned that to look at the plates would mean instant death. After the last words of the "translation" had been written, and after Smith had succeeded in demonstrating the authenticity of the tablets to the satisfaction of three selected followers, the angel Moroni appeared again to sweep the golden tablets and the magic stones to heaven.[22]

Subsequently, Smith and others developed from the "translation" the guide-

Oliver Cowdery, an early convert, became one of Joseph Smith's most devoted and most valued followers. *Courtesy Utah State Historical Society.*

lines by which Latter-Day Saints of a new religion were to live. The golden tablets became the Book of Mormon.[23] In rambling, often disconnected fashion, this story tells a tale of an epic power struggle between forces of civilization and forces of destruction.

The story in the Book of Mormon is set on the continent of North America; the lost tribes of Israel and the earliest American Indian tribes are its cast of characters. In a Bible-like pattern of books and chapters and verse, and in a phraseology of scriptural dimensions, the story of the Book of Mormon became a model for the latter-day incarnation Joseph envisioned. It introduced prophets, persons, and customs; among others, Nephi, son of the prophet Lehi. Nephi experienced a vision showing him the course of the next 600 years. Thus informed, Nephi left the Holy Land of Israel with his brothers and followers a few hundred years before the coming of Christ. To escape the destruction of Jerusalem by the Babylonians, Nephi and his company sailed for America. In resonance with the Old Testament story of Cain and Abel, some of the brothers and followers labored righteously in their new land. But Laman and Lemuel inclined toward evil, choosing riches and pride over obedience to the will of God.

A mighty struggle between these factions ensued. Because they had incurred God's wrath, the wicked brothers and their descendants were condemned to become red skinned. But those who followed God's precepts, those descended from the chosen of Israel, and so from Nephi, would reach lasting blessedness in heavenly kingdoms. Joseph conceived his story in classic prophetic tones and in limitless realms of suggestion and imagination. In Joseph's mind, every facet of this story lingered in dreams of glory: Joseph saw models for colonies of the righteous, models for temples, models for great cities. No idle dreamer, Joseph reached into ancient ages for models appropriate to fuel his own visions for the future, his fictions.

The guidelines for the new religion were based on this story and on continuing, enabling revelations; they were based as well on Smith's search for more ancient, more tried, more fulfilling practices, practices that would prove suitable for his purposes.[24] Smith provided a story as poignant, a vision as compelling, a poetic fiction as potent as that of any beginning of any cherished religion of the world.[25]

Smith became the prophet of this religion, the teller of this story, the agent of these fictions. He devised means to actualize them. On April 6, 1830, just eleven days after he offered the Book of Mormon for sale, Smith organized his first "Church of Christ," at Fayette, New York. In time it became the Church of Jesus Christ of the Latter-Day Saints. It took two months for membership to grow to twenty-seven, but in eight months Smith moved his church to Kirtland, Ohio; soon it numbered 100 converts.[26] In Kirtland, the doctrine of chosen-ness came into play. As historian Jan Shipps put it, this meant that the Saints were to see themselves as "citizens of an elect nation." This concept of chosen ones has characterized the thought of numerous religious groups, including that of the Massachusetts Bay Pilgrims, who came to New England just about 200 years before Smith founded his church in New York. Chosenness became a significant feature of the new religion.[27]

In the heavily scriptural climate of the times, some disheartened persons saw hope in the new religion; some saw new resources in the communitarian ethic that emerged. Everyone was to contribute as much as possible on a regular, escalating basis in return for inclusion, protection, and guidance; members were to respond selflessly to "callings" for service to the church. From the beginning, a tandem emphasis on financial and personal commitment to the church characterized the new religion.[28]

Upon moving to Kirtland, Smith and the Saints attracted some dedicated converts, among them persons who took an interest in long-term plans for the church-society.[29] Joseph especially welcomed Sidney Rigdon and his entire

Sidney Rigdon led a communitarian group in Kirtland, Ohio, then switched to Mormonism. Joseph Smith rejoiced that "The Lord has sent me this great and mighty man." *Courtesy Utah State Historical Society.*

communal-minded Kirtland following. In words of David Whitmer, a farmer Joseph had known from childhood, Joseph and his trusted early associates Oliver Cowdery and Martin Harris rejoiced because "the Lord had sent to him this great and mighty man [Rigdon] to help him in his work."[30] "Behold verily, verily I say unto my servant Sidney," Joseph himself exclaimed, "I have looked upon thee and thy works. I have heard thy prayers, and prepared thee for a greater work. Thou art blessed, for thou shalt do great things."[31]

What doctrine there was in the earliest days was primitive and millennial, for Joseph and the Saints believed that worldwide disaster was imminent and that only they would survive to inherit the earth. Some of their new converts held revival meetings, choice examples of emotional excess. Joseph Smith disliked the excesses, however.[32] His church disavowed those camps. One historian commented that "special visions were to be reserved for the Prophet and Revelator; they were not for the common herd."[33]

Over his lifetime, Smith repeatedly demonstrated that in matters of spiritual leadership he would brook no challenge. He made this explicit in the text for the most controversial of his revelations, the revelation sanctioning polygamous marriage, that of July 12, 1843: "All covenants, contracts . . . [must come from God] through the medium of mine whom I have appointed on the earth to hold this power (and I have appointed unto my servant Joseph to hold this power in the last days, and there is never but one on the earth at a time on whom this power and the keys of this priesthood are conferred)."[34] Since for Joseph spiritual leadership meant domination over worldly as well as otherworldly affairs, he would brook no challenge on any front.

On many occasions Smith experienced revelations that seem immediately related to everyday events, not only those of his church but also those of his personal life. When his young wife Emma grieved over the loss of her infant sons, it was revealed to Joseph that if the babies were entered posthumously into church membership, Emma would be reunited with them through eternity. When some of his new followers tried to establish camp meetings as undertakings of the true religion, Smith's revelation showed the meetings to be evil in inspiration. That Smith was able to convince so many of the divinity of his revelations measures the persuasive quality of his character. It reveals the sensitive insights of his leadership.

In contrast to the zeal of converts, persons outside the new communities experienced suspicions. They remained unpersuaded, often resentful. But regardless of furious repudiations, the Saints settled in several areas; regardless of savage persecutions and upheavals, or perhaps because of them, the Saints drew closer together.[35] In the eyes of many, the new religion gained credence and the stature of their leader grew as assaults escalated. Repeatedly Joseph demonstrated a capacity to weather storms from within and without his church.

Gradually Smith's apostles began to develop order in the doctrinal tenets. Sidney Rigdon and disciple Orson Pratt published a Book of Commandments in which they edited the prophet's revelations: An unshakable faith in the new religion would assure life everlasting through the priesthood given to every man; through the possibility for every man and, through him, every woman, to grow Godlike in an eternal kingdom of his own; and through the "sealing" of marriages as eternal relationships, in which the man was to provide direction. Though debates over their authoritative nature and over ways to implement these classic promises occurred within the Mormon religion, as they occurred within Islam and elsewhere, the foundation fictions prevailed.[36]

The promise that faithful men and women would reach eternal divinity characterized this religion and expressed fictions common in other religions;[37] but in the implications of its development, the promise that the faithful could become Godlike in limitless celestial estate came to distinguish Mormonism from other religions. One historian has suggested that although the new religion started as a branch of Christianity, and although it almost consciously patterned itself on the Old Testament "exodus" of the Jewish people, it became an original creation in the ancient search for spiritual comfort.[38]

All who accepted these tenets and the controlled social and economic designs for conducting earthly affairs that went with them were assured eternal exaltation in the celestial kingdom, reunion with those whose deaths brought sorrow, and for "time," that is, on earth, a life of good fellowship.[39] Not incidentally, this created fiction-story, based as it was on marital relationships, underlay the institutionalizing of Mormon beliefs.[40] It began to attract converts.

The new community soon encountered problems; many of the early converts deserted the Saints, but newcomers to the faith more than replaced them.[41] As the church grew over the next half-century, the Mormon Apostles took over the agency for the fiction. They set up a "Kingdom" on earth, a hierarchical structure of stakes and wards under bishops, the whole to be directed by the prophet-president, his counselors, a quorum of twelve apostles, and a Council of Fifty.[42] Like the structures of other fundamentalist theocracies, this structure projected no separation of ecclesiastical and non-ecclesiastical principles. In the nineteenth century, the behavior and religious loyalty of the Saints were strictly controlled by this means; this became the way of empowering the founding fictions.

With this understanding, missionaries began a quest to proselytize others.[43] We can make no mistake about it: From the start, Joseph envisioned that a global church would grow from his "restoration" of the gospel. Planned for international distribution, his own new translation of the Hebrew Bible became a project of major proportions.[44] In a charge to the Council of Twelve, Oliver Cowdery inspired members: "You are to go to nations afar off—nations that sit in darkness. . . . You must prepare your minds to bid a long farewell to Kirtland, even till the great day come. . . . All nations have a claim on you . . . You can part and meet, and meet and part again, till your heads are silvered over with age."[45]

The missionaries started in England, in the coal-mining regions. Strengthened by his status of priesthood, almost every Mormon man could also claim a title in the church: Young Mormon "elders" received "calls" to serve without remuneration or salary, with "neither purse nor scrip"; they were to support themselves by attracting converts and by founding churches. Despite few successes in England, members of the Council of Twelve and numbers of the "elders" were soon sent to Europe to further plans for building a universal church.[46]

These arrangements proved taxing, often heartbreaking, for wives in England, France, and Switzerland; they proved very strenuous for wives in Ohio who found themselves alone and responsible for their own survival and that of their children. Still, most women willingly endured grievous hardships. In the words of Fanny Stenhouse, wife of a Mormon "elder" missionary, "There were dark clouds on every side, and in moments of despondency we almost feared that they would never clear away. Yet in all this trouble, our faith remained unshaken; and even in the darkest hour of trial, we felt happy in the belief in the divinity of Mormonism."[47]

The plans for church government and civil government became indistinguishable. Tight control of personal and public activities resulted. Though a "free agency" to make choices belonged to everyone, to exercise one's free agency dissidently could, and often did, bring revocation of rewards and excommunication.[48]

Joseph felt no hesitation in ostracizing personal or doctrinal or business dissenters or those who grasped authority for themselves. W. W. Phelps joined the church in Kirtland in the early years, became a printer for the church, and was chosen for leadership in Missouri. But then he disagreed with the Council over finances. He testified against Joseph Smith in a legal trial. He was excommunicated in March 1838 and readmitted only when he begged for forgiveness.[49] In response, Joseph wrote that "believing your confession to be real and your repentance genuine, I shall be happy once again to give you the right hand of fellowship, and rejoice over the returning prodigal."[50] In most circumstances, however, expressing dissent in an altercation that Joseph might not win meant ostracism from fellowship.

Mormon women were to be included in all church undertakings and were to partake of all rewards—except hierarchical office and the holding of the priesthood.[51] This situation characterizes many religions. Here lay the most potent, the prevailing fiction in the Mormon theocracy: Only men could communicate directly with God through the priesthood, and only men could be assigned the direction of personal and public affairs.[52] In effect, we see the beginning of a powerful and male lay priesthood. Strongly patriarchal, it could exercise an absolute authority over those who did not hold the priesthood.

Women could share in celestial rewards—that is, achieve eternal exaltation—but only through connection with men. Since marriage became a necessary and eternal covenant, neither could men reach exaltation or progress in the quest for divinity without women. It testifies to the spiritual urgency of the times and to the motivating force of the utopian dream-fiction, as well as to the power of ancient patriarchal fictions, that women accepted these designs.[53]

These dictates clearly relegated women to second-class status. While this was typical of almost all religions of the time, it is clear that for women, economic ease on earth as well as political and social standing depended on their acceptance of a lesser religious stature.[54] In a graph showing the official Mormon power structure, Humboldt University professor Lowell C. Bennion drew by far the largest block to show "Members without Priesthood." These members were women and children under twelve; they were located separately and at the low end of the structure. Only children under age 8 occupied a lower position.[55]

Women were assigned definite responsibilities. They shared in the management of the family, and, especially in the period of late-nineteenth-century expansion, women shared in civic and religious projects; the church expected them to carry out local and national enterprises.[56] It is true that men could, and often did, find it expedient to delegate executive decisions to women. But however extensive women's projects became, the male priesthood wielded authority. So powerful was the whole religious ideology—the fiction and the established means of carrying out the fictions—that the women eventually remanded to male church leaders control of their undertakings, public positions, news organs, and finances.[57]

But as the Church expanded, one revelation, a key revelation, became so controversial in the larger American society that while Joseph Smith and his apostles practiced it secretly, they refrained from officially disclosing it to their own laity and to the public.[58]

Polygamy is denounced in passages in the Book of Mormon: "There shall not any man among you have save it be one wife; and concubines he shall have none"; again in the Book of Commandments, a guiding principle emerges that "thou shalt love thy wife with all thy heart, and shalt cleave unto her and none else."[59] Originally, therefore, monogamy was the expectation of Mormon men and women who entered the marriage state, and marriage was an article of the faith. This was a basic fiction of the Mormon religion.

Much of the rest of nineteenth-century America also exhibited Victorian marriage commitments. Generally people had been taught to believe that by nature men were licentious and women virtuous, that by nature men were sexually inexhaustible while women were sexually through at about 50 years of age. Although they seldom spoke about it, many also believed the double standard for sexual morality was as reasonable a resolution as could be expected.

It is also true that those who felt uncertain about the role of sexuality also felt concern for the importance of the home and the health of its occupants. They thought that in the less settled communities of the West, frontier conditions produced a weakening of moral restraints and an increased sexual looseness. Some believed that unbridled lust, prostitution, and violence were inevitable results; they attributed what they saw as moral degeneration not only to unsettled, transient circumstances but also to a weakening of male authority. They advocated a return to patriarchal guidance; occasionally, if less conspicuously, someone suggested a return to the polygamous arrangements of biblical days.[60] Plainly Joseph Smith believed with the Victorians that men possess far greater sexual powers than do women; it appears that he came to believe that this must be accepted in any stable society, especially in marriage arrangements.

Smith—and his successors—must also have shared the common perception that women were less endowed than men both physically and intellectually, the belief that physically they were constantly incapacitated and that mentally they simply could not deal with difficult concepts. Men who believed this tended to feel that despite their physical and mental shortcomings, women could be depended upon to hold society together by caring for children, serving their husbands, and tolerating the consequences of the greater male sexual drive.

Soon after the publication of the Book of Mormon, Joseph Smith began a new translation of the Old Testament. He immersed himself in the study of lives of such biblical figures as Solomon and David; he apparently concluded that their polygamous marriages had brought society to an attainable standard of virtue and had therefore received divine sanction. If he wanted to establish priesthoods to rebuild the kingdom of God upon earth, he must look to these revered figures and look as well to their domestic and social customs. Smith thus became increasingly drawn to Old Testament practices; he planned a Kingdom of God for his Mormon religion, a kingdom that paralleled the social structure and the Israelite theology of the ancients. He justified his departure from American marriage protocol by his reading of the Old Testament and by new revelations. He became the new agent for the ancient polygamy-fiction.

In an 1861 letter to Smith's successor, Brigham Young, W. W. Phelps remembered that Smith had revealed to five others in Jackson County, Missouri, on July 17, 1831 that "it is my will, that in time, ye should take unto you wives of the Lamanites and Nephites [Indians, descendants of the brothers of The Book of Mormon], that their posterity may become white, delightsome and just."[61] Twelve years after he reputedly uttered these words, Smith announced the revelation on polygamy to his followers; as his brother Hyrum recorded it, it began:

> Verily, thus saith the Lord unto you my servant Joseph, that inasmuch as you have inquired of my hand to know and understand wherein I, the Lord, justified my servants Abraham, Isaac and Jacob as also Moses, David and Solomon, my servants, as touching the principle and doctrine of their having many wives and concubines.[62]

After the announcement, church members were to adhere to this newly revealed theory of plural marriage. It came to stipulate four conditions: the Lord's approval through Brigham Young, succeeding First President; consent of the first wife; consent of the new wife's parents; and acquiescence of the new wife herself.[63] There is no official indication that consent of second, third, fourth wives, and so on, would be necessary as marriages proliferated, and there is no mention of economic arrangements.

Polygamy became a matter of acknowledged Church policy only after Smith's death, however.[64] Apostle Orson Pratt announced it on August 29, 1852.[65] Thereafter, officials preached it to church members, promoted it in church publications, and practiced it openly.[66] Before the 1850s, and even during the overland "exodus" from Kirtland to Missouri to Nauvoo to Illinois to Utah,[67] a movement toward plural marriage was carried on secretly, for Mormon leaders realized that polygamy violated moral, legal, and religious standards of established authorities.[68] Though Utah was about to become a territory, Mormon leaders apparently thought that church law could exist apart from, even if in opposition to, the law of the United States.

Joseph had enunciated his plans for a "City on a Hill," his new Zion. He had dreamed of mansions, of great temples, of communities monolithic in belief and practice, of a religious yet earthly empire separate from the government of the rest of the nation. He had provided the most promising of fictions. He seems also to have persuaded himself of the righteousness of polygamy as the way to implement his fictions.

Polygamy was indeed an ancient custom.[69] According to one historian, "When Brigham Young led the Saints across the plains, he led them not only out of the hands of their midwestern persecutors but backward into a primordial sacred time."[70] For more than forty years, Mormon adherents (1840s?–1890), many of whom were Church officials, explained that famous biblical figures lived polygamously: Abraham took many wives. The wise Solomon, it was said, lived with 700 wives and more than 300 concubines, while David's large harem and Rehoboam's eighteen wives and sixty concubines were not unusual.[71] Even before biblical times, Hebrew men, who left many records, were permitted total sexual liberties in and out of marriage. While wives were strictly controlled, husbands enjoyed unlimited sexual freedom, including unrestricted access to concubines and slave women.

The figures of Sarah and Rachel, both of whom lived as subservient plural wives, and Ruth and Dorcas, who delivered unquestioning obedience to Old Testament wisdom, were to became models for the sisterhood of the Saints.[72] The revelation not only revealed a rather transparent plan to control women, it contained an unmistakable threat to women who might not comply: "And as ye have asked concerning adultery, verily, verily, I say unto you, if a man receiveth a wife in the new and everlasting covenant, and if she be with another man, and I have not appointed unto her by the holy anointing she hath committed adultery and shall be destroyed."[73] "Plurality of wives was not peculiar to the Mormons," noted historian B. Carmon Hardy, "but they gave the practice a new and exalted status, considering it a prescription for health, an antidote for immorality, and a key to history and government."[74]

It is impossible to determine whether Smith's advocacy of polygamy arose at least in part from rationalizing the early adventures to which he inclined or whether he involved himself in as many as forty-eight concurrent marriages because of the new revelation.[75] Certain it is that his vision for a universal church turned on unlimited population increases and that he thought polygamy could best achieve this goal. Still, rumors about his pre-revelation liaisons proliferated, as did scraps of news about his affirmations of spiritual sanction.[76]

Beginning about the year 1832, he disclosed his various alliances to some of his followers.[77] If the rumors of his liaisons were true, and a great deal of testimony confirms that they were true, the spiritual solution of an enabling revelation would exonerate Smith in the eyes of the troubled faithful. Beyond this, whether or not the rumors were true, the polygamous family could be viewed as the defining aspect of a developing worldview. It could be understood to enhance exponentially the human potential in the limitless universe.

In effect, Smith predicted that the polygamous family would, by its extension, achieve dominion over time and space and spirit. Not unrelated was the prophet's interest in earthly dimensions of political power. He had encouraged Mormons to run for local offices and, as a matter of good faith, to cede their property to the church; Joseph himself had dabbled in the Kirtland election of 1835. He then staked out a position favoring individual nominees for state offices but offering allegiance to neither party. For this, he had tasted some acclaim in the national press.[78] On January 29, 1844, he announced his candidacy for president of the United States.[79]

Smith seems to have abandoned that path toward earthly advancement, but he and his successors did create a vision, a fiction, and a modus operandi that endowed polygamy with political resonance. On a scale never before articulated, perhaps never before conceived, polygamy became the pathway to power, to limited power on earth but to celestial dominion more extensive in time and place and impact than any earthly triumph could ever achieve. Polygamy became surpassingly political.[80]

Clearly, however, Emma Hale Smith, the first of Smith's wives, deeply distrusted the religious authenticity of polygamy. She had felt a profound commitment to Mormonism upon her baptism two months after Joseph organized his church. She and Joseph married in January of 1827; they became parents of eleven children. But Emma seems to have felt uneasy for many years. Historians Leonard Arrington and Davis Bitton report that the revelation touching polygamy enraged her. "Allegedly," they wrote, she "burned the revelation on plural marriage first recorded by Smith's scribe, William Clayton."[81] It is re-

Emma Hale Smith, first wife of Joseph Smith, knew privilege and experienced despair. She became a leader of Mormon women, up to and including her break with the orthodox church. *Courtesy Utah State Historical Society.*

ported that when Sister Eudocia Baldwin Marsh asked "Where did polygamy come from?" Emma Smith snapped, "Straight from hell."[82]

In a special "Revelation to Emma Smith, Wife of the Prophet," Joseph appears to have taken notice of his wife's intransigence; the revelation commands Emma to act "in the spirit of meekness," and to "murmur not because of the things which thou has not seen." The revelation also promised Emma that she would be allowed to select the sacred hymns and that if she were faithful and walked in the paths of virtue, the Lord would "preserve thy life and thou shalt receive an inheritance in Zion." "Keep my commandments continually," the revelation read, and "a crown of righteousness thou shalt receive. And except thou do this where I am you cannot come."[83]

Though she was angry and disturbed, Emma did twice "accept" "the Principle." But she attacked "sexual sin" by reading to the women an epistle warning of practices "contrary to the old established mores and virtues and scriptural laws regarding the habits, customs and conduct of society." Tortured by anxieties she could never resolve, she and other dissenters finally formed their own branch of the Mormon Church. This "Reorganized Church of Jesus Christ of Latter Day Saints" opposed polygamy, basing their opposition on the original Book of Mormon and the 1835 Kirtland edition of the Commandments.[84] According to John Taylor, a member of the 1880 governing Committee of Twelve, Emma Smith "made use of the position she held to try to pervert the minds of the sisters [with reference to plural marriage]."[85] For most, however, challenging polygamy stood tantamount to challenging Mormon authority itself.

Other early wives suffered intense emotional crises when polygamy was introduced. Eliza R. Snow wrote, "The subject was very repugnant to my feelings so directly was it in opposition to my educated prepossessions, that it seemed as though all the prejudices of my ancestors for generations past congregated around me."[86]

A little later, when at age 40 she considered marriage for the first time, parts of verses in her journal read:

> O, how shall I compose a thought
> When nothing is compos'd?
> How form ideas as I ought
> On subjects not disclos'd? . . .
> *This principle* will bear us up—
> It should our faith sustain,
> E'en when from "trouble's" reckless cup
> The dregs we have to drain.[87]

Despite these doubts, Eliza became a plural wife of Joseph Smith and, after that, of Brigham Young. At a later date, she wrote that polygamy promised a "more perfect type of manhood mentally and physically," and she warned the American people not to forbid it.[88]

The journals of many Mormon women recorded severe emotional suffering as the practice gained religious credence.[89] Jane Charters Robinson Hindley related in her diary of December 22, 1862, that "he has returned and brought two—I cannot call them wives, yet it seems so strange. . . . My God help me in my weakness and forgive me if I falter in my duty and affection to him I love." A few days later, on December 29th, she recorded her feelings: "The house is full of company, music and dancing, but there is a void in my heart and my eyes are full of tears. Oh I am very unhappy, and my pride will not suffer me to appear so." Ann Eliza Webb Young wrote a book detailing her anxieties. Though she believed herself to be Brigham Young's reluctant *Wife No. 19,* and though she so titled her 1875 manuscript, she appears instead to have been the twenty-seventh of the prophet's reputed forty-eight wives.[90]

In 1873, Fanny Stenhouse, wife of a "disfellowshipped" (excommunicated) Mormon elder, wrote her memoirs, *A Lady's Life Among the Mormons;* Sten-

Eliza Roxey Snow. Despite her doubts about polygamy, Eliza Snow became a plural wife of Joseph Smith, and later, of Brigham Young. *Courtesy Utah State Historical Society.*

house told her tale as well as tales involving many Mormon women she knew. Her stories spanned many years. Her words about the tortures of polygamy carried a ring of emotional honesty: "I would sometimes almost rave with anger. Then I would pray, then cry. . . . I never knew at that time what it was to smile. . . . But even up to that time [the coming of a second wife], I almost believed that all this might be right; although I saw so much wrong connected with it."[91] Janet Snyder Richards, a new Mormon and a 19-year-old bride, told her husband that polygamy was "repugnant to my idea of virtue."[92] But three years later, she consented to other wives. Lucy W. Kimball, a wife of Joseph Smith and then of Heber C. Kimball, wrote that "there was not any love in the union between myself and Kimball. . . . It was the principle of plural marriage that we were trying to establish . . . and if we had established it, it would have been for the benefit of the whole human race."[93]

Despite anxieties of a religious nature, despite secrecy and economic hardship, despite personal humiliations, many Mormon women who entered plural marriage or found themselves involved did endure it for over half a century.[94] It is probably true that more men took several wives and that more women and many more children were involved than we previously believed.[95] It is also true that anxieties of other descriptions worried non-Mormon monogamous women in the nineteenth century: For much of that time many suffered every legal, political, and economic disadvantage.

But most Mormon women—those who entered plural marriage and those who did not—believed that Church doctrine—polygamy—stemmed from a new revelation in a stream of "continuous revelations" of divine truth and that religious dictates derived therefrom superseded all else and could neither be questioned nor ignored.[96] To Mormon women, God's truth was more important than earthly ease, though one suspects that God's truth was important for varying reasons.[97] Since threats and banishments were fairly common, some may also have dreaded the possibility of estrangement from Mormon fellowship.[98]

In point of fact, Mormon polygamy reinstituted a cultural imperative for an old ill, the patriarchal double standard for sexual morality; it did so by nearly mandatory programs from early youth to late adulthood. It is true that other religious denominations indoctrinated children in their faiths in the nineteenth century, and it is certainly true that most religions in the western world insisted on monogamy.[99] In the Mormon theocracy, however, women were officially coached to persuade other women of the morality of polygamy—a practice outlawed from the beginning by the marriage laws of the United States.[100]

Presented in regular children's church-school assemblies and in Female Relief Society gatherings, defended in *The Woman's Exponent*, which was the Society's news organ, polygamy was preached routinely on Sundays and at weekday meetings.[101] Elders insisted that "everything must be used as it was intended by nature," that reproduction was nature's supreme mandate, that plurality of wives furthered this law. Writers in church publications explained and supported the practice. Leaders of the church told how polygamy extended sexual potency. One of them bragged of having fathered a child in the 88th year of his life; another asserted that he remained sexually vigorous in his 90s. Romantic notions aside, the fathers of the church insisted they had discovered in polygamy the roads to health and dominion.[102]

Apparently Mormon men experienced fewer doubts than did Mormon women. In the nineteenth and more aggressively into the twentieth century, church-school publications among Mormons became businesses of large proportions.[103] Much of the later effort seems to have been directed toward easing the doubts of Mormon women. In her book *Why We Practice Polygamy*, Helen Mar Whitney, an orthodox Mormon, envisioned such a need. She wrote that "from these mountains is to roll the little stone that will bring to pass the purposes of the Almighty and settle this social question by a practical reform in the marriage system."[104] Eliza Snow came to a resolution about the matter. She wrote "We are at the head of all the women of the world."[105] Margaret A. Smote wrote that "I have had a voice in my husband taking more wives; for this I am thankful. I have taken pleasure in practicing this pure principle, although I have been tried in it. Yet since the birth of our first child by the second wife, I have never felt to dissolve the ties thus formed."[106]

For her, as for the sisterhood, the whole community and religious setup prescribed a fiction of greater promise than a fiction that treated women equitably and allowed women earthly comfort.[107] It became, therefore, *the* fiction by which they would abide. Right up to the moment in 1890 when the Mormon church appeared to disavow polygamy as a religious principle, Mormon women never officially refused to practice it.

This mindset explains the anomaly that while some Mormon women accepted polygamy reluctantly, others appeared to, and finally did, accept it willingly. Probably no one knows for certain how many Mormon women lived in polygamy; recent scholarship suggests the number was larger than leaders indicated. Among those women who did accept the practice, including the plural wives of officials of the church, some found polygamy helpful in the sharing of child care and daily duties.[108] And some found friendships among their "sister wives." Some wives, believing in "the Principle," and desiring the benefits that would accrue in the celestial kingdom, helped their husbands acquire other wives.[109] Most believed that men are "naturally" licentious and women pure and that the new arrangements would contain men's sexual fervors. All believed that spiritual hardships well endured brought rich rewards in the celestial kingdom.[110]

As time passed, the new authentic polygamy became embedded in expanded frameworks of the old monogamous orthodoxy. The merged orthodoxies exerted so powerful an influence over the sisterhood that their leaders even championed the new custom in public pronouncements—probably at the behest of church leaders, but also because in the end they believed in its possibilities.[111] The polygamy-fiction as a means to implement the greater purposes of the Lord had become the most formidable institution of the establishment religion. Whatever their misgivings, whatever their personal sufferings, Mormon women supported it.

But as they drew together to live the polygamy-fiction, Mormon women began to experience unforeseen consequences.[112] Many had grown up in strict New England homes where Puritan religious trappings blended with a respect for education and with dreams of a perfect society on earth; they had come earnestly to the utopian-communitarian ideas implied in Mormon theology.[113] As Mormons, their endeavors displayed a spectrum of social concerns that at times focused upon the suffrage for themselves.

Historian Julie Dunfey explained how, though polygamy provoked "conflicting emotions," it set the stage for discovering benefits in close female alliances and for achieving increased independence.[114] Joan Iversen's thoughtful study showed further "Feminist Implications of Mormon Polygyny." Polygamous living, she suggested, and the pains and pleasures and political visions it encompassed, "resulted in an assault upon the ideology of romantic love." Zena D. H. Young, a wife of Joseph Smith and then of Brigham Young, put the matter plainly: "A successful polygamous wife," she observed, "must regard her husband with indifference." Love, she continued "must be regarded as a feeling which should have no existence in polygamy."[115] No one could afford too exclusive an investment in her husband's love; indifference to his alliances became a protection, and children became more important as sources of emotional satisfaction. In many economic and civic endeavors, polygamy pushed women toward self-sufficiency.[116]

At the same time, Mormon women were particularly encouraged to endorse the polygamy-fiction as the custom came under attack in the wider American society. For forty years polygamy was a sanctioned, insisted-upon religious practice among Mormons. During the years after the official acknowledgment of 1852, its image was zealously upheld in public by church members of both sexes.[117]

So confident was the male Mormon hierarchy of the compliance of women, so powerful was the story that dictated compliance, so certain was the leadership of divine approval that the Utah legislature felt safe in granting women the suffrage in 1870.[118] This, in the view of historian Marilyn Warenski, was "perhaps the ultimate example of how women have been coerced, in the name of God, to participate in their own oppression."[119]

Certainly their compliance also demonstrates that "oppression" can produce unexpected results: Individual women found emotional support and learned economic independence, and women's groups gained influence. In both cases, Mormon women's public support of the marriage arrangements of polygamy, their public insistence that they were well pleased with polygamy, provides a striking example of the power of a fiction to influence behavior and belief. While it seemed to observers that the women became agents of their own afflictions, it seemed to Mormon women that they reaped and would reap substantial benefits.

Whatever the complexities, Mormon religious authority was superseded in this telling case. A fiction powerful enough to overcome another powerful fiction emerged from prevailing trends in the wider American society. Though relations between the sexes weren't always the most paramount concern, the succeeding fiction legally and religiously had long sanctioned only monogamous marriage.

As industrialization intensified in the middle and later nineteenth century, reformers called for improved conditions in America's slums, for legislation to protect factory women and children, for an expanded democracy. Among the earlier crusaders for the abolition of slavery, for temperance, for moral reform, networks of women across the country had begun to work for women's property rights, for the extension of women's civil rights, for women's education, for the inclusion of women in democratic processes. In the East their activities coalesced in the first women's rights convention in Seneca Falls in 1848,[120] while in the West some states began seriously to consider, then to implement, women's suffrage demands.

These women contributed to the superseding fiction; their struggles and their activities carried connections, muddied as some connections may have been, to the wider struggle for social justice that grew in strength in the United States throughout the period of Mormon polygamy.[121]

While it is difficult to assess internal pressures, especially those pressures on Mormon women that may have contributed—however obliquely—to the downfall of polygamy, we know that after Joseph's death, Emma Smith and her supporters left the established church to form a new organization. We know from their records, their books, and their diaries that many women involved in polygamy suffered from it. It is probably true that Mormon women became pacesetters in matters of women's rights because polygamy pushed them in that direction.

Not long after the practice of polygamy became common knowledge, persecutions on account of it erupted. Some hostility may have arisen from other objections: When the U.S. government was subduing Native American Indians, it was thought that Mormons supported Indians. As the struggle over slave labor escalated, it was believed that Mormons sometimes "agitated" Negro slaves and Negro freedmen. In the wake of the surge to the West, it was resented that Mormons acquired property.[122]

But the deepest enmity sprang from the perception of a majority of Americans of predominantly Protestant religions that polygamy was evil, that it was undemocratic, that it denigrated women. It sprang as well from the suspicion that Mormon theologians perceived that gender arrangements stood at the center of social equanimity and that they took merciless advantage of this perception. As one Mormon woman wrote, "The dominant principle of Mormonism is marriage and the theory that men and women are not perfect without each other. . . . The woman ought to be married but once; the man may be married as often as he pleases, if he can provide for his wives and their families."[123]

The fiction that non-Mormon Americans lived had long rejected polygamy. As historian Nancy F. Cott has pointed out, "Wielders of public authority in the Christian West since the early modern period have seen monogamous marriage as the most crucial precondition of public order."[124] The new fiction that arose from non-Mormon discomfort with polygamous Utah never flirted with polyandry, but it displayed yearnings toward rights for women. From whatever convictions, these non-Mormon Americans purported to see polygamy as most damaging to women; they felt it disgraceful that Mormon women had publicly supported polygamy. Even if sometimes subconsciously, many non-Mormons in Utah and in the rest of the nation may also have begun to see women's deprivations as bearing connections to democracy's shortcomings.

So it happened that while a fiction derived from continuous revelations and a return to ancient patriarchal practices permitted a reinstitution of polygamy in the Mormon theocracy, another old political and religiously driven fiction—monogamy—combined with a surge of democratic drives to enable the United States to outlaw the polygamous principle.[125] Would polygamy have been outlawed if there had been no rising tide of American displeasure? Probably not, had its exclusion depended on Mormon women. But with the arousal of American outrage, Mormon female dissatisfactions may have contributed to its suppression. For deeply religious Mormon women, for children—and for some men—hurtful adjustments accompanied each shift in marriage custom. Each alteration of the fiction to be accepted, then lived, brought uncertainties and hardships.[126]

Not the least difficult may have been the spiritual confusion attendant to the changes. How was it possible that God would shift positions so drastically in the fundamental matter of the relations between the sexes? Was it possible that God had made no changes but that Mormon men had failed in transmitting God's commands? Or could women trust Mormon men because they had grasped a "Principle" that would some distant day assure everlasting bliss? Should men as priests be trusted despite the cost to women, or could women no longer hold faith in the religious and social arrangements they had believed to be righteous? Could they no longer feel a safety in the privileged priesthood of Mormon men? Was the celestial escalation to be achieved by the polygamous family worth the emotional cost on earth? To this day, much of the public-relations effort of the Mormon Church centers on attempts to answer questions to the satisfaction of Mormon women.[127] The Church itself enlists the services of public relations experts among its adherents in order to address these concerns.

For many, a devastating confusion must have pervaded daily life. Some women must have lost confidence as younger women replaced them. Some learned reluctantly to share their husbands and their homes with "sister wives." Some women supported the male hierarchy with an earnestness characteristic of the power-hungry in any situation. Many must often have felt unsure of what they ought to feel.

Some seem to have flourished, to have developed nourishing support systems in women's activities, to have made strides in new directions. Others must have felt the economic deprivation occasioned by multiple households, both through the arrival of additional wives and additional families from the 1830s on and through the deterioration of arrangements after the Woodruff Manifesto disestablished polygamy as a state-sanctioned religious principle in 1890. At the least, this terminating manifesto disoriented families and necessitated painful domestic and legal rearrangements. B. Carmon Hardy has shown that polygamy did not die gently with the Woodruff Manifesto; Mormons of stature in the church continued to embrace it, however unofficially, well into the twentieth century.[128] Recently on National Public Radio, a Mormon First President referred to the high quality of leadership that had resulted from polygamous marriages.[129]

Nancy F. Cott has observed that the institution of marriage "is and has been a public institution and a building block of public policy," and that marriage obligations and benefits have "always been built into many legal and governmental structures in the United States."[130] Monogamous marriage had indeed become a fiction legally and socially entrenched by the later half of the nineteenth century. During the years when Mormons practiced and attempted to institutionalize polygamy, the American determination to obliterate it escalated and operated on many levels. There were sneak attacks. There were denigrating newspaper articles and humiliating cartoons.[131] There was open mob violence, openly supported. Smith and leaders of his church spent time in jails for alleged polygamous practices—as well as for financial irregularities. Finally, gangs dragged Joseph Smith and his brother Hyrum from their jail and murdered them.

Offended that Mormon women could vote while they could not, offended at what seemed the arrogance of the Utah Legislature in bestowing this privilege, angered because Mormon women supported polygamy, non-Mormon women organized an Anti-Polygamy Society in 1878; it launched an attempt to disfranchise Mormon women.[132] Driven by the belief that the achievements of western civilization itself rested upon the sanctity of the monogamous family and by the fear that Mormon polygamy corrupted the nation's homes, Protestant women's groups drew together to take up the cause. American policymakers and legal experts shared their views and, as it turned out, stood ready to implement them.

Eastern women's rights leader Elizabeth Cady Stanton had spoken with suffrage leaders in Utah in the course of attempts to build a national suffrage coalition.[133] But after a suffrage conference in 1879, she summarized her thoughts about the situation of the Mormon women: "When women understand that governments and religions are . . . emanations from the brain of man," she wrote, "they will no longer be oppressed by the injunctions that come to them with the divine authority of 'Thus saith the Lord.'"[134] In a sense, if from a female point of view, Stanton echoed the Enlightenment philosopher

Charles-Louis de Montesquieu. Montesquieu suggested that "religion doesn't come from God; like politics, it is a creation of men. It is their response to their anthropomorphic idea of God."[135] Nor did the Mormon fictions or their methods of carrying them out come from God. They were the creations of men and women. They came from the spinning of fictions and the weaving of means to implement those fictions.

So it happened that non-Mormon women became agents of a different fiction. Even as these opponents of polygamy challenged the practice on grounds that it was anti-democratic, irreligious, and denigrating to women and to the family, they organized further efforts to deprive Mormon women of the franchise. In the monogamous American society, women were struggling to possess the franchise. It outraged their sense of propriety that women in polygamous Utah could vote. Thus they demonstrated the very anxieties to which they objected in the Mormon women.

In 1880, the new Anti-Polygamy Society conceived a political party and mounted a legal challenge with the object of forcing the voting registrar in Salt Lake County to remove the names of all women from the registration lists. But when the Society asked for a writ of mandamus to force compliance with U.S. law, Utah officials denied the request. There were several other failed attempts to disfranchise Mormon women, and there was a great deal of agitation.

The Society next joined forces with Protestant reform women eager to extirpate polygamy. They worked together to collect an anti-polygamy petition of 250,000 signatures, which they sent to Congress. Prominent eastern suffragists opposed this move, for they feared it would jeopardize their own chances to win the suffrage. But by 1882 there was enough agitation in the country and in Congress to achieve passage of the Edmunds-Tucker Bill; it disfranchised all polygamists, reflecting the national temper on the matter of plural marriage and giving legal substance to the preferred fiction. More enabling legislation followed; it permitted the imprisonment of polygamists and placed restrictions on the right of plural wives to refuse to testify against their husbands.[136]

In March of 1886, a remarkable gathering of Mormon women to protest the Edmunds-Tucker law and to promote polygamy took place in Salt Lake City; in vain did Mormon women attempt to roll back the tide of American displeasure. To other Americans, it only appeared that the women enthusiastically participated in their own oppression.

To many Mormon women, the protest represented some suppression of anxieties by formally supporting Church doctrine. Perhaps it also represented—if subconsciously—Mormon women's appreciation of benefits they felt they had attained: strong female friendships, effective alliances, some degree of economic independence, some effective political representation. And surely some women thought of the polygamous way of life and their support of it on this earth as a pathway to eternal celestial ease, even to some measure of domination. Overall, this mass demonstration displayed the power of the fictions they accepted and the principles by which they lived their fictions.

Whatever the sources or the strength of their convictions, the Mormon women made no impression on the wider American determination. They never impacted the preferred fiction. Not insignificantly, however, they did gain a great deal of grassroots political experience from this performance. That experience proved an apprenticeship for the coming struggle over an equal rights amendment.

More than they cherished celestial and earthly polygamy, Mormon male leaders desired the advantages of statehood. Six times over forty-seven years, Utah solicited admittance to the union, finally presenting a constitution prohibiting polygamy. Even this and other concessions failed to persuade Congress. Not till after 1890, when Mormon First President Wilford Woodruff drafted an apparently official document—his Manifesto, his Advise—terminating polygamy as a religious principle did Utah come into the union as a state.[137] A revelation legitimizing monogamy never happened. Even though polygamy was officially if reluctantly abandoned as a religious principle in earthly dimensions, Mormon leaders secretly practiced it; they also advocated it for Mormons willing to live in Mexico and other places.[138]

The legal triumph of the monogamy fiction thus followed a tortuous trail. In shifting its religious marriage arrangements from monogamy to polygamy and then back again, Mormon society entertained dramatic changes, each reversal driven by the fiction that won acceptance. From sordid beginnings involving mob violence, treachery, and assassination to sophisticated legal maneuverings at powerful levels of government, the world of American monogamy demonstrated the force of its chosen fiction.

Eleanor Roosevelt
Changing Fictions in the Life of an Individual

Inheritance

Nowhere is the complex operation of fictions for living more visible than in the life of Anna Eleanor Roosevelt, first lady of the United States from 1933 to 1945. This is her story according to *my fictions*: The continued prominence of national and international issues she confronted, the choices she made, the responses her name still evokes reveal what I believe to be *her fictions*. Her choices and the styles of her living measure her growth. They measure as well the impact of her life.

What inherited fictions shaped the consciousness of this dynamic woman's childhood? What elements of her personality, what chances of her education enabled her to supplement those first fictions until they became scarcely recognizable? Which fictions impeded her development? Which faded away? How did she discover fictions lying deep beneath the frameworks of her family? How did she then create her own fictions? Did she meet opposition?

Eleanor Roosevelt began life in a world that thought it understood which fictions would prove desirable for her roles-to-be. She was to be educated to personify a great family name; as an upper-class woman, she would be educated lightly, not too much. She was to marry appropriately and become a wife who would serve her husband, who would overlook his shortcomings, who would forever treat his needs and his moods and his views as superior to her own. She was to become a mother who would stay at home, raising children, attending church, and running a household. She was to regard these precepts as her duty. She was to forego any interests that might conflict with these demands.

Participation in public affairs would be scarcely imaginable, but she could follow the noblesse-oblige fictions of her family, perhaps to become a lady bountiful. Eleanor herself remembered perfectly: "You were kind to the poor, you did not neglect your philanthropic duties, you assisted the hospitals and did something for the needy."[1] She understood she had a "duty" to exemplify "definite ideas . . . which had been put before [me] . . . as the only proper existence for a lady."[2] These standard Victorian American principles—fictions—governed the outlook of upper-class ladies of this era.

But another agenda lay at the foundation of this set of fictions. The other agenda reflected intimate relations in people's lives; it set two standards for sexual conduct and two standards for social morality. It displayed a conspiracy to keep silent about both. This agenda implied views of men and women: Men were, and could be permitted to be, licentious; women were, and could only be permitted to be, chaste. For men, sex could be pleasurable, random, unfreighted; for women, sex must be loaded with moral precepts, must be a carefully guarded service, must be considered a duty.

In social arrangements, the rich were entitled to opportunity, and the poor ought to appreciate what they got. Taken together, the whole array dominated the circumstances of Eleanor Roosevelt's birth. "I was for many years," she wrote, "a sounding board for the teachings and influence of my immediate surroundings. The ability to think for myself did not develop until I was well on in life."[3] How, then, did this woman, born into an established, well-to-do but deeply troubled family, become a revered, compassionate figure of the twentieth-century world?

Eleanor Roosevelt never discarded all the establishment fictions of nineteenth- and early twentieth-century upper-class America. She never escaped all the reaches of those fictions; increasingly, however, she did modify them. She retained some. She rejected some. Some she merged into her own designs for living—her own fictions. And some she created. On an everyday level, she lived them according to her own standards, her own choices.

Eleanor Roosevelt's childhood could scarcely have proved lonelier or emotionally more desolate. "I was a shy, solemn child even at the age of two," she wrote, "and I am sure that even when I danced I never smiled."[4] On a more intimate note, she remembered that "I was an exceptionally timid child, afraid of the dark, afraid of mice, afraid of practically everything."[5]

She was born in the year 1884 in the month of October on the eleventh day. Like imagined heroines of fairy tales, and like real-live heiresses in Europe and America, this young American princess lived in houses staffed with servants—cooks, maids, butlers, laundresses, nurses, governesses, gardeners, coachmen.

On her father's side, she began life as a descendant of seventeenth-century Dutch traders; in the New World, they became successful bankers, real estate dealers, manufacturers of construction materials, and politicians. The family branched into two lines, one emanating from Oyster Bay, Long Island, the other from Hyde Park on the Hudson River. Both branches retained their wealth and influence to the time of Eleanor's birth.

On her mother's side, Eleanor came from a family of southern merchants and New York bankers, some of whom had become prominent political figures, and one of whom had signed the Declaration of Independence.[6] Another had administered the oath of office to George Washington. The joining of these families through the marriage of Eleanor's parents, Elliott Roosevelt and Anna Ludlow Livingston Hall, seemed a significant event in the Knickerbocker society of old New York.

As time passed, Eleanor's parents led a privileged existence in Hempstead,

Long Island, and in New York City, where Eleanor, their first child, was born. Quite often they traveled abroad and to other residences; in New York, they moved among the reigning elite.[7] It would seem impossible to conjure a more cushioned childhood than that which this little girl inherited.

Yet as events and the fictions of her daily life shaped an awakening consciousness, Eleanor felt lonely, insecure, betrayed, and angry. In the richly thoughtful words of her biographer Blanche Wiesen Cook, hers was "A Childhood of Tears and Loss."[8] She believed that she was a "plain" person—not a surprising belief in a child whose mother called her "Granny." "Come in, Granny," her mother would say. This might be followed with "She is such a funny child, so old-fashioned that we always call her 'Granny.'"[9]

That same mother, a famous beauty, quite openly lamented her daughter's appearance and quite obviously found her two younger sons more congenial. Damaging as these circumstances were, they could scarcely have suggested the most hurtful happenings of Eleanor's childhood.[10]

Appearances to the contrary, Eleanor's mother, Anna Hall Roosevelt, had married into a difficult situation. Her husband Elliott Roosevelt, whose older brother Theodore was soon to make his way toward the presidency, seemed to have been born to charm. Elliott had been an appealing, favored child. He grew into a rather disengaged adolescent. After one year at fashionable St. Paul's, a preparatory school for boys, he became ill. In a postscript to a letter to his father, he wrote "Yesterday during my Latin lesson without the slightest warning I had a bad rush of blood to my head, it hurt me so that I don't remember what happened."[11]

Elliott withdrew from the school and went with a family friend, a physician, to a frontier post in Texas. There his friends were the young officers of Fort McKavit; there Elliott accompanied the soldiers on hunts for wild game and hostile Indians.[12] Elliott wrote to his mother that "our life during the days in camp was of course but one continual hunt and I am sorry to say very little shoot."[13]

Elliott never returned to his school, and he seems never to have attempted seriously to qualify for a profession or any other life work. He did dabble in writing verses and, later, in banking and in real estate, but his commitment to the sporting life, the life of the bon vivant, took clear preference. Quickly he became known in New York society as a dashing young bachelor, a charmer, a good catch. By the time Elliott was 21, his father had died.[14] That father, Theodore Roosevelt, Sr., had been concerned by his second son's difficulties. Writing of an early episode in Elliott's life, the senior Roosevelt had thought that "a pillow fight was perhaps the principal cause. . . . It produced congestion of the brain with all its attendant horrors of delirium, etc. The doctor says that there is no cause for anxiety as it is only necessary to avoid all excitements for 2 or 3 years."[15]

After his father's death, Elliott took his inheritance and departed to hunt big game in India. Though he contracted a fever there, he returned to meet and marry the lovely Anna Hall—Eleanor's mother—and to make a stab at carrying on the charitable work his father had begun among disabled newsboys of the city.

But soon after the marriage, both Elliott's beloved mother and his sister-in-law, Alice Lee Roosevelt, died, as it happened, on the same day.[16] While riding in a Long Island society circus, Elliott broke his leg; it had to be rebroken and reset.[17] He had been a popular youth, affable in manner. But despite luxurious surroundings, despite the friendship of the sporting elite at home and abroad, despite his reputation for grace in social situations, Elliott suffered from a persistent ennui, occasional fainting spells, depressions, accidents, and physical seizures. Before and after his marriage he lived at the edge of inner confusion, prey to tempests of wrath and self-pity.

Elliott Roosevelt seems to have made efforts to connect with fictions that guided wealthy young people of his social position. He early wrote to his father that he wanted to be "as good as you, if it is in me. But it is hard."[18] One biographer, Eleanor's friend Joseph P. Lash, has noted that Elliott's "private papers, especially his letters as a young man, are full of vivid images and sensitive observations." But Elliott never could carry off the establishment fictions of his class—those fictions which elevated masculine vigor, aggressive focused behavior, the discipline of business enterprise, Victorian sexual codes.

Nor could he discover fictions that would work for him; he lived with many doubts. On one of his trips to India, Elliott described his impressions: "How easy [it is] for the smallest portion [of us] to sit down in quiet luxury of mind and body—to say to the far larger part—lo, the poor savages. Is what we call right, right all over the world and for all time?"[19]

He grew progressively less focused. Life became so unbearable that he began to seek solace in a mistress and in alcohol. He never escaped this fetish; he grew more dependent upon it and less dependable in every relationship. In a pitiable understatement of his state of mind, he wrote to his mother-in-law "I am not, I fear, particularly well."[20]

Although Elliott strove sporadically to connect with fictions of his boyhood, his efforts came only to further defeats. Why was he troubled? For a time, no one seems to have realized that he faced mental illness, that while others could confront the harsh happenings of life without damage to their personalities, without shattering the fictions they needed to live, Elliott might require long-term professional care. He grew increasingly irascible, accident prone. He spent time in sanitariums.

Perhaps no one could have understood the rending anxieties Elliott knew; his struggles with his inadequacies and his reckless behavior alienated his friends and his family—all except his daughter Eleanor. "I acquired a strange and garbled idea of the troubles around me," she remembered. "Something was wrong with my father and from my point of view nothing could be wrong with him."[21]

Anna Hall Roosevelt could comprehend neither her husband's difficulties nor the behavioral responses of their daughter Eleanor. Perhaps the fictions that determined this southern-oriented beauty's experience left her unable to conceive of anything but a life of ease and perpetual social activity. She "belonged," according to her daughter, "to that New York City society which thought itself all-important."[22]

On the surface, Anna Hall Roosevelt embraced that elite life, those fictions. To her friends, she seemed to have been made for the daily round of lunches and dinners and charity balls of late-nineteenth-century New York. But she lived with an undercurrent of discomfort, especially in her relationships with her husband and her daughter.

In efforts to excuse her husband's inappropriate behavior, she became a bitter, aloof person. Always religiously oriented, she conformed through the eight short years of her marriage to prevailing fictions about women's roles. To the world, she hid her dismay. She suppressed her anger. She tried to cover for her husband's lapses, concealing her anger in disabling headaches. She wrote to her sister-in-law that

> Elliott has been a perfect angel since he left Arles & he never tried to take anything more which I think shows how very much better he is and how much more control over himself. But Bamie I have *never* been so worried about him as for the past week he has settled into a melancholy from which nothing moves him.[23]

At the cost of her own equilibrium, Anna Hall Roosevelt sought to preserve the establishment fictions of a happy marriage and a settled, balanced, well-appointed home for her children, Eleanor, Ellie, and Hall. Alternately, she longed for her husband's company and suffered when she had it. The stressful situation in which she lived doomed her efforts.

She never understood her daughter's deprivations, for she believed that Eleanor's attention-seeking behavior arose from an unfortunate disposition. She scolded her daughter for childish shortcomings: Eleanor became defensive. She showed signs of an ungovernable disobedience. She told little lies. Sometimes in Eleanor's hearing her mother spoke of her daughter's unpleasing appearance or her intractable temperament. From her earliest years Eleanor could find no comfortable place at the heart of establishment fictions.

Never able to face her husband's predicament, Anna Hall Roosevelt grew tense, troubled, and distant. After a surgery, she contracted diphtheria; she died in December 1892 at 29 years of age.[24]

To the little girl whose mother made it clear that she thought her homely and whose father delighted, then deserted, her, life was puzzling. That father emerged in this child's mind as the mainstay of her existence. He called her affectionate pet names—"my own little Nell." He played with her. She remembered a trip to Italy when she was very small: "In Venice, my father invited me to ride in a gondola, and he paid the gondolier to sing. Some sort of fiesta was going on at the time and people were tossing flowers."[25]

When he traveled or stayed away from the family—often not by choice—her father wrote to her. He brought her presents. He made elaborate promises of wonderful excursions they would share. He gave her a pony. He encouraged her efforts; in his exile, he even invented study-games for her. Through years of pathetic attempts to survive in an uncomprehending world, Elliott seemed always to have cared for his daughter. But on one notorious occasion, he left her in the charge of a doorman. She stood for hours in the rain while he enjoyed a drinking round with friends at the New York Knickerbocker Club. She watched several men carry him out.[26]

For Eleanor this sort of treatment must have precipitated an emotional roller-coaster. Small wonder that she became in some situations willful and unmanageable, in others defensively protective of the father whose love meant everything to her. She always adored him. Late in life she revered his memory. He brought love and excitement and wonder to his daughter's life; he provided the only strong emotional support of Eleanor's childhood. She clung to the belief that he wanted to share his life with her, that he cared what became of her.

So despite an appearance of protection and privilege, despite an actual situation of economic comfort, Eleanor Roosevelt's childhood passed in a turbulent, emotionally threatening environment. She lived with the fiction that all was right in the best of worlds, that the stage was set for prescribed roles and lasting ease. This was a fiction well understood; it made small sense to the confused but striving child. After her mother died, 8-year-old Eleanor was sent to her maternal grandmother Hall. There she lived for the next six years. Both families virtually banished Elliott from the rearing of his children.

As Eleanor entered her grandmother's house, a different life began. In her seventies, Eleanor recalled that "the world of my grandmother was a world of well-ordered custom and habit, more or less slow to change." Elitist to the core of her being, Eleanor's grandmother lived as a vessel conveying aristocratic attitudes, aristocratic fictions. But Grandmother Hall did bring this sad, deprived child to the center of the stage.[27]

Later, Eleanor realized that her stern grandmother believed she had failed to provide discipline for her own children and that she must now insist that her grandchildren obey. "She proceeded on the theory that it is wiser to say 'no' than 'yes' to children," Eleanor thought.[28] "She so often said 'no' that I built up a defense of saying I did not want to do things in order to forestall her refusals and keep down my disappointments."[29]

A sad little girl who lost both parents and her brother before she was 10 years old. *Courtesy Franklin Roosevelt Library.*

Soon after her mother's death, Eleanor's younger brother Ellie passed away. Prevented from close contacts with his children, ill, almost ostracized, and fatally alcoholic, her sometimes wonderful father died. It was August of 1894. Eleanor would reach her tenth birthday in another two months. In less than two years, this little girl lost her mother, her father, and her brother.

The many traumatic losses turned the child's world upside down and presaged change. Despite the rules of her grandmother's household, despite the underlying attitudes that characterized an elitist, sexist, often anti-Semitic, anti-immigrant, and racist America, Eleanor no longer lived on the peripheries and sometimes at the center of her parents' dilemmas, at the center of the fictions that characterized their lives. For Mrs. Hall, Eleanor, and Eleanor's development, became "the real business" of each day.[30] This meant an even more thoroughgoing exposure to the fictions of America's most traditional families. It also meant insulation from much of the folklore other children glean. "I said to my grandmother," Eleanor wrote, "'What is the meaning of whore? It is in the Bible.'" The only answer her grandmother gave her—"severely"—was that "whore" "is a word little girls should not use."[31] Still, though distant from many realities of American life, the arrangements at Grandmother Hall's house provided for Eleanor a consistent fiction-frame.

Eleanor's relationship with her grandmother can scarcely be said to have been warm. Late in life, Eleanor wrote that "I wondered then and I wonder now whether, if her life had been less centered in her family group, that family group might not have been a great deal better off. If she had some kind of life of her own."[32] But Eleanor seems to have retained an affection for this grandmother who, in her own fashion, cared about her bereaved young granddaughter.

Eleanor did experience the interest of her mother's siblings, her lively, unstable, sometimes caring, sometimes tempestuous aunts and uncles, some of whom still lived at home. They taught her tennis and offered her a family. Though she could scarcely be depended on, Eleanor's Aunt Pussie introduced Eleanor to the worlds of theater, music, and art. Eleanor little cared that her grandmother usually decided on old-fashioned clothes or that she insisted on the strictest supervision. Eleanor seemed at first to withdraw, to flounder, to suppress her feelings, to live in a dream world, a world in which her father had become the leading figure. She needed him, for, as Blanche Wiesen Cook perceived, her "mother's disapproval, dominated [her] childhood . . . [and] permanently affected her self-image."[33] Because of this, she could never believe that she could be accepted for her own sake.

Eleanor could scarcely have realized what was going on; but gradually she came, through some gifts of her nature, through some talents, some deep energies, to reach for new and viable life fictions. Even then, she seemed to be seeking a mental-emotional center, an equipment and a confidence that could work for her.[34]

A turning point in the development of fictions for Eleanor's living came with her entry at age 15 into Allenswood, a school in Wimbledon Park, near the center of London.[35] At the turn of the century, this school was remarkable for the quality of education it offered girls in a still-Victorian England. Most girls there and in the United States had been denied higher education in the belief that their minds were fragile and would suffer damage.

The creation of Marie Souvestre, daughter of a distinguished French philosopher-novelist, the Allenswood school reflected the personality of its headmistress. Knowledgeable in the ways of scholars, intellectually agile, and committed to liberal, often radical, causes, Mlle. Souvestre also provided a model of social grace. Most important, she offered caring guidance. "I imagine her methods were more like those of a college professor," Eleanor thought.[36] For Eleanor Roosevelt, Mlle. Souvestre and her methods and her choices of fictions as well as her manner of living them made a crucial difference. She taught Eleanor to express herself—mentally and emotionally. She offered Eleanor approval for her own sake; she valued those qualities of character and intellect she perceived in her young student.

Speaking of some of her English classmates, Eleanor noticed that they were apt to repeat in their papers what their teacher said. "You are giving me back what I gave you," Mlle. Souvestre exclaimed on one such occasion. "It does not interest me. You have not sifted it through your own intelligence. Why was your mind given you but to think things out for yourself?"[37] With the encouragement her own papers earned, Eleanor's confidence rose.

A special, loving relationship developed between Eleanor and her teacher. Eleanor often sat at the head table with Mlle. Souvestre. In vacation periods, she was invited to travel about Europe with Mlle. Souvestre. For Eleanor her teacher became a model of achievement, warmth, and creative expression. She demonstrated the possibility of living graciously, thoughtfully, and independently. With Mlle. Souvestre, Eleanor experienced a different set of fictions. She observed that they could be implemented. In Mlle. Souvestre's company, everything seemed possible. Eleanor blossomed. She became the best-loved girl among her classmates. To Eleanor, Mlle. Souvestre became "one of the people whom I cared most for in the world."[38] Eleanor's whole outlook changed.

After three of the "best years" of her life at Allenswood, she returned to New York. Had she absorbed only the fictions of her class and her family, Eleanor might have followed the debutante trail from society life to immersion in marriage and children. She nearly did. But because of her inner needs, indeed because of her strengths, because of the chances of life and love, and because of the good fortune of having encountered Mlle. Souvestre, she discovered different fictions.

On returning to New York at age 18, she found the round of debutante parties anxiety provoking. Any young woman who from childhood had believed herself "old-fashioned," ungainly, almost ugly, would have dreaded an empty dance card. Any young woman who found she couldn't measure up to the fictions about who she should be would have felt anxious. Eleanor hated the "Assembly" and its cruel protocols. "I went into that ballroom not knowing one single man except Bob Ferguson," she wrote. "I do not think I realized beforehand what utter agony it was going to be." But "gradually I acquired a few friends." Still, "by no stretch of the imagination could I fool myself into thinking that I was a popular debutante." In these remembrances, she expressed discomfort and something less than acceptance of the fictional role laid out for her.[39]

Actually Eleanor had become an attractive young woman who didn't fare

At the age of 19, Eleanor Roosevelt became a debutante in the Knickerbocker society of old New York. *Courtesy Franklin Roosevelt Library.*

badly in the social whirl. But she found the parties boring. In the autumn and early winter of 1902, the social round of a debutante's life seemed hollow, unfulfilling. The fictions implied in the debutante ritual never suffused this young woman's horizons.

Nor did the parties provide escape from the embarrassments of living at Tivoli, her grandmother's home, with Vallie and Eddie, her ominously alcoholic uncles. The alternative was living in her grandmother's 37th Street house in the city, alone or with her troublesome Aunt Pussie. The family fortunes were falling apart because the family itself was deteriorating. Eleanor nearly had to take charge of the 37th Street house. "I ran the house as far as it was run by anyone," she wrote. "Pussie was even more temperamental than she had been as a young girl." While members of Eleanor's family suffered the ravages of alcoholic self-destruction, she tried to take on responsibilities. Her native strength and vitality began to come into play.

When her grandmother decided to close the town house, Eleanor began to cast about for a more rewarding way of life. So during the summer and fall of 1903, she went to live with her godmother and cousin Mrs. Henry (Susie) Parrish at 8 East 76th Street.

By then, she had become attracted to voluntary settlement house work and to causes associated with problems of the poor. She had joined a group of young women—the newly organized Junior League. Through the group's interest in social improvements, she had become aware of the floods of immigrants and of the struggles of working people. She had begun to take an interest in their lives. She saw that all was not well in the slums of the city.

To the concern of her family, she followed these new interests for a time. Accustomed to a comfortable distance from those who received their largesse, her family warned that she would find herself in danger on the streets of the city, that she would bring home diseases. Their warnings failed to deter her.

She visited the Rivington Street Settlement House regularly. There she taught classes for the children of immigrants. Because the children loved them, the classes became, for Eleanor, "the nicest part of the day." At Rivington Street, she also came face to face with the shameful conditions in the tenement slums of New York. She enrolled in the New York Consumers' League, where Florence Kelley was the leading figure; as the League carried on investigations, she began to learn of twelve-hour workdays and sweatshop labor and piecework; she saw with amazement the deplorable situations of young women workers in garment manufacturing and retail industries. She walked alone in the streets, and she took public transportation. "I was terribly sensitive to what people would think and feel," she wrote, meaning that she was aware that she was not conforming to her family's cherished principles—their chosen guidelines, their fictions. "But my desire to taste all of life and try to understand it was so intense that I went ahead, regardless of whether or not people were watching me or approving, and so slowly acquired a new sense of freedom and confidence."[40]

These excursions began to give her a realistic understanding of the needs of people whose situations differed from her own. Rather than commit herself to the debutante track, she was choosing to explore interests akin to her grandfather's and her father's interest in the newsboys of New York as well as to Mlle. Souvestre's commitment to dreams of a kinder world. "Give some of your energy, but not all, to worldly pleasures," Mlle. Souvestre had written. On another occasion, she had said "Dear child, my mind is so divided in respect to you. I should like to know that you are happy, and yet how I fear to hear you have been unable to defend yourself against all the temptations which surround you, evenings out, pleasure, flirtations. How all this will estrange you from all that I knew you to be!"[41] Eleanor listened. She was developing a selective engagement with the fictions of the old elite.

Historian Lois Scharf has noted that "the habits of patronizing benevolence were not easily changed," that some of Eleanor's activities were traditional, such as playing hostess at the annual Christmas party or raising money for a clubhouse.[42] But whatever the sway of the entrenched fictions, Eleanor had begun the alteration of one of them. In retrospect, her new interests might be considered foundation-stones in the building of fictions for the rest of her life. Though a realization of this turn in her activities would be deferred, the period formed an apprenticeship for concerns she came to consider paramount. In a sense, and in *her* sense, Eleanor began to take over the fiction that to dispense charity should be a leisurely, aristocratic undertaking of choice. In years ahead, she would alter that fiction beyond recognition. She would make an involved concern for the less fortunate a requirement for a civilized society.

In Eleanor's hands, charity would become not the occasional gesture of the rich and the first line of defense in maintaining an old order of privilege; it would become a different fiction, the priority and obligation of an individual and of a society. She would redefine it; it would become her challenge, and ultimately, that of everyone. This was the beginning of her ventures toward reaching a separate identity, an identity powered by fictions new to her; it also began a restructuring of a fiction that was basic to her class.[43]

On one mellow autumn evening in the year 1902, one of her cousins invited her to join him for dinner at Sherry's and the horse show. Eleanor was 18. A remote cousin noticed Eleanor among the guests. Though as children these fifth cousins—Franklin and Eleanor—had taken part in one or another of the family gatherings, this meeting proved portentous. During Franklin Roosevelt's junior year at Harvard, they began to see each other in a different way. She found him genial and charming, possessed of assets rather like those of her father, though more directed. She probably never consciously compared them.

At Groton, and then at Harvard, Franklin Roosevelt had been less than successful in a social sense; despite an engaging personality and an agreeable, if somewhat condescending air, he had failed to make the Porcellian Club to which members of his family had belonged. "This," wrote his cousin Corinne, "was a blow to his pride and a frustration to a very ambitious nature."[44] Some years later, Franklin told his friend Sheffield Cowles that this failure had been "the greatest disappointment in his life."[45]

Nor had he been popular with girls. Among his Oyster Bay cousins he was considered a mama's boy; they had nicknamed him "Featherduster" because of the nature of his relationship with his mother; from childhood, she had dominated his every move, leaving him little room to make choices or take on responsibilities. The nickname stuck because of the seeming superficial nature of Franklin's involvements with everyone else.

Eleanor and Franklin Roosevelt in the early days of their courtship.
Courtesy Franklin Roosevelt Library.

But Franklin Roosevelt's biographer Geoffrey Ward believed that Franklin early understood that he would have to learn every manipulative skill to accomplish any purpose of his own.[46] He would have to learn every subtle method of controlling the behavior of others in order to succeed in his own desires. Franklin managed to counter his disappointments at Groton and Harvard; he involved himself in campus political activities and he became editor of the *Harvard Crimson*.[47] He found Eleanor encouraging, intelligent, acceptable in the coin of the fictions he knew, and genuinely interested in him and his hopes.

They became engaged, but secretly. Franklin's mother Sara Delano Roosevelt was determined that his graduation should come before all else. More significant, she seemed unlikely to welcome any intruder in the intimacy between herself and her son. Since the death of her husband, her son Franklin had become her reason for living. For her part, Eleanor looked for acceptance and love in her future mother-in-law. But from the start, she experienced difficulty with Sara Roosevelt's determination to cling to her son.

Eleanor couldn't deceive Franklin's mother. During the courtship, she took the first tentative steps toward controlling her own emotional life. She tried a course more in tune with her needs than with establishment fictions. When

Franklin planned to tell his mother that he would be visiting a "Mr. Marvin," Eleanor let him know that she wanted him to tell his mother the truth, that he planned to visit her: "I never want her to feel that she has been deceived," Eleanor wrote. "Don't be angry with me Franklin for saying this and of course you must do as you think best."[48] The last clause in her letter asserts the superiority of male judgment, according to approved fictions. Though it would take a long time and more than one traumatic experience to set her feet on another path, Eleanor had managed to request in definite terms that Franklin tell his mother his plans. He did.

They overcame Sara's intransigence. But she exacted conditions. She asked Eleanor to keep their engagement secret for a year; then, at Franklin's invitation, she and her son and a friend from his Groton days traveled to the Caribbean.[49]

Meanwhile, Eleanor seems to have been schooling herself in the techniques of a life of service to others, most particularly to Franklin. She seldom thought of her own possibilities, except as they would serve Franklin. If she did think of herself, she downplayed her desires. She became a very model of establishment decorum; to the letter, she exemplified the fictions the Victorian American elite approved for young women: "I felt that I must acquiesce in whatever he might decide," she wrote, remembering. "I took it for granted that men were superior creatures."[50]

So devastating had been the experiences of her childhood, so deep had been her longing for a loving family that she spared no effort to please her fiancé and his demanding mother. Beyond doubt, her love for Franklin was real, lilting: "You know dearest all that I wish you," she wrote, "and I only hope that your Christmas will be very, very happy dearest & that the New Year will bring you more joy than you have ever known before. I can never tell you how much happiness you have brought to me my dearest boy, but I can never remember feeling half so happy before."

Remarkably, Eleanor understood Franklin's situation with his mother. She lavished attention on Sara. "I know just how you feel and how hard it must be," she wrote to Sara, "but I do so want you to learn to love me a little."[51] The sorrows of Eleanor's childhood had rendered her sensitive to other people's discomforts. She embarked on a nearly obsequious relationship with Sara.

Eleanor and Franklin were married in her godmother's home with the rituals attendant to the fictions of the elite, with an added flourish.[52] The president of the United States, Eleanor's Uncle Theodore, gave the bride away. The only flaw was that the president attracted more attention than the young couple; they were left standing nearly alone as guests scrambled to shake the president's hand and listen to his stories.

Eleanor had lived with the feeling that she had no home of her own. That day she may have felt that she had no wedding of her own. She was fond of her

Uncle Theodore and may even have resembled him in some respects. But to that time she had developed little interest in politics. She later recalled that on her honeymoon, an English hostess had asked her to explain the difference in America between national and state governments. "I had never realized," she recorded, "that there were any differences to explain."[53]

The young Roosevelts began life together in a small New York apartment as Franklin continued his law studies at Columbia. But as soon as the older Mrs. Roosevelt went to her summer place, they moved to her Hyde Park home. The thought of housekeeping chores seemed another world to Eleanor, for she had never undertaken them. The fictions of her childhood had led her to believe that one needed servants to prepare meals, go to market, clean house, pay bills, tend to the laundry and the ironing, do daily household tasks.[54] As soon as Franklin completed his law classes, the couple left for a honeymoon in Europe.

In the early years of her marriage, a feeling of helplessness gradually replaced the confidence Eleanor had gained at Allenswood and on visits to her Aunt Bye, the president's older sister in Washington.[55] Eleanor soon ran into perplexing situations for which she felt unprepared. The simplest solution seemed to be to avail herself of her mother-in-law's resources to solve problems. Sara's expertise was pressed upon her. She felt that she was constantly making foolish mistakes, a feeling that did not bolster self-confidence. She would find herself in tears, seemingly without reason.

Upon her return from a trip to Europe, Sara Roosevelt decided she must now care for two people instead of just one. She proceeded to do so capably—but smotheringly, and on her terms. She rented a house for the young couple in New York, a house very near her own. She selected furniture and employed servants. Until the house was ready, Eleanor and Franklin were to live with her in New York and in the big house at Hyde Park or at Sara's summer home at Campobello, off the coast of Maine.

The effect was to replay an old scenario in Eleanor's heart and mind, the "outsider" scenario, the feeling that she didn't belong, that still she had no family and no home of her own, that she had become an accessory to other peoples' arrangements. "For the first year of my married life I was completely taken care of," Eleanor wrote. "My mother-in-law did everything for me."[56]

Valiantly, Eleanor tried to please her mother-in-law, to cater to her every wish. This amounted to a near-slavish obeisance to the most burdensome of the elite fictions, those fictions pertaining to a young woman's role. It meant conducting her life according to Sara's views and deferring to Sara's wishes in matters large and small. Sara wished to maintain control over everything pertaining to her son—and very soon, to her grandchildren. Eleanor had acquired precious little knowledge about planning details involved in living anywhere and no experience in caring for babies and young children. In the face of Sara's determination, she couldn't find support for taking control of her life. According to old fictions, Sara even insisted that most outdoor activities—tennis, swimming, horseback riding, golf—were harmful and that one certainly should not engage in any of them during pregnancy. Nor should a pregnant woman appear in public.

In 1908, the Roosevelts moved into a New York town house Sara built for them, a house adjacent to another she built for herself. The houses were so designed that the dining rooms and drawing rooms could be joined. Sliding doors and connecting hallways allowed Sara to come into the house, any floor, any time. Eleanor wrote that one never knew "when she [Sara] would appear, day or night."[57]

Sara wanted to remain Franklin's most intimate connection; systematically, she excluded her daughter-in-law. Through it all Eleanor found herself dominated by the way Franklin's mother propelled the fictions of the elite. Both Eleanor and Franklin had inherited independent annual incomes of amounts sufficient for them to live apart from Sara: Franklin's came to about $5,000, Eleanor's to about $7,500. It didn't occur to either of them that a lesser standard of living could be preferable.[58]

So Eleanor never had a voice in the selection of furnishings or servants. One day in 1908, she found herself weeping in front of her dressing table. "I did not know what was the matter with me," she wrote. But "when my bewildered young husband asked me . . . I said that I did not like to live in a house which was not in any way mine, one that I had done nothing about and which did not represent the way I wanted to live."[59] Franklin thought her "quite mad." Disinclined to participate in his wife's feelings, he simply disengaged himself. At this moment, though she would scarcely have seen it in these terms, Eleanor must have been realizing that the fictions of her childhood were not working for her. Thinking back, she wrote that "I was beginning to realize that something within me craved to be an individual."[60]

By the time there were several children, Sara had moved the young family to "the big house" at Hyde Park. There Sara arranged and directed all the details of living—two chairs by the fireside, one for herself, one for Franklin, herself at one end of the dinner table and Franklin at the other.

Eleanor found that Sara and the nurses made decisions about the care of her babies, how to clothe them and even whether she should nurse them. "For years I was afraid of my nurses," Eleanor wrote. They were "usually trained English nurses who ordered me around quite as much as they ordered the children."[61] Of the six children born to the Roosevelts, one died in infancy. In the circumstances in which she found herself, Eleanor never learned to relate as she would have wished to her young children.

The situation became less and less tolerable to the intelligent, vigorous Eleanor. Nevertheless she lived in this pattern, with these fictions, for fifteen years. Thinking over her life of this time, she realized that "I was not develop-ing any individual taste or initiative. I was simply absorbing the personalities of those about me and letting their tastes and interests dominate me."[62] This meant that up to then, the fictions that characterized their lives had to become her fictions. It meant that their customs had to become her customs. It also meant that she would pay a price for repressing her own inner needs; she didn't complain, but for many years she suffered painful migraine headaches. At Sara's insistence, Eleanor had even given up the ventures into social service which had opened worlds for her in the year of her coming out. She had learned, she said, that "almost everyone had something interesting to con-tribute to my education." But

> I had lost a good deal of my crusading spirit where the poor were concerned
> because I had been told I had no right to go into the slums or the hospitals for
> fear of bringing disease home to my children. . . . I had fallen into the easier
> way of sitting on boards and giving small sums to this or that charity.[63]

So powerful was the operation of the fictions into which she had been born and into which she had married that for all that time she didn't realize that she could have any choices. She lived with the old feelings of being an outsider in other people's homes, of possessing no powers over her own life.

We would today think her prudish, anything but responsive and joyous in her relations with her husband; in this area, old fictions proved crippling. Physical contact for women within marriage had been looked upon as a duty, a duty "to be borne," never a matter in which one could experience pleasure, never a matter in which a woman could have a choice. Imprisoned in a cluster of fictions that exacted self-control of women, as it accomplished the repres-sion of sexual desire in many of them, Eleanor probably found it difficult to achieve a pleasurable physical intimacy in any caring relationship.

She suffered depressions. My "Griselda moods," she called them. When one of her babies died, the depressions became severe. Franklin had already begun to take dinners at the Harvard Club and to stay late for poker games. He would return to a gloomy, uncommunicative wife.

But Franklin found his excursions into the life of New York clubs intriguing. He found the traditional sex-role fictions of the old elite congenial. He had al-ways considered his cousin Theodore a man to emulate. He began to think in political terms. Though the president was a Republican, Franklin's father had been a Democrat. When he was asked if he would run for a seat in the New York Assembly on the Democratic ticket, Franklin demurred. Then he replied that he would ask his mother! Up to then, politics, like charity, had been for most Roosevelts an occasional interest. According to old fictions, gentlemen were appointed, not elected. Only Theodore had made politics a prime concern, carrying his activities into the crowded centers of New York City politics. There Theodore Roosevelt sought not only a base for political power but also lasting connections with a politics of reform.[64]

If Franklin had succumbed to Sara's guidance, he never would have become president. Eleanor might have missed her callings. But Eleanor encouraged her husband. At a friend's suggestion, he discarded the pince-nez he was wont to display. Franklin, too, was altering old fictions. He was beginning to enjoy his own talents. With Richard Connell, the Democratic candidate for congress, he planned an unorthodox campaign in districts known to vote solidly Republican. He was friendly and innovative, and he avoided issues. He courted people. He campaigned in a showy motor tour of upstate villages where it was difficult to find a Democrat. To the surprise of the faithful, he won. The family moved to Albany.

Childhood fictions had profoundly fueled the life passages of Eleanor and Franklin. So too had fictions by which they had related to each other in the uneasy first fifteen years of their marriage. But with this turn, they began to develop fictions of their own. For both Franklin and Eleanor, the new fictions altered the directions of their lives.

Franklin could have remained a country gentleman, living safely and elegantly as his father had lived. He decided instead to enter politics—not as a Republican in the fashion of his cousin Theodore, but as a Democrat in a style of his own. Eleanor realized Franklin's situation perfectly. Looking back, she wrote "It would have been easy for him to have become just a nice young society man who, after his work in the department was over for the day, sat around in the Metropolitan Club."[65]

Eleanor herself could have remained the martyred lady housekeeper and mother, subordinating her life to the fictions of others. Instead she became a woman of public and political consequence. Both Roosevelts showed themselves willing to take risks that would alter the fictions with which they had lived; so began two portentous political careers. For a time their marriage benefited.

Franklin continued and escalated a quest to become his own person; the fictions he developed grew from those he had learned at his mother's knee. Skillfully he honed them. His top priorities became the urge to gain power and the determination to do the decision-making himself. He parlayed an art of getting his way into an abiding domination of the Democratic Party.

Eleanor longed for warmth and for approval. She began to discover new fictions to express her talent and her individuality. As her husband became more involved in politics, she also became interested. For some time she leaned on the fiction that, whatever her inclinations, a woman should support her husband. But on her own, she enjoyed it all. She scarcely expressed her discoveries, not even to herself. But she found that she could organize, that she could run her own households. She began to make new friends, friends from whom she learned to reconnect herself with fortunes of those less favored.

Thus Eleanor Roosevelt, mother of three children, came to a landmark in the development of fictions for the rest of her life. "For the first time," she remembered, "I was going to live on my own: neither my mother-in-law nor Mrs. Paris [the housekeeper at Hyde Park] was going to be within call."[66]

She began by dismissing a French nurse the children disliked and employing three new servants. Next, the day after she arrived in Albany, she found caterers for a reception—an Inaugural Day open house at the new residence—for 250 of Franklin's constituents. Whether by chance or by design, she had stumbled into situations she could manage well. This paved the way for her to become mistress of fictions that would guide her the rest of her life.

In an astonishing display of energy and ability, she began, that same day in Albany, after that "interminable" reception, to unpack boxes and arrange furniture in the house at 248 State Street. That same night, she managed to go to another reception in the home of John Alden Dix, the new Democratic governor. With this, Eleanor Roosevelt set the pace of activities that would become her pattern, the wonder of all who beheld it, for years to come.

For Eleanor, the move to Albany presaged an awakening, a quickening of latent talent. She had always felt a need for warm emotional connections with those about her. She had always shown a capacity to listen to others, to care deeply about their needs. Easily and quickly she became involved in the life of the New York capital and its people. To that time, she had not realized that she liked to organize the enterprises around her—the running of her home, the planning of political gatherings, the management of her children, the mechanics of political ventures for her husband.

She discovered a gift for relating to people of disparate backgrounds. "Anyone who came [to my house] was grist to my mill," she wrote, "because I was beginning to get interested in human beings." But she still, in her words, "lived under the compulsion of my early training" and "looked at everything from the point of view of what I ought to do. . . . So I took an interest in politics. . . . It was a wife's duty to be interested in whatever interested her husband."[67] In the past, she had supposed that meant anything from seeing that his favorite foods appeared on the table to espousing his notions of how she should do things and even his notions of what she should think. It had meant living his fictions.

But Eleanor discovered that *she* could connect with politicians of motley origins. She could make them feel comfortable. Political people began to notice her. Now she could use the social skills she had accumulated at Allenswood, in New York, and under her Aunt Bye's tutelage in Washington. She could use her special gifts of relating to people. Eleanor understood how to leave political opponents feeling warm toward her and tolerant toward her husband. She even knew how to remain on good terms with Franklin's mother; she wrote to Sara daily. In a lingering fashion, she still hoped to please Sara.

Prominent among the people around Franklin was one person Eleanor did, for a time, find difficult. Louis Howe, a newspaperman, had become a knowledgeable political strategist. He presented a rough exterior, the result, in part, of a childhood accident. "I was not favorably impressed with Louis at the time," Eleanor wrote, "because he smoked a great many cigarettes! . . . I was very disapproving whenever he came down to report on the campaign."

But Louis Howe sensed the mighty possibilities of Franklin's appeal. He realized the attractiveness of the Roosevelt name, the Roosevelt charisma. He also perceived Eleanor's abilities—as well as her falterings. "Louis was entirely indifferent to his appearance," she thought. "He not only neglected his clothes but gave the impression at times that cleanliness was not of particular interest to him." For years, Eleanor preserved a distant air. But despite her feelings, she couldn't deny his knowledge of political realities, above all, his political skill. Later she revised her impressions and even gathered him into the fold of her new fictions: "The fact that he had rather extraordinary eyes and a fine mind I was fool enough not to have discovered," she wrote.[68] Fortunately for both Roosevelts, Howe became manager of Franklin's campaigns. In her seventies, Eleanor reflected again. She wrote that "this little man was really the biggest man from the point of view of imagination and determination I have ever known."

A group of Tammany Hall reformers became important among her new acquaintances. Franklin too identified with their goals to fight corruption and promote conservation. He became an insurgent, the leader of the insurgents vis-à-vis the Tammany establishment of New York City. The deeper interests of influential members of this group had to do with Tammany's powers over the lives of people, however—over places where they lived, where they went to school, where they worked, the peril of their streets. These issues interested Eleanor. She came to know Al Smith, Ed Terry, Robert Wagner, Thomas Grady, and the legendary political boss Big Tim Sullivan. She entertained them in her home. She listened to their deliberations. She developed warm personal relations with them, whatever their political loyalties.[69] Historian Blanche Wiesen Cook believes that "ER was largely responsible for smoothing FDR's path to better relations with the Tammany reformers."[70] The forging of new alliances, as of new fictions, was a delicate task; Eleanor began to do it sensitively. In that time, in that climate, New York belonged to Tammany.

On a sea trip from their summer home in Campobello to New York, where Franklin intended to help plan Woodrow Wilson's campaign strategy, both Eleanor and Franklin contracted typhoid fever. Both faced a depressing period of convalescence. For a while, both were unable to take part in political concerns. But Franklin called Louis Howe to save his reelection campaign, and from that time Howe became a fixture in their lives. Because he understood politics, he became invaluable in the careers of both Roosevelts. With sharp insight, he analyzed events. He briefed Franklin. He arranged meetings and speech opportunities. He created and placed news releases. He planned trips and conferences.

Very tactfully, he helped Eleanor overcome her shyness. "To this day," Eleanor ruefully mused after years of experience, "feelings of panic sweep over me occasionally when I face a crowd, and I wish the ground would open and swallow me."[71] But Louis Howe sought her opinions. As the campaigns progressed, and in years that followed when they traveled with Franklin across the country, Howe would knock on her door to consult with her. He would ask if he might discuss a speech or a policy. He convinced her of her value to her husband's hopes. When Franklin could not appear at a political event, Howe persuaded Eleanor to take his place. He sensed her moods. He coached her on speaking in public: Prepare only the beginning and the end of your remarks. In the middle, say what you have to say, say it from your heart, and stop.

At a deep level, Eleanor cared about Franklin's campaigns; had she felt no genuine involvement, she could never have reassigned the priorities of her childhood fictions, particularly the fictions which affected women of her class: Ladies did not interest themselves in politics. They did not spend time listening to sessions of the Albany Legislature. They did not lobby for causes. They scarcely expressed any views. They never spoke at public gatherings. To her reporter friend Lorena Hickok Eleanor later confided that she had been "brought up by a very strict grandmother, who thought no lady should ever have stories written about her, except in the society columns."[72] Surely no lady should allow herself to be seen with the likes of Louis Howe. It is also true that the attachment she felt to her husband—a husband who exemplified many of her father's more captivating traits—sustained her efforts. Still, some of the fictions of Eleanor's childhood were slowly giving way.

The Wilson campaign for the presidency in 1912 determined the rest of their lives. It precipitated an altering of priorities, a major shifting of fictions. This was their first national convention. Eleanor disliked it. She couldn't bear the noisy, smoke-filled rooms, the strident delegates, the whole boisterous performance. In the middle of this, she felt lonely and bored. Speaking of her convention experience in later years, she wrote "Most of the time at the convention I sat and knitted, suffered with the heat, and wished it would end."[73] Before this one ended, she did leave. But both Roosevelts learned; this was an important step toward becoming the seasoned politicians they would need to be.

Despite Theodore Roosevelt's Bull Moose campaign to recapture the presidency, despite Eleanor's quiet sympathy with its goals, Woodrow Wilson won in 1912. Or perhaps he won because there *was* a third party and a split. Wilson then offered Franklin the position of assistant secretary of the navy. Though

Eleanor felt misgivings, Franklin joyfully accepted. The family moved from Albany to Washington, D.C. Even then, her own explorations caused her to fear being cast in the supplementary, ceremonial position political wives occupied.

To both Roosevelts, and especially to Eleanor, the complexity of living in the nation's capital became evident soon enough. A sense of rising hurdles, of tests, of values challenged, of old fictions displaced, politically and personally, sprang from every unfolding event. The life of a cabinet official in prewar Washington exacerbated every tension. "I could have learned much about politics and government, for I had plenty of opportunities to meet and talk with interesting men and women," Eleanor thought. But "as I look back . . . there was the social aspect, which then seemed to me most important." She remembered that "nearly all the women at that time were the slaves of the Washington social system."[74] This meant endless calls on officials' wives, planning entertainments, planning political gatherings, learning Washington ways from the top down.

It meant accomplishing all this while bearing two more children and caring for the three she already had. By March of 1916, the United States was becoming deeply involved with the war in Europe. Because of this, Eleanor changed her ways at the Washington scene; she plunged into war-related activities. In March 1916, she gave birth to their last child, John. Looking back, Eleanor realized that her ability to respond to the many different calls upon her time and energies was "just a symptom of developing executive ability."[75]

There were emotional dimensions. For Eleanor, the physical expressions of marriage had been associated with a sacrosanct concept of a woman's duty. This was a fiction of her world and, pointedly, of her class: Women were supposed to be available at all times, though they were not supposed to feel the sexual urges that possessed men. It was expected that they would overlook their husband's "indiscretions."[76] Nevertheless, when Eleanor learned of her husband's affair with Lucy Mercer, her own secretary, she felt devastated.

When Franklin returned home ill after a trip to England, Eleanor came upon a packet of love letters to Franklin from Lucy Mercer. In that instant, the boundaries of Eleanor's emotional life dissolved. Perhaps she could have allayed her feelings by calling forth the Victorian fictions of her childhood. To some extent, she did. Perhaps she never quite made sense of the situation. Beyond doubt, this was more than the flirtations of other days. This was a troubling, close attachment. Franklin loved politics. He loved the challenges of appealing to many kinds of constituents. But Franklin wanted a certain festive frosting to his days. Flirtations had been frequent—and fleeting. It is said that Franklin and Eleanor even came to a kind of accommodation in their Albany and Washington days—that Franklin might go his way as long as Eleanor could be spared the evenings of drinking and cavorting.

Whatever her concerns, the physical aspects of Eleanor's relations with

Franklin ceased when she read Lucy Mercer's letters. She never again shared a marriage bed with her husband. She could no longer travel with the fictions that men are licentious, women pure, and that women ought to believe in and protect these fictions. Perhaps physical relations unofficially ended before the discovery of the letters; their children noticed that the Roosevelts did not share a bedroom after the birth of their last child.[77]

Whatever their relationship, agonizing discussions ensued after the discovery of the letters. The discussions involved Franklin's mother and, reportedly, his mother's threat to disinherit her son. They resulted in the decision not to divorce. Franklin promised not to see Lucy Mercer. Some observers believe, however, that from the time of his involvement with Lucy, Franklin became less superficial, less self-centered, more capable of emotional depth.[78]

And some believe that the seeds of Eleanor's future took root in these moments, that Franklin's infidelity propelled her toward activities for which she became known, that Eleanor's loss of faith in her husband's allegiance brought a compelling need for new attachments. Historian William Chafe has insightfully suggested, however, that Eleanor had always experienced strong emotional connections with those involved in her endeavors, that this had been and continued to be her distinguishing style.[79] Whatever the explanations, Eleanor embarked, albeit painfully, on the defining ventures of her life, the quest to decide upon the fictions that mattered most for her, then to implement them.

Still, Eleanor's goals—and Eleanor's public fictions—increasingly became those Franklin preferred. Perhaps this happened because, in a political sense, Eleanor understood his approaches and his needs. Apart from the turbulence between them, and from whatever different motivations, Franklin and Eleanor still shared concerns and in some measure operated along each other's wavelengths. Without putting a name on it, they formed a political partnership. They learned from each other. Eleanor expressed this. Once she remarked that "from him I learned how to observe from train windows; he would watch the crops, notice how people dressed, how many cars there were and in what condition, and even look at the washing on the clotheslines."[80] She noted that there were occasions when Franklin told representatives "to act not according to the arguments he had given me but according to the arguments that I had given him!"[81]

Though Franklin's ambition seems to have played a dominant role, the political goals of both arose from issues of economic reform, education, the suppression of the Nazi tyranny, always the anguish of widespread poverty, always the effort to achieve a just society. They were goals that involved choosing different fictions than either had known in the circumstances to which both were born. They shared each other's discoveries. "I . . . have learned from my husband that no leader can be too far ahead of his followers," Eleanor wrote.[82]

Franklin genuinely liked and listened to Eleanor's female friends, those whose careers had expressed Eleanor's commitments.

The nation's participation in World War I and its aftermath provided painful verification of Franklin's insight that it would be difficult to lead Americans to bring all their resources to defeat the Nazi tyranny. Before the United States declared war on Germany, Eleanor believed, with many Americans, that "only our financial resources would be needed" and that the navy would be the only branch of the service likely to become involved.[83] She wrote that "many foolish people like myself" shared this belief. So in that prewar summer, Eleanor noted that "I did little war work . . . beyond the inevitable knitting which every woman undertook and which became a constant habit. No one moved without her knitting."[84]

Invention

Like women of patriarchal societies everywhere, Eleanor turned increasingly to women friends and to women's organizations. Up until then, she had concentrated her energies on the challenges of her husband's career. She had been the stellar helpmate. Now, in her own right, she turned toward causes that attracted her; she looked to relationships with new friends for emotional satisfactions.

William Chafe has pointed out that Eleanor became a "center for an ever-growing female reform network."[85] In itself, this didn't require a radical shift in fictions. But as Eleanor's development progressed, changes in direction occurred. After the crisis in her relationship with her husband, Eleanor turned not to former society friends but to new connections. In the years after her discovery of Lucy Mercer's letters, and despite the emotional trauma she suffered, she did shape a different life.

She made the acquaintance of two Democratic Party workers, Marion Dickerman and Nancy Cook. Both were educated, professional women. Both had been suffragists. Deeply committed to reform causes, both had traveled with fictions unlike those Eleanor had known. Both had sought labor laws for women and children, both were committed to world peace. Though Cook and Dickerman had lived together in an arrangement then called a "Boston marriage," the three became close companions. They shared interests and projects and, often, living arrangements. Franklin appreciated Eleanor's stimulating friends; he absorbed information and ideas from conversations with them. He, too, shared their interests. For both Roosevelts, Dickerman and Cook provided a focus for a shifting of fictions, certainly an enhancement of fictions already redirected.

Eleanor met labor organizer Rose Schneiderman. On a cold winter day in 1926, she accompanied Schneiderman to picket a garment factory. She also

Eleanor flanked by Nancy Cook and Marion Dickerman. *Courtesy Franklin Roosevelt Library.*

joined the Women's Trade Union League and came to know its gifted leader, Mary Dreier. At the National Consumers' League, she became acquainted with Molly Dewson, the League's research secretary. At this time in her life, Eleanor longed for companionship and for support. She found it among the networks of women interested in moving toward a just society. She came to know women who followed careers, women who broadened her horizons, women who opened doors to new fictions, women who cherished goals similar to her own.

She also developed a warm friendship with Earl Miller, a bodyguard from the Albany days. For many years, Earl Miller enhanced the living experiences of "the lady," the name by which he referred to Mrs. Roosevelt. He seems to have cherished more belief in her abilities than she had been able to muster. He suggested, for instance, that she take up horseback riding; he convinced her that she could shoot a gun and drive a car. He believed that her views deserved respect. His confidence in her abilities contributed in important ways to Eleanor's self-assurance. She even seems—with Earl Miller—to have modified the fiction that women must feel subservient and, to some extent, that male-female contacts were, as once she had told her daughter, only meant to be "borne." Eleanor's friend Marion Dickerman thought that Earl Miller "gave something to Eleanor. . . . It was a very deep attachment. . . . Eleanor played with the idea of marriage with Earl. . . . How seriously she ever considered it I cannot honestly say."[86] As for Earl Miller's thoughts, "You don't sleep with someone you call Mrs. Roosevelt," he said in an interview he later gave to Joseph Lash. But he always appeared more than professionally interested in protecting "the lady."[87]

Thus a painful period in Eleanor's life became a pathway to self-reliance and to new experiences involving emotional dimensions. She learned that others could be interested in her feelings. Though she could no longer relate to her husband in the style of the old fictions, she did continue to share his interests as they both turned to new fictions. Remarkably, she continued to appreciate his talents.

She developed wondrous executive abilities: "I was accustomed to managing quite a small army on moves from Washington to Hyde Park and to Campobello and back," she wrote.[88] She did this routinely, as often as four or five times in a year. She engineered many a political gathering. She traveled extensively— so presaging an investigative career unique in the lives of American first ladies. After Franklin could no longer walk through hospitals and state institutions to uncover information, Eleanor undertook such trips, then reported to him. From him, she learned to see more than the surface disclosed.

By intervals, she found herself with the children at Campobello, away from the political spectrum. An epidemic of infantile paralysis precipitated a long stay; Eleanor wrote that she felt "marooned" on that island. But on returning to Washington, she realized the ominous drift toward war. She realized that attacks on our merchant marine were straining relations with Germany, and that atrocity stories were inflaming public opinion.

When war was declared in April of 1917, Eleanor found herself entertaining many members of visiting diplomatic missions. They came, she wrote, "to talk over the type of co-operation that we were to give the Allies."[89] She also joined Red Cross Service groups and navy groups distributing wool for knitting. She astounded fellow workers by her energy and her dedication. Inevitably, this turn of affairs and these activities modified whatever fictions she brought from earlier experiences. Sometimes her thoughts and her fictions changed abruptly, as when she visited hospitals for the wounded. She came to know many situations of desperate peoples of the wider world; as a direct consequence, she experienced a shifting of priorities she would assign to the fictions by which she lived.

Meanwhile, Franklin's career progressed. After a defeat as a candidate for the Senate, he returned to his desk at the navy department. He traveled far on matters related to war participation, while Eleanor kept a demanding schedule of war work in Washington. She did this even though she realized that she differed with members of her family on questions of war and peace and even though she well knew that she stood in the middle of conflicts between Secretary of State William Jennings Bryan's passionate "stand on peace" and her family's participation in international power politics. "My time," she said, "was completely filled with a variety of war activities."[90]

The very circumstance of becoming involved in the European conflict meant that old connections dissolved as new issues preempted public attention. Private concerns reflected the turbulence of public events. For her part, Eleanor seems still to have felt discomfort as Franklin's personal involvements continued. Old alliances shifted or expired, old fictions evaporated, sometimes leaving empty spaces and confused human hearts. It may be that Eleanor and Franklin and those about them were involved in an enormous realigning of basic social fictions about gender-role assignments and the necessity for reform. Eleanor sought consolation. She spent lonely hours in a secluded park, gazing at "Grief," a statue of Henry Adams's wife, Clover, who had committed suicide.

Whatever her emotions, whatever the upheavals, Eleanor Roosevelt stepped into the future with greater confidence than she had achieved in the past. Her brother Hall enlisted in the aviation service. When Grandmother Hall couldn't understand why he did not hire a substitute, as gentlemen had often done in earlier wars, Eleanor told her grandmother that Hall was "no different from any other kind of citizen." Having expressed this radical opinion to her grandmother, Eleanor felt more trust in her own "changing point of view." In reality, she was changing more than her point of view. In her thirties, she had altered fictions basic to living. "This," she said, "was my first really outspoken declaration against the accepted standards of the surroundings in which I had spent my childhood."[91]

Franklin's dashing personality found echoes in wartime Washington. Affable, high-spirited, good-looking, politically and festively inclined, he relished the clubs, the excursions on the Potomac, the dinners with diplomats. While Eleanor often remained home with the children, he spent time with Harvard friends and Washington acquaintances; he played with whatever light love affair might come his way. Eleanor knew all of this. It must have hurt her, continually, but finally it did not deter her. She carried the multiple obligations of her large family and her daunting schedule of wartime service, even in the heat of the Washington summer.

Eleanor did, however, possess access to assistance unavailable to most women; her household consisted of seven family members and ten servants. This meant that she could involve herself in public activities, that she could entertain, that she could travel, that she could carry on extensive correspondences. In an immediate sense, class privilege insulated her from daily concerns of ordinary people. In the wake of some embarrassing publicity when she told a reporter that she was setting an example of wartime economies in her household, her husband wrote her that "I am proud to be the husband of the Originator, Discoverer and Inventor of the New Household Economy for Millionaires!"[92]

After the armistice, Eleanor and Franklin traveled together to Paris to take part in President Wilson's presentations at the peace conference. Two months later, they returned to another Washington, the Washington of the president's tragic attempts to obtain congressional approval for the League of Nations.

Years afterward, Eleanor wrote about Wilson's defeat. "Perhaps the answer is," she thought, "that these agreements should be worked out in conjunction with the leaders of Congress instead of by the Executive alone." This proved a realization that would be important some twenty-five years later as Franklin Roosevelt planned to bring his country into the United Nations.[93]

Eleanor's activities did not diminish with the conclusion of the war. Rather, they veered in another direction. "In October," she wrote, "I had my first contact with women's organizations interested in working conditions for women. . . . I liked all the women very much indeed, but I had no idea how much more I was going to see of them in the future."[94] Nor did she realize how extensive the political influence of women's networks would become.

Franklin's career progressed almost inexorably. By June of 1920, he had been nominated as running mate for presidential candidate James M. Cox. In the conduct of this campaign, Franklin displayed a disregard for principles that had dominated Progressive-Democratic views and a willingness to cater to questionable factions. For example, he heartily endorsed the Legionnaires of Centralia, Washington, even though they had lynched a Wobbly, in an unspeakably cruel way, for his antiwar views. Through this campaign, Franklin seems to have laid bare the fictions that were taking precedence for him. He probably also learned the dynamics of communicating with audiences; in this respect, the indulgence of the press and others on the campaign train assisted him vastly.[95]

He invited Eleanor to accompany him—not, it seems, to enjoy her company but to take political advantage of her presence. She was to keep a diary, she was to take notes. She was to appear adoringly on the platform when he spoke. "I was glad for my husband, but it never occurred to me to be much excited. I had come to accept the fact that public service was my husband's great interest," Eleanor said.[96]

She said this in deference to old fictions, ignoring, as she said it, her own inclination to serve the public. She ignored as well the persistent painful exhibitions of her husband's flirtations. So far as anyone can tell from her memoirs or any public record, she may never have accorded herself leeway to express her feelings about Franklin's dallyings. But she did learn to laugh a little with her reporter friends on occasions when those dallyings were obvious to all. There can be little doubt that her feelings played an important role in her choices of fictions for the rest of her life.

The political dynamic had become her great interest, but no longer because it happened to be her husband's. In early days of their marriage, she had believed it a wife's duty to follow her husband's interests unquestioningly. Now she would have her own thoughts, her own "great interests." They would become her chosen fictions. Years later, she could muse about the importance of developing one's individuality: "This is your life, she wrote, "not someone else's."[97] She had learned that the war had rendered a life of "teas, luncheons and dinners . . . an impossible mode of living"—the expression of fictions with which she no longer felt at ease.

She described Franklin's acceptance of his nomination for the vice-presidency as "the first really mammoth meeting to be held at Hyde Park."[98] Eight thousand people tramped over the lawns of Sara Roosevelt's estate. Typically, Eleanor understood her mother-in-law's difficulties in welcoming so many of Franklin's supporters, for the rally also signaled a change in Sara's style of living.

The disastrous defeat in this vice-presidential campaign dampened Franklin's spirits somewhat. Yet the campaign increased his public visibility. During this campaign, Franklin first met Marguerite LeHand—"Missy"—the woman who became his longtime private secretary, his manager of White House schedules and occasions, his close companion.

Knowing defeat was likely, Franklin made plans to resume the practice of law in New York. Since the war had rendered society rounds trivial for Eleanor, she considered briefly whether she should learn to cook and take a course in shorthand and typing. Wasn't this what women were expected to do? Weren't these the guiding solutions—the fictions—women had been taught? Would these activities put her in closer touch with realities of most women's lives?

But before long, Mrs. Frank Vanderlip (Narcissa Vanderlip), chairman of the New York State League of Women Voters, persuaded her to join the league's board and be responsible for reporting national legislation. Thus she came in contact with two remarkable feminist women, Elizabeth Read, a lawyer who possessed "a keen and analytical mind," and Esther Lape, whose "brilliant mind" produced a "driving force, a kind of nervous power." "It was the beginning of a friendship" Eleanor wrote, "which was to be lasting and warm. I remember many pleasant evenings spent with Elizabeth and Esther in their little apartment."[99] Both women became members of Eleanor's female reform network. And though it would take her a while to feel comfortable with a fiction alien to her earlier life, Eleanor Roosevelt learned from them the new importance of the feminist approach to the political landscape.

In the fateful summer of 1921, Eleanor took the children to Campobello. Franklin joined them in early August. In retrospect, Eleanor realized "that he had had no real rest since the war."[100] Delayed in returning from a sailing excursion by the discovery of a forest fire, then by taking a swim, Franklin sat around in his bathing suit reading his mail. He felt a chill. This proved the onset of the illness that disabled him. Paralysis set in. "The use of his hands and arms came back completely," Eleanor wrote.[101] But Franklin never regained the use of his legs.

Nor did he ever lose his belief that there was a way to surmount every obstacle, that he would walk again. He lived this fiction. He spent days in hospitals, in therapy. He struggled through long hours every day. He learned to carry heavy metal braces on his legs. He went through many fittings, many brace alterations, many discouraging failures. In the autumn of 1924 he traveled to Warm Springs, Georgia, where the climate might be beneficial. He never backtracked, he never gave up. For the rest of his life, and throughout his career as governor and president, and even though his efforts to move his legs went nearly unrewarded, he strove for improvement in his physical condition.

Some have noticed that his interest in the problems of others grew with the magnitude of the physical difficulties he faced. The fiction that he could improve served him well. Probably he did cling to the fictions of his early life, but he expanded those fictions. In the exigencies of his physical limitations, Franklin enlarged exponentially his understanding of deprivations that crippled other lives. He also deepened his concept of the possible reaches of politics. He increased his capacity to concentrate, to face the philosophical implications of political actions, to feel for the misfortunes of others. In the swings toward progressivism and internationalism, he came to oppose money in politics, private control of national finances, starvation wages, the treatment of human beings as commodities.

Trying as it must have been, Eleanor accepted his situation with grace. She never gave up. She made every arrangement for Franklin's care and comfort. "People have often asked me how I felt about his illness," she wrote. "To tell the truth, I do not think I ever stopped to analyze my feelings. There was so much to do to manage the household and the children and to try to keep things running smoothly that I never had time to think of my own reactions. I simply lived from day to day and got through the best I could."[102]

In the face of the new obstacle, Louis Howe demonstrated his commitment to Franklin's career. At that point, Eleanor entered the lists in earnest. On the surface, she did this in her husband's behalf. In reality, she did it in harmony with her own brilliant political abilities. She did it because she had grasped and widened, independently, the fictions by which she wanted to live. Though her accommodations sometimes carried a certain frantic quality, those fictions that were becoming her priorities reflected a deepening commitment to the needy of the nation. They reflected her understanding that one might look for change through political channels.

With the help of Louis Howe, Eleanor Roosevelt took over the organizing of the state of New York to deliver female votes. She served as a stand-in for her husband, keeping the Roosevelt name in the forefront of political life. She had come to know it was crucial to her own survival to develop meaningful activities.

The long struggle for woman suffrage came to a conclusion in 1920; this was the first year in which women everywhere in the United States could participate in a national election. At first, Eleanor had shown only a peripheral concern for votes for women; that position reflected old values, old fictions. But when she and her husband had learned more about the idea from Eleanor's friends, they developed an interest. When Franklin backed the idea, surely for political considerations, Eleanor came to the realization that women's votes mattered to every woman, that women's votes could make a difference, and that she could scarcely hope to find steadier support for causes important to her. Women's concerns, especially the welfare of working women and of children, became fixtures of her changed fictions. Eleanor's efforts proved successful, and they impressed Democratic Party regulars.

She learned in detail the personal and public derelictions of politicians of President Warren Harding's Republican administration. She campaigned zestfully: Recalling the general corruption, and in particular the Teapot Dome scandals of the 1920s, she at one time arranged for a teapot built on top of an automobile to trail the Republican candidate—who happened to be her uncle.[103] By then cleavages in the Roosevelt family had become irreparable.

About this time, Eleanor became interested in building a "cottage" of her own. Partly this reflected old yearnings, old dissatisfactions with fictions of her class; partly it reflected a new independence, a search for fictions viable for her. Whatever her deepest needs, Val-Kill Cottage did enable Eleanor to live apart from her mother-in-law. With Franklin's help, she built Val-Kill Cottage beside Val-Kill Brook on the Roosevelt estate. Eleanor's friends Marion Dickerman and Nancy Cook lived there. The three entertained and spent pleasant evenings by themselves; often they picnicked there with Franklin. From there Nancy Cook directed a furniture factory—an enterprise which survived the Depression but not the stresses resulting from Cook's simultaneously holding another position as executive secretary of the women's division of the Democratic State Committee.

Eleanor had also associated herself with Marion Dickerman at the Todhunter School; she joined her friends in purchasing the school. There Eleanor taught courses to the older girls in American history, English, and American literature and current events. Partly as a fulfillment of her new independence, she continued to teach there after her husband became governor of New York.

Eleanor was also beginning to earn money from writing and from radio talks. These activities certainly confronted old fictions, for upper-class Victorian "ladies" didn't and often couldn't support themselves. Her success was especially galling to her mother-in-law. Eventually Eleanor took over the furniture factory and converted it into "a fairly comfortable if somewhat odd house."[104]

Franklin's condition improved, but there were extended periods when he wasn't up to participating. When it looked as if Al Smith could be the Democratic nominee for president in the spring of 1928, Franklin intended to support him; he delegated Louis Howe to represent him full time at headquarters.

Franklin and Eleanor both believed, in Eleanor's words, that Al Smith "sought the welfare of the average man and woman." At this convention, Eleanor, who also spoke for her husband, soon realized as well that "the kind of propaganda [against Smith] that some of the religious groups, aided and abetted by the opposition, put forth" would utterly disgust her.[105] Disillusioning as that experience proved, the realization contributed to the development of a political expertise Eleanor Roosevelt would need.

Despite such disappointments, she worked tirelessly for Smith and the party at local levels and on the national scene. Louis Howe delegated her to represent him; she was to bring women's groups into the fold. She put in "prodigious hours of work," for "work is easier to carry if your heart is involved."[106]

All the while, Eleanor's growing experience and her astute, fair judgments of people and ideas escalated her influence. As time went on, her insights became valuable to her husband: In 1928, Smith won the nomination but lost the presidency. After the election, Eleanor believed Al Smith wanted her husband to appoint Belle Moskowitz to an important New York State position in order to perpetuate Smith's authority in New York; although Eleanor appreciated Belle Moskowitz as a talented woman, she told Franklin she thought this would interfere with his plans for New York.

She thought, for example, that Al Smith's "memory and his knowledge of New York State were phenomenal. . . . Had he been elected president, he would have chosen his Cabinet well, even though his knowledge of the country as a whole was slight and his advisers in the state knew little of the nation," but "I never felt sure he could have handled our foreign relations. . . . Also, I thought him less of a humanitarian than most people did."[107] In her judgments, Eleanor was selecting the political skills and insights—the fictions—of her family as well as the fictions she had developed herself. She couldn't forget that Smith refused to endorse a child labor amendment.

Rapidly this upper-class lady became indispensable not only to her husband but to the Democratic Party. Whatever her private thoughts, and she was constantly extending them, she never uttered or wrote one critical word about her husband or the party. Nor did she display her sufferings from Sara's and Franklin's indifference to her feelings. But to a friend she wrote that "it is new for me to have anyone know when I have 'moods' much less have it make any real difference."[108] She signed this letter "Much, much love dearest, Eleanor."

Though Eleanor protested that she "knew very little about the 1928 campaign for the governorship," she helped the committee to get in touch with Franklin at Warm Springs.[109] Franklin accepted the nomination for governor with the clear intention of acting without recourse to Smith or anyone else. This was his first venture back toward the active political scene. Because of Eleanor's efforts, and in spite of his mother's disapproval, he had kept his hand in; now he would return.

Eleanor was still finding that many of her interests dovetailed with those of her husband. For different reasons, they shared commitments. But they traveled divergent paths. Still, neither really wanted to function without the other; this situation led to a style of marriage not unlike those of some career patterns of later days. Eleanor and her friends exercised a strong influence upon Franklin's positions—partly, it seems, because they took care never to appear to dictate to him.

During the 1928 campaign, she found a new secretary, Malvina Thompson; they became lifelong friends. For both, the 1928 campaign proved a trial by fire. Both labored into the small hours. Eleanor remarked that she had found out where women stood when it came to national campaigns: "They stood outside the door of all important meetings and waited."[110] "If I needed anything to show me what prejudice can do to the intelligence of human beings," she wrote, "that campaign was the best lesson I could have had."[111]

Al Smith met defeat at the national level, but Franklin Roosevelt managed to win enough votes to become Democratic governor of New York. Eleanor told a reporter that she felt no excitement about her husband's election as governor. "What difference does it make to me?" she asked. Her historian-friend Joseph Lash perceived the reason: "For almost a decade she had built her own life, developed her own point of view,"[112] he wrote. Lash understood that Eleanor had feared being obliged to conform to entrenched fictions, to ritual duties, to the public notion of how a governor's wife should behave, and to Franklin's idea of how a decorous political wife should act.

This role would conflict with progress toward her goals. Lash knew that Eleanor's well-being lay in her right to express her own opinions, act in accordance with her own lights, and, though he wouldn't have expressed it this way, choose and live by her own fictions with all of her heart and mind. It cannot have been easy to replace old, taken-for-granted fictions, even upon understanding that they had been damaging, that they had caused pain and frustration.

Yet Eleanor Roosevelt found ways to supersede those early fictions. A decade before, in 1919, she had written in her diary the she had "never felt so strangely as in the past year. All my self confidence is gone and I am on edge though I never was better physically."[113] She had lived through a despairing time. But she had grown. Now she was ready to explore the challenges her hard-won new fictions were displaying. She couldn't welcome built-in restraints.

Eleanor lived as if she were walking a tightrope. As Franklin progressed toward the presidency, Eleanor realized the escalating danger of becoming a figure of ceremony. Her realizations of her abilities were precious; every day brought a growth in her powers, every day strengthened her connections with the most fundamental needs of people. Every day clarified the fictions by which she wanted to live. No longer could she be willing to give up her self or forsake the horizons of her future for those of her husband. But at some deep level, she knew the role of political power in attaining her goals. She had found guiding principles—fictions—that would work for her in her life as it was. She had formed close friendships and lasting emotional connections. She had begun to walk the high-wire more confidently, gracefully.

Still she shared goals with her husband. From mixed motives, in which ambition played a dominant role, Franklin wanted political power; he intended to achieve it. He intended to exercise it on his terms. From the strongest of motives—her own psychic survival—Eleanor needed constantly to prove her worth to herself. But her motives, too, were mixed. She needed to use her own powers. She felt a dedication to the welfare of others in need; she intended to devote the rest of her life and her energy to that ideal. But she wanted political power so that she could implement her endeavors as she saw fit. Still, in her view, and for her at that time, the White House loomed as an obstacle. "I was deeply troubled," she wrote. "As I saw it this meant the end of any personal life of my own."[114] When she wrote rather frantically to her friend Marion Dickerman that she could not live in the White House, her friend showed the letter to Louis Howe. Howe "tore it into a thousand pieces."[115] Eleanor's friends neither understood nor approved her reluctance.

But in the throes of the presidential campaign, Eleanor found a friend who did understand her concern. Lorena Hickok was a reporter who had made it to the top of a profession in which men ruled supreme. She was assigned to cover the Democratic nominee's wife during the campaign. Even in early meetings, Lorena Hickok sensed that Eleanor Roosevelt felt "unhappy about something."[116] Because of Hickok's sensitivity and because of her trustworthiness in reporting campaign events, Eleanor allowed "Hick" to become her friend.

Over the course of the campaign for the presidency, the two women grew close. They shared many a train ride. They told each other about their childhood experiences. Eleanor learned of the terrors of Lorena Hickok's early life, of the handicaps Hickok had overcome. Hickok learned about Eleanor. They came to trust each other. Both needed closeness, both needed affection, Eleanor in part because of her reactions to Franklin's rovings, Hickok because the woman with whom she had lived for several years had abruptly left her. So it appears on the surface.

Yet the two expressed deeper needs in the many letters they exchanged. "Only in the last ten years or so," Eleanor wrote to Hick, "have I made friends to whom I have talked!" In the first few of her letters, she described details of her life at the White House. She soon began to share family concerns with Hick, who responded sympathetically. To the degree that she could speak of her feelings, Eleanor's anxieties lessened and her confidence grew. Hickok's friendship strengthened Eleanor's belief in her own abilities.

The letters became more intimate, more expressive of their feelings for events and people, more expressive of their feelings for each other. "I miss you greatly my dear" Eleanor wrote. "Oh! How I wanted to put my arms around you in reality instead of in spirit. I went & kissed your photograph instead & the tears were in my eyes. Please keep most of your heart in Washington as long as I'm here for most of mine is with you! A world of love & good night my dear one."[117] Again, Eleanor wrote "Hick darling, All day I've thought of you. . . . Oh! I want to put my arms around you. I ache to hold you close. Your ring is a great comfort. I look at it & think she does love me, or I wouldn't be wearing it!"

The two longed for time together. "Only eight more days," Hick wrote to Eleanor. "Most clearly I remember your eyes, with a kind of teasing smile in them, and the feeling of that soft spot just northeast of the corner of your mouth against my lips. I wonder what we'll do when we meet—what we'll say when we meet. Well—I'm rather proud of us, aren't you?"[118] Their relationship had evolved into expressions of the fundamental emotions of their lives. For some years, Hickok lived in the White House.

Perhaps most loving interactions between people take account of the fictions those involved have known. While fictions encompass intense relationships that are not physical in character, they also set stages for physical expressions of deep emotional significance. Monogamous marriage between the sexes was ingrained in the fictions from which Eleanor's values arose as well as in the custom of the wider world of her experience. It was far and away the usual fiction. But deviations were known; some, though sub rosa and unofficial, were more or less tolerated. Homosexual and lesbian relations were known, but no one in the young Eleanor's circles had thought them appropriate.

But in a desperate search for guiding fictions that took account of emotional dimensions, Eleanor looked for love where she could find it. Certainly the tone of Eleanor's letters expresses the warmth and the vibrancy of a personality capable of love. But because of sexual expectations for women of her time and class, giving love physically often proved troublesome, even according to accepted fictions. Giving physical intimacy as an expression of love in any pattern different from that acceptable in her childhood would have been most difficult.

Female networks arose in Victorian England and elsewhere. Women in repressive societies have looked for love in female networks and have sometimes passionately expressed the yearnings human beings feel. By and large, their societies have tolerated and even encouraged such expressions. This may be the situation we read in Eleanor Roosevelt's letters to Lorena Hickok. In the end, and because of the fiction-patterns of her early life, Eleanor was probably unable to live with this friend's need for physical intimacy. As Hickok became more needy, Eleanor began to withdraw. Hickok came to feel that she could no longer handle her reporting assignment objectively. She resigned, leaving a legacy by suggesting the publication that became Eleanor's trademark, her column, "My Day." Out of the precariousness of her own experience as a reporter, Hickok also suggested that Eleanor hold White House press conferences for women reporters. The conferences became news events and landmarks of women's political participation in the national life. Thus this talented, intimate friend helped Eleanor cope with the traditional role of First Lady.

We shall probably never know the extent to which Hickok benefited and suffered in her career or in her personal life. Although the two communicated for many years on a level Eleanor scarcely accorded to others, it seems that a measure of emotional fulfillment escaped both women. Attesting to the substance of their relationship, Hickok burned many letters. Of the letters that remain, many are cast in a rhetoric historian Carroll Smith-Rosenberg has shown to be typical of upper-class female relationships in Victorian societies of England and America. And many letters express commitment and longing. Still, both Hickok and Eleanor experienced other relationships as their lives progressed. It may be wise to view this friendship, with Smith-Rosenberg, "within a cultural and social setting rather than from an exclusively psychosexual perspective."[119]

Certain it is that the fictions Eleanor and her friend brought to their intense relationship affected its course. It also seems clear that by fostering the play of intellect and love, their relationship deepened the living of both. "You taught me more than you know," Eleanor wrote to Hick. "I bring unhappiness & if I didn't think in the end it would make you happier I'd be desperately unhappy for I love you & you've made of me so much more of a person just to be worthy of you—je t'aime je t'adore."[120]

During the hot summer of 1932, despite, in her words, "the turmoil in my heart and mind," Eleanor Roosevelt had persistently, patiently, and skillfully worked on her husband's behalf. By then, depression had suffused the land. Appalling numbers of Americans had joined unemployment lines. The very fictions that underpinned and sustained the republic were coming into grave scrutiny. As families confronted specters of starvation and despair, it had become clear that immediate political change would prove the least of the upheavals. Ironically, this had worked to Franklin's advantage.

During this time Eleanor Roosevelt suffered anxieties occasioned by the circumstances of her life. She also experienced a strengthening of fictions arising from the underside of American life she had been learning to know, arising as well from her deepest beliefs. It was almost as if the anguish in American life found expression in the personal conflicts of Eleanor Roosevelt's experience. Both called for resolution.

As wife of the governor of New York, Eleanor had continued her teaching at the Todhunter School. "I really had for the first time a job that I did not wish to give up," she wrote. "From the personal standpoint, I did not want my husband to be president."[121] But by the bleak fall of 1932, Franklin had won the Democratic nomination and was intently seeking the presidency. In the climate of suffering and despair, it was nearly certain that a Democrat would win the election. In her activities on Franklin's behalf before and after the nominating convention in Chicago, Eleanor Roosevelt often had to submerge her inclinations. Motivated in part by the sense of duty ingrained in the old fictions, in part by her own political talent, as well as by her growing expertise, she made herself available.

To play a political role was no departure for Eleanor Roosevelt. She had become a personality of note. She had become a key figure of the Democratic National Committee. She had held positions at the Todhunter School, in the Women's Trade Union League, in the League of Women Voters, in the Non-Partisan Legislative Committee. She had created radio programs, she had contributed to newspaper columns; she had expressed opinions through many interviews, speeches, and magazine pieces. She had worked for causes such as eliminating child labor, improving educational opportunities, and bettering working conditions for women. She had expanded her personal acquaintance. She had participated in election campaigns as speaker and organizer. She had been learning to use the sources of power available to her. As she had gained confidence in her newer fictions, she had accumulated a following.

She had, however, developed a habit of downplaying her own importance, especially with respect to that of her husband. Historian Allida M. Black suggests that Eleanor Roosevelt realized that such an unthreatening approach could increase her influence.[122] At this juncture, and in consonance with lingering fictions, she listened to the advice of party regulars: Maintain a low profile. When speaking or writing for magazines or when giving interviews, choose non-controversial topics such as "Responsibilities of Citizenship," or "Building Good Character." Eleanor thus displayed the fictions expected of a candidate's wife. But she did sometimes disagree with her husband's positions. When that happened, she skillfully overcame the difficulties that ensued. When asked to comment on election issues, she did so constructively and with such competence that she satisfied questioners. She impressed her audiences—and the party regulars.

After the election Eleanor scarcely rejoiced. "For myself," she wrote, "I was deeply troubled. As I saw it, this meant the end of any personal life of my own."[123] She tried to resolve her feelings. Acting in accordance with the fictions she had developed for herself, she asked for an opportunity to take part in the new administration, for a real job. She suggested that she be given the task of reading and reporting on the president's mail. Never dreaming that her own mail would exceed his, she longed for an opportunity to serve. But the president denied her request. He said, and it must have troubled her, that this could offend "Missy" LeHand. Even though "Missy" had become Franklin's close companion, over the years in which she often acted as Franklin's hostess and White House confidante, Eleanor treated her with acceptance and grace.

So Eleanor Roosevelt found herself occupying the ceremonial role she had dreaded. But not exclusively, not for long. Over the next few years she effected a miracle: She transformed the role of first lady. She moved it away from the realm of ritual and into the arena of issues that mattered to people. She developed a set of fictions wholly new in the popular concept of first lady. With the informed support of Lorena Hickok, Eleanor began to see that her position as the president's wife could accord her opportunities she had scarcely envisioned: In the face of opposition, it could accord her the chance to affect the life of the nation. It was again as if the turmoil in Eleanor's life reflected both the anxieties of the American people and their ability to surmount disasters.

The first few of her ventures set the tone. She mastered the details of keeping house in the White House. With a staff of more than thirty and her own housekeeper, Mrs. Nesbitt, she established a sufficient routine, a routine that could accommodate visiting officials and visiting crowds as well as the enormous culinary demands of the White House. The fictions of her family and her husband's family had always held that upper-class ladies should know how to manage a household, even a large household. But the social side of the White House now "seemed to me rather unimportant; indeed there never came a point when I felt the world was sufficiently stable for us to take time to think very seriously about purely social matters," she wrote.[124] This comment mirrored the new directions of her personal fictions, the fictions by which she desired to live. Almost irrelevantly, she remembered that a few years back when she had come to the capital as wife of Assistant Secretary Franklin Roosevelt, she had believed that social activities carried a foremost importance. She had traveled far. Her personal fictions—her commitments to herself—had evolved almost beyond recognition.

Her press conferences required another approach; they took careful planning on an official level and negotiating as to whether she should even introduce them, whether they should include women only, which issues could be discussed. "It was new and untried ground and I was feeling my way with some trepidation," she wrote.[125] She discovered a channel through which to introduce to the Washington scene many talented and committed women. She also discovered a medium for influencing the direction of press activities and a resounding forum for drawing attention to projects of the New Deal. Sometimes in the early days she slipped a little, sometimes there were indiscretions. But so grateful were the female reporters to find themselves significantly included that they protected the new first lady. From time to time, they reminded her that some matters would best be considered off the record.

Once again, Louis Howe steered her toward a course of her own. He supported the idea of press conferences for women reporters. He invited her participation in developing a plan to aid the miners of West Virginia, in particular the miners of the little town of Scott's Run. As Eleanor Roosevelt became aware of the nearly hopeless circumstances of these American workers, an innovative project took shape. The project required large amounts of money as well as a different philosophy of social well-being. Since mining would provide only desperate poverty for the families of Scott's Run, the planners would establish and finance a new community at Arthurdale. It would provide health care, modern schools, and an industrial base adequate to the needs of the community. Since Eleanor could not persuade Interior Secretary Harold Ickes of the value of such a program, she turned next to Assistant Secretary of the Department of Agriculture Rexford Tugwell, then to financier Bernard Baruch. She undertook a series of radio programs, using her radio money to aid the deprived children of that district. She had been accustomed to giving "small sums to charity." Now she worked for money she could use for a project of importance, a project in which she had become deeply involved.

All of these measures, sustained as they were by Eleanor Roosevelt's commitment to her new fictions, proved insufficient to propel this idea to viability. The project called down upon itself every invective; it was even reviled as communist and un-American. But it grew into the Resettlement Administration. Eleanor desperately wanted Arthurdale itself to flourish, but she finally had to admit that it lacked a firm economic base and that it surely lacked political support. She learned that without these attributes, no venture can survive. Still, she wrote, "Such experiments, changing for the better the life of the people, would be a mighty bulwark against attacks on our democracy." Later projects of the New Deal, especially the Tennessee Valley Authority (TVA), did secure sufficient financing and sufficient political backing to survive.

On one pleasant afternoon, Howe invited Eleanor to drive with him to the Veteran's Camp, a location adjacent to Potomac Drive. By assisting the desperate veterans to occupy this location, the Roosevelt administration avoided a costly showdown like that of the previous administration: Veterans had built "Hoovervilles" all over urban America and within sight of the president's office during the Hoover administration. On arriving at the new encampment, Howe said that he would remain in the car while Eleanor walked among the veterans.

She walked among them and spoke with them, and she joined them in their eating hall. When they invited her to say a few words, she mentioned that she had gone over the battle fronts in 1919 and walked about them at the close of the war. She managed to relate to these indigent ex-soldiers. In the big hall, they sang for her. When "I got into the car and drove away," she remembered, "everyone waved and I called, 'Good luck,' and they answered 'Good-by and good luck to you.'"[126] She had conveyed the message that someone close to the sources of power cared about them and their sufferings. They believed in her concern. At her next press conference, she made it a point to notice that she had seen fine boys, a clean camp, a fine spirit, and that she had been "most courteously treated." Her experience with the veterans and the effective political repercussions initiated a program in harmony with her new fictions. In succeeding years, she would enormously expand that program; we remember it as the National Youth Administration (NYA).

As Eleanor Roosevelt extended her visits, first to nearby areas, then around the nation, and finally overseas she met warm receptions among those to whom she spoke. She traveled extensively. Wherever people were in trouble, wherever disaster struck, her presence became important. Over and over, the sincerity of her concern impressed people—the young, the poor, the wounded, the bereaved, the desperate, the powerful. She contributed most of the money she earned to organizations seeking the betterment of the nation's communities.

She became deeply interested in the problems of young Americans. Franklin Roosevelt realized the depression despairs of the young, those to whom education was denied, those who could find no work. He had promoted his Civilian Conservation Corps (CCC) to deal with their needs. It employed some, paid them a little, gave them a place to live, and taught them forestry. Eleanor conceived of their situations on a broader canvas. She believed that teaching forestry barely began to prepare young men for productive lives and that it ignored the needs of young women. She believed that a much broader and deeper education would be crucial, and she altogether disapproved the militaristic character of the CCC. Realizing that the government ought to develop a comprehensive program that addressed the many ways in which young Americans were unprepared for the future, she studied economic, vocational, and educational theories. In efforts to arouse public awareness, she wrote of her concerns. "I live in real terror," she told the New York Times, "when I think we may be losing this generation. We have got to bring these young people into the active life of the community." Stressing benefits society would reap, she met with officials in government and other fields. Out of these endeavors, and the efforts of those she lobbied, the National Youth Administration came into being. In its program young people themselves were to have a say.

Years later she wrote in This I Remember that "One of the ideas I agreed to present to Franklin was that of setting up a National Youth Administration. . . . It was one of the occasions on which I was very proud that the right thing was done, regardless of political consequences." Despite the mutterings of hardline opponents, she extended her full support and she persuaded the president to change directions; when he signed the executive order creating the agency in June of 1935, the president authorized five areas of operation: work projects, vocational guidance, apprenticeship training, educational and nutritional guidance camps for unemployed women, and student aid. Eleanor managed to find positions for close friends in the new National Youth Agency. At one

Franklin Roosevelt visiting a CCC camp with (*from left to right*) Louis Howe, Harold Ickes, and Robert Fechner. *Courtesy Franklin Roosevelt Library.*

point she telegraphed her husband that "you are going to make an appointment to see Charles Taussig and you are going to ask Myron Taylor to serve on the NYA Advisory Board." Franklin did, in fact, ask his aide to arrange an appointment with Taussig that week.[127]

She made suggestions to officials. She offered her husband names for appointments, frequently the names of women. Increasingly, she came to champion those most in need—poor white people and poor black people of the South and the cities, jobless young people, refugees from Nazi horrors. Sometimes her activities led to difficulties, especially in her support of youth organizations; for her efforts, she was accused of communist leanings. But through everything that happened in her life, her feeling for the genuine needs of all kinds of people increased. Her own new fictions stayed firmly in her heart and mind. They became the determining features of her personal identity.

Touring the area where later the TVA Administration would operate, she wrote that "the crowds at the stations were so poor; their houses were unpainted, their cars were dilapidated, and many grownups as well as children were without shoes or adequate garments."[128] Because she found herself in a position to draw attention to such conditions and to bring them to the notice of policymakers, Eleanor Roosevelt was able to direct the fictions of her choice toward the priorities of the nation. Everywhere, people believed she cared. This rendered her credible and effective.

In those moments of unprecedented American suffering, her caring became crucial to the president's efforts. She kept him informed. She often directed his attention toward projects she thought pressing. By the president's bedside she placed an "Eleanor basket" so that as every day began he would first turn his attention toward her findings. Her skills increased. She exercised her own well-earned political wisdom. She undertook crusades inside and outside the White House on behalf of the downtrodden, on behalf of women and children, increasingly on behalf of international understanding.

Nor did she fail to arrive at sophisticated appraisals. There seems little doubt that she influenced the development of the New Deal philosophy. But in her unassuming fashion she noted that "*my husband* [italics added] had frequent run-ins over the new theory that government had a responsibility to the people."[129] This is the theory that in a democracy, economic planning by the federal government on behalf of all the people will produce a more stable economy than random operation by individual entrepreneurs on behalf of themselves. It is the theory that the federal government can better operate with justice for all than can individual states. This is the theory that represents the fruition of Eleanor Roosevelt's political fictions.

In her public—and private—statements, however, Eleanor continued to insist that she was acting on behalf of her husband. This amounted to a denial of her own involvement in projects they undertook as well as a denial of her own contributions. Did she do this because she felt the need to let Franklin know she did not compete with him? Or because she learned to shun personal recognition in order to attain political leverage? Or because she could never overcome the traumas of her childhood? Or because she sensed just below the surface a consensus that resented a woman's competence? Or for all of these reasons? Neither she nor her husband ever admitted the extent of her influence.

Eleanor understood the reaches and the limitations of this philosophy— that the federal government can and should take responsibility to protect and assist those who suffer most. She cherished individual freedoms. Yet she also believed that only the federal government can curb big-business abuses. "The so-called New Deal was, of course, nothing more than an effort to preserve our economic system," she wrote, thinking perhaps, of the Communist system of total control of its citizens as well as of the explosive situation in her own country. "It was the rebuilding of those two qualities in the people of the United States—[confidence, a sense of security]—that made it possible for us to produce as we did in the early days of the war [against the Nazis], and to go into the most terrible war in our history and win it."[130]

Over the years in which she lived in the White House, Eleanor Roosevelt set an example of concern for the needs of a stricken nation. She displayed a nearly unprecedented capacity for personal involvement at every level. She drew on a boundless energy. She channeled her considerable abilities. She graduated away from fictions taken for granted in her childhood—anti-Semitism, racial prejudice, social elitism. Indeed, she became an advocate for the very people her family had routinely denigrated. The fictions that fueled her activities expanded to champion victims of the Holocaust, African Americans, veterans of the war, the disadvantaged of every situation. She had long cared about the exploitation of women workers. She had always understood the importance of nourishing the nation's children. She knew that education makes a difference in a person's life and that the level of education can define the character of a society.

On a public level, Eleanor Roosevelt expressed the nation's need to involve itself with conditions of those disadvantaged by race or sex or age or poverty; on a private level, she lent a hand to thousands who believed she could solve every problem. Letters to her and pleas from unknown correspondents escalated. Sometimes the writers took advantage of her. Sometimes in the fluctuating areas of public relations, she stumbled; learning to replace old fictions can be fraught with difficulties and can prove treacherous. But her new awareness of those caught up in high-stakes political adventures and in international power plays tilted the axis of her efforts toward the core of the deepest concerns of her time. She had entered an arena for which she was superbly endowed.

In tandem with the scope of this first lady's interests, her ability to withstand the slings and arrows of the political scene grew. Since her endeavors discomfited many establishment regulars, she drew criticism. She found herself the butt of tasteless jokes. But by the year 1936, this is some of the advice she was able to offer to women who chose to work in politics:

> You cannot take anything personally.
> You cannot bear grudges.
> You cannot get discouraged too easily.
> Women who are willing to be leaders must stand out and be shot at.
> Above all, women in political life must develop skin as tough as rhinoceros hide.[131]

She learned personal survival and she learned to use power at high levels in small and large and innovative ways. As the New Deal progressed, her activities took on a wider latitude. Never did she allow herself credit for what she did. Nor did the president credit her. Eleanor actually denied her influence when somebody realized or even suspected it or when it became apparent. Late in her life on a trip to India, she expressed surprise that vast crowds turned out along the route she traveled. "I didn't realize the extent to which they cared for Franklin!" she exclaimed. The extent to which Eleanor Roosevelt affected New Deal activities has long remained hidden.

Yet Eleanor Roosevelt became a power in other countries. She became a student of America's role in foreign relations. She began to take part, both as the woman who accompanied, and sometimes spoke for, Franklin Roosevelt, and as an independent person. She became painfully aware of international tensions that were becoming ever more insistent; she brought to the center of attention the concern for human rights that most characterized her activities and the fictions of her choosing: What about education in deprived countries and in her own? What about unemployed mothers? What about revoking their food allowances in the wake of Depression? Ought their distress to be permitted anywhere on earth? What about fingerprinting aliens in democratic America? What about programs for sheltering and caring for aging persons, for their minimum health and happiness needs? Were not these concerns in her own country as urgent in every country, in some more devastatingly urgent than in ours?

In reply to many criticisms, Eleanor let her work speak for itself. To those who contended that the activities of domestic agencies came only to patching serious wounds with Band-Aids, that New Deal measures were stopgaps, she replied with the thoughts of Harry Hopkins, FDR's confidante and director of the largest relief program in the country's history: "People don't eat in the long run," Hopkins said. "They eat every day."

As time passed, Eleanor 's column "My Day" increasingly became her channel of communication with the people and their representatives. It was widely read before and after she left the White House. She talked about her garden and her family and her dog. She talked about her many trips and the people she met. She talked about the concerns of those who wrote to her. She talked about daily occupations to which everyone could relate.

Frankly and knowledgeably and frequently she also talked about the actions and opinions of those who run government. Feelings of shyness and a tendency to withdraw—feelings prominent in her personal life—never determined the content of her columns. She could discuss the actions of senators or ambassadors and the effects of their actions. She could castigate the witch-hunting Senator Joseph McCarthy or she could disagree with President Truman or President Eisenhower. She brought ordinary Americans into a kind of personal contact with their leaders. Her readership expanded so enormously that she influenced the opinions of large constituencies and the actions of officials. For many years, "My Day" served as a vehicle for transporting her fictions and her precepts for living them to the notice of Americans. Eleanor Roosevelt's choices of fictions to determine her thought and her activities became models and ideals.

At the same time, and not surprisingly, her work and her thought and the depth of her influence aroused powerful enemies. They made their opinions clear. It became a parlor game in some circles to tell the latest unflattering stories about the president and, even more disparagingly, about the president's wife: He was a spoiled rich boy who was betraying his own class. She was a meddling old busybody with buck teeth. Eleanor felt the brunt of the least lovely aspects of fictions of her establishment opponents. And this happened just as she grew more confident in her own convictions and just as success in many ventures strengthened her trust in the fictions by which she wanted to live.

When the president died on April 12, 1945, Eleanor realized that our nation had yet to recover from the effects of the Great Depression. At that time, she wrote movingly that the children and the dogs would think of Franklin's burial place at Hyde Park as "a place where flowers grow and where the hedge protects them from the wind and makes the sun shine down more warmly." "I have always felt, she continued, "that one could have a certain sense of resignation when people die who have lived long and fruitful lives. My rebellion has always been over the deaths of young people; and that is why I think so many of us feel particularly frustrated by war, where youth so largely pays the price. It seems as though youth was so much needed to carry the burdens of peace."[132]

One month later, the war in Europe was over. While others joyfully took to the streets, Eleanor wrote that "I cannot feel a spirit of celebration today." She was glad that the killing in Europe had ended but distressed that the war in the Pacific raged on. "It is far more a day of dedication for us, a day on which to promise that we will do our utmost to end war and build peace," she thought.[133] "Europe is in ruins and the weary work of reconstruction must now begin. Freedom without bread has little meaning."[134]

In spite of inevitable readjustments, the energy behind Eleanor's efforts to build the peace and the range of her concerns in doing so increased after the president's death. She continued her column. She used it to help Americans see the problems of their own land and their own government and she began to help them understand the relation of their problems to those of other lands.

Increasingly she became outspoken about international affairs. As first lady, she had of necessity restrained her opinions. Now she was free to express them. As if building for the role she would play for much of the rest of her life, she almost systematically considered in her columns the policies that outlined U.S.

postures. She would write about the hardships of American migrant workers, their needs for housing, education, the bare necessities of life. Then she would write about children in Russia, in other lands, about refugee children, about their comparable needs. "I don't believe that greed and selfishness have gone out of the human race," she wrote. "I am quite prepared to be considerably disappointed many times in the course of cooperation."[135]

And she was disappointed. But not always. Remarkably enough, her life took on an even richer emotional coloring. Her home at Hyde Park and her apartments and living quarters wherever she traveled had become second homes to those who formed her friendship circles. Many friends lived or visited wherever Eleanor lived and had even done so while she lived in the White House. Her hospitality had become legendary.

Prominent among them was a new friend, Dr. David Gurewitsch. Once, at the behest of another friend, she had helped him obtain passage for an overseas trip. On that occasion they had become acquainted. "We all got to know each other well and I think he enjoyed it," Eleanor had written to her friend Trude Lash.[136] This beginning barely suggested the scope of Eleanor's coming attachment to David. Over many years they met and talked and corresponded.

There were happy times and, for Eleanor, there were troublesome times. David was fifteen years younger than Eleanor. At 63, she had become a figure known over the world. Born of Russian parents, his father a Jewish philosopher, his mother a strong woman who became a physician, David had grown up in Russia and Berlin. Handsome and accomplished, David had looked into the movie industry in Germany. Then he had become interested in farming and in ceramics; he had formed a wide acquaintance before he had decided to begin the study of medicine. A mutual friend of Eleanor and David had helped him with prerequisites. After receiving his medical degree and completing his internship, he served in Jerusalem during Hitler's ascendancy, married an English woman, then went to the United States to study pathology. Polished and continental in style, David found himself at 45 in a difficult marital situation and in somewhat precarious health.[137]

Soon their letters took on an intimate air. "I love your letters," Eleanor wrote. "Don't tire yourself ever for I will understand." This chatty letter ended with the words "May your strength grow and with it our friendship. . . . My thoughts turn to you often."[138] She began to send him copies of her books and manuscripts of chapters she was writing. David responded sensitively: "If one considers how many 'mistakes' were made with you, and what a difficult youth you have had and compares it with the result, in which balance and absence of neurosis are so prominent, one begins to wonder. In how many people the greatest protection and psychology do not prevent weakness and neurotic trends, yes they even seem to breed it," he wrote.[139] David's insight into the psychological facets of personality attracted Eleanor. The volume of their correspondence grew. Over the years she came to address him as "David dear," and as "Dearest David." They confided in each other, often about David's wife Nemone and his daughter Grania. Eleanor made plans to see him, to dine with him whenever they might find themselves in the same cities. She invited him to Campobello and to Hyde Park. For Eleanor, this friendship proved a fascination and a commitment. She grew to love David, not passionately, perhaps, as in earlier relationships, but constantly. It is more difficult to gauge David's dedication to Eleanor; he remained to an extent involved with his wife, then later with other women. But he did appear to remain intimate with Eleanor.

Eleanor did much more than write the books for which she is known. She conducted the most extensive of human rights campaigns. From the vantage point of her tenure as U.S. ambassador to the United Nations, she discovered new levels of action and interaction. Tireless and confident in the fictions she had chosen, she explored every avenue. There were many. In the complexity of foreign relations exchanges, the issue of human rights often got pushed aside. But in Eleanor Roosevelt's lexicon, that issue took preference. The 198 boxes of her human rights papers recently released by the State Department testify to this paramount concern. Just as convincingly, the multiplicity of documents showing FBI intent to discredit her portrays the actions of her enemies. Both collections testify as well to the dedication and the strength Eleanor Roosevelt poured into implementing the fictions she chose.

Since her departure from the international scene, the Declaration of Human Rights achieved under her leadership in the United Nations has too often been shoved from the center. It stands, however, as a monument to Eleanor Roosevelt and as a promise that cannot be ignored.

Eleanor Roosevelt derived the fictions of her mature life from her fund of personal endowments and from her need to be loved, to contribute, to find fulfillment. She needed to be needed. She became a loved—and hated—figure in American public life. Though blessed with intelligence and talent adequate to every intricacy of international politics, she never lost touch with the needs of ordinary people. She wanted from life, in her words, "the opportunity for doing something useful, for in no other way, I am convinced, can true happiness be obtained." Yet she became no starstruck "do-gooder." She learned, as her life went on, the tensions and the conflicts that arise because so many disparate people live together on this planet. Since the world is populated with people in need, the fictions she chose became beacons. Endowed with intelligence, energy, and sympathy, she channeled her political talents into serving those more needy than she.

How poignant that Eleanor Roosevelt found her way from a heartbreaking childhood and the traumas of her early marriage to become so compassionate a figure of the twentieth century! If it is sad that many personal satisfactions eluded her, it is miraculous that a father in psychic collapse and a strained and despairing mother could give the world such a woman. Of the three stellar Roosevelts, Eleanor Roosevelt most notably chose fictions that reflected deep dimensions of experience—her own and those of her world. On intellectual levels she cultivated a capacity to understand, to think, to grow, to act. On emotional levels, she struggled to come to abiding satisfactions. And she experienced an expanse of human feelings. She lived passionately and she interacted with men and women of all ages and the most diverse life situations. By combining her selections of fictions on moral levels, by living them according to her own choices, she affected the climate of her time. She lived richly.

Epilogue

Musings on Fictions: A Time for Another Beginning?

Perhaps it is fitting here to relate a little story. When my sister and I visited our Aunt Charlotte for a Thanksgiving vacation, she met us at the door. "Now girls," she said, "there are three subjects we don't discuss: religion, politics, and the recipe for turkey dressing." I have tried, not often successfully, to bear this wisdom in mind.

In learning about my own fictions, I came upon myriad ways that people directed their thoughts and their acts. I suspected that discovering our fictions would reveal the engines that drive our interactions with ourselves and with others. I saw fictions playing out in the lives of persons and of societies; I saw them influencing the stories historians have told. I did not suppose, however, that striving to define an idea or ordering a few stories as I saw them supporting that idea could present so daunting a challenge. I did suppose the concept of fictions would precipitate into focusing on the relativities in human motivations.

Beyond this, I came to believe that these flights of mine would become beginnings toward understanding a personal experience, a larger society, the largest social arrangements, and the far-reaching influences historians exert. I saw that we are justified in no absolute mental conclusions, no absolute emotional positions in the perceptions we draw from our daily experience. This situation happens because we are evolutionary creatures and because our information depends on where we are and when we find it. This is clear in each life, in the societies we build, in the stories historians tell.

But in order to live, we must construct fictions. By looking we can discover them. The favorable outcome is that we need not stay entrapped in shallow perceptions or ill-taken judgments. A wonderful gift comes to us from whatever gods may be: We can evolve. We can develop. We can grow. Above all, and within our circumstances, we can choose. We may look to the future with hope.

It seems that points of view—our fictions—rise from our situations, that we cannot avoid them, but we can select them. Out of our lives and our longings, we can form fictions. As we venture along, we can direct them. It seems that our fictions shift as purposes crystallize, as horizons expand.

It seems that by choosing to look at who we are in the ways that we do, we often understand events and people in distinctive dimensions. By choosing fictions we take stands. Taking stands need not mean rejecting all aspects of other people's histories or fictions. It does mean more than a token participation, and it does suggest a penetrating relativity as we live the stories of our own pasts. Looking at fictions opens windows on vast, established influences that play over our lives as we evaluate ourselves and our thoughts, as we read or write the stories of history, as we perform experiments, as we paint pictures, as we make music, as we take everyday decisions.

I hope that my thoughts about fictions and histories may enter the spectrum of historical approaches. Perhaps they may escalate; they may even lead to more reappraisals of our own heritages. Fictions are powerful, driving ideas; they are vital for existence. Because of the density of the whole human experience and the strength of human institutions, our fictions require constant readjustment. These few stories come to one attempt to assess the value of my fictions.

For each of us there stretches a vista. At the start of this adventure, I related the story of a hunter who spent the better part of his life following a fiction. If, as in the tale of the Brantingham hunter, it becomes possible to undertake a search, we may create another story.

Notes

1. Fictions and the Missions of History

1. See John Bodnar, *Remaking America: Public Memory, Commemoration, and Patriotism in the Twentieth Century* (Princeton: Princeton University Press, 1991).

2. See Michael Kammen, *Mystic Chords of Memory: The Transformation of Tradition in American Culture* (New York: Knopf, 1991).

3. See Thomas Kuhn, *The Structure of Scientific Revolutions* (Chicago: University of Chicago Press, 1970). See also Natalie Davis, *Fiction in the Archives: Pardon Tales and Their Tellers in Sixteenth-Century France* (Stanford, Calif.: Stanford University Press, 1987).

4. Davis, *Fiction in the Archives*, 3.

5. *Book of Mormon* (Salt Lake City, Utah: Church of Jesus Christ of Latter-Day Saints, 1986), Jac 1:15; 2:23–27; 3–5; Mos. 11:2–4; Eth. 10–5.

6. *The Book of Mormon: Another Testament of Jesus Christ* (Salt Lake City, Utah: The Church of Jesus Christ of Latter-Day Saints, 1927), Introduction, n.p.

7. The text of the revelation on polygamy is given in Philip R. Kunz, "One Wife or Several? A Comparative Study of Late Nineteenth-Century Marriage in Utah," in *The Mormon People: Their Character and Traditions,* ed. Thomas G. Alexander (Provo, Utah: Brigham Young University Press, 1980), 54.

8. Thomas A. Bailey, *The American Pageant: A History of the Republic,* 3rd ed. (Boston: D. C. Heath and Company, 1966).

9. Thomas A. Bailey and David M. Kennedy, *The American Pageant,* 9th ed. (Lexington, Mass.: D. C. Heath and Company, 1991), 785.

10. Ray Allen Billington, Bert James Loewenberg, and Samuel Hugh Brockunier, *The United States: American Democracy in World Perspective* (New York: Rinehart & Company, 1947).

11. John A. Garraty, *The American Nation: A History of the United States since 1965,* 3rd ed. (New York: Harper & Row, 1975).

12. Arthur S. Link with the collaboration of William B. Catton, *American Epoch: A History of the United States since the 1890's* (New York: Alfred A. Knopf, 1963).

13. Theodore J. Lowi, *American Government: Incomplete Conquest* (Hinsdale, Ill.: The Dryden Press, 1976), ix.

14. Eleanor Roosevelt, *Autobiography of Eleanor Roosevelt* (New York: Harper & Brothers, 1981), xvi.

15. Carl Becker, "What Are Historical Facts?" in *Detachment and the Writing of History: Essays and Letters of Carl H. Becker,* ed. Phil L. Snyder (Ithaca, N.Y.: Cornell University Press, 1958), 41–64.

16. William H. McNeill, *Mythistory and Other Essays* (Chicago: University of Chicago Press, 1968), 3–42.

17. Bernadette Fort, "The French Revolution and the Making of Fictions," in *Fictions of the French Revolution,* ed. Bernadette Fort (Evanston, Ill.: Northwestern University Press, 1991).

18. William Cronon, "A Place for Stories: Nature, History and Narrative," *Journal of American History* 78, no. 4 (March 1992): 1347–1348.

19. Cotton Mather, "The Wonders of the Invisible World," in *The Annals of America,* ed. Mortimer J. Adler. Vol. 1, *1493–1754* (Chicago: Encyclopedia Britanica, 1976), 297–

298. This is a description of the "witchcraft delusion." It is Mather's discussion of spectral evidence that comes close to noticing that fictions of one kind or another prevail in the world at hand.

20. Lawrence W. Levine, "Clio, Canons, and Culture," *Journal of American History* 80, no. 3 (1993): 865. Levine refers to the histories of George Bancroft, James Ford Rhodes, Henry Adams, Frederick Jackson Turner, Charles Beard, and their peers.

21. Michael Kammen, "History as Lightning Rod," Organization of American Historians *Newsletter* 23, no. 2 (May 1995): 1, 6.

22. I have in mind the publications of the Institute for Historical Review, a political organization that first sought incorporation in California and, upon being refused, sought and gained incorporation in Texas. This group insists that Hitler's Holocaust never occurred. Another example: Polygamy is given no mention in a manual to educate young and prospective Mormons about church history and principles. According to Craig Manscill, chairman of the committee that produced a new 370-page manual of the Female Relief Society for the instruction of new converts to the Mormon faith (edited by John A. Widtsoe), the purpose of the committee was to "[introduce] Brigham Young to a church member throughout the world who is not familiar with the historian's perspective." Manscill and Widtsoe tell us that polygamous practice was never approved or engaged in by Brigham Young and other church officials. Editorial, "Changed Man," *San Jose Mercury-News,* 23 May 1998.

23. Nancy Mairs, *Voice Lessons* (Boston: Beacon Press, 1994), 118–119.

24. Graham Swift, *Waterland* (New York: 1983), 53–54. Quoted in Cronon, "A Place for Stories: Nature, History and Narrative," 1147.

2. The Grandest Fiction

1. A note on usage: I define "patriarchy" as the exertion of male control over women and children in families and in social activities; it entails the exclusion of women from major institutions that educate children, develop industrial capacities, form societies, and manage public policy, the result of which is the exploitation and often the rejection of women from participation in projects in all areas. I define "gender" as the different established roles of the sexes in social situations, while I define "sex" as characteristic biological inheritances of men and women. Though overlapping occurs in the categories of sex and gender, these broad delineations serve my present purposes.

2. For an instance of looking at one situation in one area at one time, see Frances Richardson Keller, "The Dilemmas of Eve in American Fiction, 1900–1970: Technocracy Realized?," in *Views of Women's Lives in Western Tradition: Frontiers of the Past and the Future,* ed. Keller (Lewiston, N.Y.: Edwin Mellen Press, 1990), 680–795. Hereafter referred to as *Views.*

3. Margaret Atwood, *The Handmaid's Tale* (New York: Ballantine Books, 1985).

4. Anthropologists, archeologists, and feminist scholars have enormously expanded our knowledge of ancient peoples and of women's roles in events of recorded history and events of history prior to the appearance of writing (approximately 3500 B.C.). I am especially grateful to historian Gerda Lerner, whose *The Creation of Patriarchy* (New York: Oxford University Press, 1986) and other works provide rich substantiation for this chapter.

5. See Kate Millett, *Sexual Politics* (Garden City, N.Y.: Doubleday, 1970), 26–39, for pioneer work in the study of the socialization of the young.

6. All dates are approximate, tentative, and suggestive. William H. McNeill, *The Rise of the West* (Chicago: University of Chicago Press, 1963), 1–28 provides guidance about dating events and movements of early periods.

7. For our purposes, Paleolithic refers to a time from approximately 750,000 years B.C. to about 15,000 years B.C., Mesolithic from about 15,000 B.C. to about 10,000 B.C., Neolithic from about 10,000 B.C. to the Christian Era.

8. See J. J. Bachofen, *Myth, Religion, and Mother Right, Selected Writings of J. J. Bachofen,* trans. Ralph Mannheim with a preface by George Boas and an introduction by Joseph Campbell (Princeton, N.J.: Princeton University Press, 1967). Bachofen was one of the first in modern times to believe that the "feminine principle" embodied the most cultivated of human developments and that it should be incorporated into patriarchal models. Bachofen's thinking is cast in evolutionary terms. See also Friedrich Engels, *The Origin of the Family, Private Property, and the State in the Light of the Researches of Lewis H. Morgan* (New York: International Publishers, 1942). Ann J. Lane discusses Engels's concepts of early evolutionary patterns in "Women in Society: A Critique of Frederick Engels," in *Liberating Women's History: Theoretical and Critical Essays,* ed. Berenice A. Carroll (Urbana: University of Illinois Press, 1976), 4–25.

9. See Lerner, *The Creation of Patriarchy,* 15–35. See also Robert Briffault, *The Mothers,* abridged by Gordon Rattray Taylor (New York: Athenaeum, 1977). Briffault sees social organization as an evolutionary development in which patriarchy is a long phenomenon and, though deeply and widely entrenched, is not the highest development to be reached. See also William H. McNeill, *The Rise of the West* (Chicago: University of Chicago Press, 1963), 1–63.

10. See Maryanne Cline Horowitz, "Introduction: Playing with Gender," in *Playing with Gender: A Renaissance Pursuit,* ed. Jean R. Brink, Maryanne C. Horowitz, and Allison Coudert (Urbana: University of Illinois Press, 1991), ix–xxiii.

11. See Nancy Tanner, "Matrifocality in Indonesia and Africa and among Black Americans," in *Women, Culture & Society,* ed. Michelle Zimbalist Rosaldo and Louise Lamphere (Stanford, Calif.: Stanford University Press, 1974), 129–156. Tanner notes that "matrifocality may be limited to the elemental mother-child unit . . . or it may be a feature of the nuclear family and more inclusive kin units . . . or the matrilineally extended family."

12. Edith Hamilton, *Mythology* (New York: Mentor, 1942), 173.

13. Abby Wettan Kleinbaum, *The War against the Amazons* (New York: McGraw-Hill, 1983), 1.

14. Ibid., 5. Kleinbaum remarks that "to win an Amazon, either through arms or through love, or, even better, through both" is to be certified as a hero.

15. Roslyn M. Frank with Susan Ayres, Monique Laxalt, Shelly Lowenberg, and Nancy Vosburg, "Etxeko-Andrea: The Missing Link? Women in Basque Culture," in Keller, ed., *Views,* 133–157. The Frank group's study of the Basque people finds that they lived continuously in a matrilineal and probably matriarchal polity for at least 10,000 years at the same location. Frank et al. find that "skull shapes and bone structures of individuals as well as purely cultural considerations" attest to great antiquity and show a matrilineal lineage and an exercise of powers (131–132). Most convincing is the discovery of a unique Rh-negative blood type long and continuously indigenous to this part of the European world. As Gerda Lerner insightfully observes, and Frank points out, however, such arrangements have eventually disappeared; they have been unable to survive the stresses of technological developments.

16. Joan Markley Todd and Joseph Cono, "After Sappho, Aspasia, and Xanthippe: Women as Equals in the Writings of Xenophon," in Keller, ed., *Voices,* 174–193. For a discussion of the overprecise dichotomies that Todd and Cono have avoided in this essay and the benefit of the interdisciplinary approach they use, see Gisela Bock, "Challenging Dichotomies and Perspectives on Women's History," in *Writing Women's History,* ed. Karen

Offen, Ruth Roach Pierson, and Jane Rendall (Bloomington: Indiana University Press, 1991), 1–23. See also Phyllis Stock-Morton, "Finding Our Own Ways: Different Paths to Women's History in the United States," in *Writing Women's History*, 59–77. See also "Introduction," in *Writing Women's History*.

17. Gregory L. Schaaf, "Queen Coitcheleh and the Women of the Lost Shawnee Nation: A Note on an American Matriarchy," in Keller, ed., *Views*, 158–165.

18. See Eleanor Leacock, "Women in Egalitarian Societies," in *Becoming Visible: Women in European History*, ed. Renate Bridenthal, Claudia Koonz, and Susan Stuard. 2nd ed. (Boston: Houghton Mifflin Company, 1987), 15–38.

19. We shall see in Chapter 4 that this situation lingered in the Mormon community of nineteenth-century Utah as Mormon leaders retained control of women's activities.

20. Elizabeth Judd, "The Myths of the Golden Age and the Fall: From Matriarchy to Patriarchy," in Keller, ed., *Views*, 68, n.7.

21. Ibid., 18–24.

22. Hesiod, *Works and Days*, in Hesiod, *The Homeric Hymns, and Homerica*, trans. Hugh G. Evelyn-White (Cambridge, Mass.: Harvard University Press, 1914), 11, 109–120. Quoted in Judd, "The Myths of the Golden Age," 18.

23. Ovid, *Metamorphoses* I, trans. Mary M. Innes (Harmondsworth: Penguin, 1955), 31–32. Quoted in Judd, "The Myths of the Golden Age." Ovid's view, though traditional and male-oriented, does look toward a different, earlier situation.

24. On the relevance of the private property concept, see Friedrich Engels, *The Origin of the Family, Private Property and the State*, trans. Ernest Untermann (Chicago: C. H. Kerr and Company, 1902). Engels believed that the quest for private property meant that one gender—men—sought dominance over the other gender—women—and that thereafter men developed control over women's sexuality and their labor.

25. W. K. C. Guthrie, *In the Beginning: Some Greek Views on the Origins of Life and the Early State of Man* (London: Methuen, 1957), 77.

26. See J. J. Bachofen, *Mother Right*, in *Myth, Religion, and Mother Right: Selected Writings of J. J. Bachofen*; see also Briffault, *The Mothers*. See also recent interpreters such as Riane Eisler, *The Chalice and the Blade* (San Francisco: Harper & Row, 1987).

27. Mary Elizabeth Perry, "The Black Madonna of Montserrat," in Keller, ed., *Views*, 110.

28. See Judd, "The Myths of the Golden Age" for a discussion of ancient concepts of reproduction.

29. Lerner, *The Creation of Patriarchy*, 141–160. For a story showing the authoritative role of the goddess Nugur in China, see Tsao Hsueh-Chin, *Dream of the Red Chamber*, trans. Chi-Chen Wang (New York: Bantam-Doubleday Dell, 1989).

30. An anthropological museum in Madrid, Spain, displays such animals in simulated cave settings. The originals are in caves in southern France and southern Spain. See James Mellaart, *Catal Huyuk: A Neolithic Town in Anatolia* (London: Thames & Hudson, 1967). Cited in Lerner, *The Creation of Patriarchy*, 249, nn. 47, 49. Lerner notes that Mellaart's later work shows greater caution than does his first description of this Anatolian town.

31. For a discussion of the implications of concluding that women are natural while men control culture, see Sherry B. Ortner, "Is Female to Male as Nature Is to Culture?," in *Women, Culture, and Society*, ed. Michelle Zimbalist Rosaldo and Louise Lamphere (Stanford, Calif.: Stanford University Press, 1997), 67–87.

32. Historian-archeologist Nancy McCauley has supervised and curated a collection of goddess figures and slides which may be viewed in the Stanford University collections. It is astonishing that male historians of many generations have overlooked the great numbers of these figurines in European collections.

33. See the interpretation of the goddess figures in Marija Gimbutas, "The Image of Women in Prehistoric Art," *The Quarterly Review of Archeology* (December 1981). Gimbutas also discusses cults and religious developments as well as rituals and carvings relevant to women's lives in prehistoric periods. See also Eisler, *The Chalice and The Blade*, 59–77.

34. Carol Field, *Celebrating Italy* (New York: William Morrow and Company, 1990).

35. See Elizabeth Gould Davis, *The First Sex* (New York: Penguin Books, 1971) and other titles. Davis dwells on the importance of the mother-goddess concept to men; she discusses the continuance of this theme into later religions.

36. Qu Yajun, associate director of Center for Women's Studies, Deputy Director of Women Culture Museum, Shaanxi Normal University, Xian, P.R., China. Lecture presented to the International Museum of Women, 1848 Pine Street, San Francisco, California, May 24, 1999.

37. Quoted in Joan Markley Todd and Joseph Cono, "After Sappho, Aspasia, and Xanthippe: Women as Equals in the Writings of Xenophon," in Keller, ed., *Views*, 180.

38. Engels, *The Origin of the Family, Private Property and the State in Light of the Researches of Lewis H. Morgan*, 1–45.

39. Lane, "Women in Society: A Critique of Frederick Engels," 7.

40. Technology neutralizes the male advantage of physical strength in many fields, ranging from office work to the use of robotics. It frees women to perform many functions they could not previously perform, for whatever reasons. The outcome is that the entrenchment of patriarchal authority prevails in areas where it is no longer necessary by any concept. In academia, one of the last bastions of male dominance, there is no requirement that females cannot perform. In the information age, it may be irrelevant, as well as impossible, to tell the sex of many with whom one works but whom one has never met.

41. For this classic, original analysis of the institution of human slavery, see Lerner, *The Creation of Patriarchy*, Chapter 4, "The Woman Slave," 76–100.

42. Alice Walker, *By the Light of My Father's Smile* (New York: Random House, 1998), 164–165.

43. See Antoinette Burton, "From Child Bride to 'Hindoo Lady' Rukhmabai and the Debate on Sexual Respectability in Imperial Britain," *American Historical Review* 103, no. 4 (October 1998): 1119–1146. It has also been suggested that some of the practices noticed in this paragraph arose as well from the deep poverty of the societies where they were to be found. This may have contributed to such customs, and to their continuance, but it does not lessen the deep injustice or the horror involved for the women victims.

44. Penelope D. Johnson, "Finding Their Place: The Rich Roles of Religious Women in the Middle Ages," in Keller, *Voices*, 219–243.

45. This information about Kuan Yin appears in "Kuan Lin," a brochure produced by the Quon-Quon Company, 843 Los Angeles Street, Los Angeles, California. The early Kuan Lin is characterized by the aphorism "Noble natures are calm and content."

46. This is an ironic circumstance in view of Plato's respect for women and his inclusion of them in his plans for state direction.

47. Maryanne Cline Horowitz speaks of the "Aristotelian intellectual habit of describing the female body as a departure from the norm of the male body." "Aristotle and Woman," *Journal of the History of Biology* 9, no. 2 (Fall 1976): 185.

48. See Maryanne Cline Horowitz, "The 'Science' of Embryology before the Discovery of the Ovum," in *Connecting Spheres: Women in the Western World, 1500 to the Present*, ed. Marilyn J. Boxer and Jean H. Quataert (New York: Oxford University Press, 1987), 86–94.

49. Horowitz, "Aristotle and Woman," 183–213; for a careful assessment of transitional interpretations by influential clergy and religious scholars, see also Maryanne Cline

Horowitz, "The Image of God in Man—Is Woman Included?" *Harvard Theological Review* 72, no. 3–4 (July–October 1979): 175–206. See also Maryanne Cline Horowitz, "The Woman Question in Renaissance Texts," in *History of European Ideas* 8, no. 4/5 (1987): 587–595.

50. Leviticus 27:3.

51. I Corinthians 11:3.

52. I Corinthians 11:9.

53. I Timothy 5:10.

54. I Timothy 2:11–12.

55. I Peter 3:1.

56. A very few notable examples: Christine de Pisan, Mary Wollstonecraft, Simone de Beauvoir, Mary Beard. The list is long. Some men find places here.

57. See Barbara Welter, "The Cult of True Womanhood: 1820–1860," *American Quarterly* 18, no. 2 (Summer 1966): 151–174. Medieval codes of chivalry also contained this fiction. See also Aileen S. Kraditor, ed., *Up from the Pedestal: Selected Writings in the History of American Feminism* (Chicago: Quadrangle Books, 1968). Saint Peter may have been one of those to initiate this idea: "Even if some husbands do not obey the word," he wrote in I Peter 3:1, "the incorruptible ornament of a gentle and quiet spirit [woman's] which is very precious in the sight of God" may win them to the word.

58. Gerda Lerner, *Why History Matters* (New York: Oxford University Press, 1997). This is a personal story that Lerner uses movingly to demonstrate the impact of histories in the life of an individual or a society.

59. See Bachofen, *Myth, Religion, and Mother Right: Selected Writings of J. J. Bachofen.*

60. Joan Bamberger, "The Myth of Matriarchy: Why Men Rule in Primitive Society," in Rosaldo and Lamphere, eds., *Woman, Culture, and Society,* 263–280.

61. Ibid., 272–274, 280.

62. Sara M. Evans, *Born for Liberty* (New York: The Free Press, 1989), 77.

63. For a biographical study of Elizabeth Cady Stanton, see Lois Banner, *Elizabeth Cady Stanton: A Radical for Women's Rights* (Boston: Little, Brown, 1980).

64. Ibid.

65. For an insightful approach to the long struggle to win suffrage, see also Ellen Carol DuBois, *Harriet Stanton Blatch and the Winning of Woman's Suffrage* (New Haven, Conn.: Yale University Press, 1997).

66. Miriam Schneir, ed., *Feminism: The Essential Historical Writings* (New York: Vintage, 1972), 132–142.

67. Couverture refers to the French (and English and early American—to the middle 1900s in the United States) legal custom that women possessed no rights by law; they were entirely "covered" by the authority of their husbands or by that of the nearest male relative. Husband and wife were one person before the law; that one was the man. Women could not own property or control their children or keep any wages they might earn or property they might inherit. They could not sue except through their husbands. They could be punished as their husbands or substitutes at law saw fit.

68. Evans, *Born for Liberty,* 103.

69. Judith Strong Albert, "Encountering Margaret Fuller," in *Margaret Fuller: Visionary of the New Age,* ed. Marie Mitchell Olesen Urbanski (Orono, Maine: Northern Lights, 1994), 203.

70. *Ralph Waldo Emerson,* vol. 1, *Conversations in Fine Arts* (Boston: Phillips, Sampson & Co., 1851), Section V. This section covers "Memories of Margaret Fuller"; from this section arose the earliest "conversations" among Fuller and her friends as well as among later groups of women and students.

71. See Mary A. Hill, *Charlotte Perkins Gilman: The Making of a Radical Feminist, 1800–1896* (Philadelphia: Temple University Press, 1980).

72. See Mary Gabriel, *Notorious Victoria: The Life of Victoria Woodhull, Uncensored* (Chapel Hill, N.C.: Algonquin Books of Chapel Hill, 1998); Barbara Goldsmith, *Other Powers: The Age of Suffrage, Spiritualism, and the Scandalous Victoria Woodhull* (New York: A. A. Knopf, 1998), quotations, 300–301. See also Lois Beachy Underhill, *The Woman Who Ran for President: The Many Lives of Victoria Woodhull* (Bridgehampton, N.Y.: Bridge Works Publishing, 1995); and James Brough, *The Vixens: A Biography of Victoria and Tennessee Claflin* (New York: Simon and Schuster, 1980).

73. Quoted in Rosalie Maggio, ed., *The Beacon Book of Quotations by Women* (Boston: Beacon Press, 1996), 432; quoted in Goldsmith, *Other Powers,* 301.

74. See Louise Daniel Hutchinson, *Anna J. Cooper: A Voice from the South by a Black Woman of the South* (Washington, D.C.: Smithsonian Institution Press, 1981).

75. See Anna Julia Cooper, *Slavery and the French Revolutionists,* trans., ed., and Interpretive Essay by Frances Richardson Keller (Lewiston, N.Y.: Edwin Mellen Press, 1988).

76. Anna Julia Cooper, *A Voice from the South by a Black Woman of the South* (Xenia, Ohio: Aldine Printing House, 1892), 144–145.

77. Jane Addams, *Twenty Years at Hull House* (New York: Macmillan, 1911).

78. Linda Kerber and Jane DeHart-Mathews, eds., *Women's America: Refocusing the Past* (New York: Oxford University Press, 1987). See essay introducing the Progressive Era in America.

79. Kathryn Kish Sklar, *Florence Kelley and the Nation's Work* (New York: Yale University Press, 1995). For information on the work of Rowena and Russell Jelliffe, see Frances Richardson Keller, *An American Crusade: The Life of Charles Waddell Chesnutt* (Provo, Utah: Brigham Young University Press, 1978), 245–248. See Kerber and DeHart-Mathews, eds., *Women's America* on Republican Motherhood and other concepts. See Linda K. Kerber, Alice Kessler-Harris, and Kathryn Kish Sklar, eds., *U.S. History as Women's History: New Feminist Essays* (Chapel Hill: University of North Carolina Press, 1995), especially Linda K. Kerber, "A Constitutional Right to Be Treated Like American Ladies: Women and the Obligations of Citizenship," 11–35.

3. The Scramble After the Civil War

1. The preferred usage at present is "African American." This has varied before and after the official establishment of the United States in 1787. At the time of the 1790s revolution in the nearby then Dominican Republic, now Haitian Republic, the preferred designation was "colored." In the 1800s, it became "negro." Due to the influence of W. E. B. DuBois, it became "Negro" with a capital N; then, "Black." Somewhat after that "Afro American" was preferred, then "African American." In each of these time periods, black people struggled to craft terms that spoke of their race with respect. I have retained these time-specific usages to express my respect for the political and social work that was necessary to bring the terms into U.S. culture.

2. Abraham Lincoln, "Gettysburg Address."

3. Winthrop D. Jordan, *White over Black: American Attitudes toward the Negro, 1550–1812* (Chapel Hill: University of North Carolina Press, 1968). See Part One, "Genesis," 3–91, for origins of American racial dilemmas.

4. See William Lee Miller, *Arguing about Slavery: The Great Battle in the United States Congress* (New York: Alfred A. Knopf, 1997).

5. Bernard Weisberger, "The Dark and Bloody Ground of Reconstruction Historiography," *Journal of Southern History* XXV (November 1959): 427–447.

6. Wendell Holmes Stephenson and E. Merton Coulter, *A History of the South,* Vol. VII, *The South during Reconstruction, 1865–1877,* ed. E. Merton Coulter (Baton Rouge: Louisiana State University Press and the Littlefield Fund for Southern History of the University of Texas, 1947), 139–161. E. Merton Coulter fits into the first groupings, though he wrote at a later date than most of those in the first three groupings. I have grouped writers according to their fictions rather than according to chronology.

7. Though some northern women suffrage leaders had earnestly worked for Negro suffrage, they were deeply disappointed that women were excluded. See the work of Elizabeth Cady Stanton and Susan B. Anthony. Even so, they probably did not envision suffrage for black women.

8. John Hope Franklin, *The Militant South, 1860–1861* (Cambridge, Mass.: Belknap Press of Harvard University Press, 1956).

9. See especially Henry L. Swint, *Northern Teacher in the South* (Nashville, Tenn.: Vanderbilt University Press, 1941).

10. Herbert S. Klein, *Slavery in the Americas: A Comparative Study of Virginia and Cuba* (Chicago: Quadrangle Books, 1971), 40–44; quotation, 41. See Jordan, *White over Black,* 44–91.

11. Theodore J. Lowi, *American Government: Incomplete Conquest* (Hinsdale, Ill.: Dryden Press, 1976).

12. See Eric L. McKitrick, *Andrew Johnson and Reconstruction* (Chicago: University of Chicago Press, 1960). McKitrick makes the point that the distinction between victors and vanquished became blurred after the Civil War.

13. See Leon F. Litwack, *North of Slavery: The Negro in the Free States, 1790–1860* (Chicago: University of Chicago Press, 1961).

14. Lawrence W. Levine, *The Opening of the American Mind: Canons, Culture, and History* (Boston: Beacon Press, 1996), 26.

15. C. Vann Woodward, "Critical Essay on Authorities," in *Origins of the New South* (Baton Rouge: Louisiana State University Press, 1951), 482.

16. D. M. [Dumas Malone], "James Ford Rhodes," in *Dictionary of American Biography* (New York: Charles Scribner's Sons, 1935), vol. 15, 531–533.

17. See James Ford Rhodes, *History of the United States from the Compromise of 1850* (New York: Harper & Bros., 1893–1928).

18. William A. Dunning, *Reconstruction, Political and Economic, 1865–1877* (New York: Harper & Row, 1907), 1–16.

19. J. G. [J. G. de Roulhac Hamilton], "William Archibald Dunning," in *Dictionary of American Biography* (New York: Charles Scribner's Sons, 1930), vol. 5, 523–524; see Charles E. Merriam, "William Archibald Dunning," in *American Masters of Social Sciences,* ed. Howard Odum (New York: Holt, 1927).

20. See J. G. de Roulhac Hamilton, "Introduction to William A. Dunning," in Hamilton, ed., *Truth and History and Other Essays* (New York: Columbia University Press, 1937); Merriam, "William Archibald Dunning."

21. John Braeman, "John W. Burgess," in *Dictionary of Literary Biography* (Detroit, Mich.: Gale Research Company, 1986), vol. 47, 69–75.

22. See Karl R. Popper, *The Poverty of Historicism* (New York: Harper & Row, 1961).

23. Quotations as noted in Braeman, "John W. Burgess."

24. Arthur S. Link, *Woodrow Wilson: A Brief Biography* (Cleveland: World Publishing Company, 1963), 9–27.

25. Woodrow Wilson, "The Reconstruction of the Southern States," *Atlantic Monthly* 87 (January 1901): 2–11.

26. Ibid.

27. J. G. Randall and David Donald, *The Civil War and Reconstruction* (Boston: D. C. Heath and Company, 1961), 543–545.

28. J. G. Randall, *The Civil War and Reconstruction* (Boston: D. C. Heath and Company, 1937), 850–854.

29. Ibid.

30. Francis L. Simkins, "New Viewpoints of Southern History," *Journal of Southern History* 5, no. 1 (1939): 49–61.

31. Ibid.; E. Merton Coulter, *The South during Reconstruction, 1865–1877* (Baton Rouge: Louisiana State University Press, 1947).

32. Michael Bordelon, "Claude G. Bowers," in *Dictionary of Literary Biography,* ed. Clyde L. Wilson (Detroit, Mich.: Book Tower, 1983), vol. 17, 86–92.

33. Shirley Graham DuBois, *DuBois: A Pictorial Biography* (Chicago: Johnson Publishing Company, 1978), 10. See the excellent new biography by David Levering Lewis, *W. E. B. DuBois: The Fight for Equality and the American Century, 1919–1963* (New York: H. Holt, 2000).

34. DuBois, *DuBois,* 12.

35. Ibid., 12–13.

36. W. E. B. DuBois, *Black Reconstruction in America: An Essay toward the Part Which Black Folk Played in the Attempt to Reconstruct Democracy in America, 1860–1880* (1935; reprint, New York: S. A. Russell, 1956).

37. W. E. B. DuBois, *The Souls of Black Folk* (Greenwich, Conn.: Fawcett Publications, 1961), 23.

38. C. Vann Woodward, *Origins of the New South* (Baton Rouge: Louisiana State University Press, 1951), 429. (Vol. IX in Wendell Holmes Stephenson and E. Merton Coulter, eds., *History of the South*).

39. Elizabeth Muhlenfeld, "C. Vann Woodward," in *Dictionary of Literary Biography* (Detroit, Mich.: Gale Research Company, 1983), vol. 17, 465–482. I have used interpretations from this excellent study.

40. Buck Colbert Franklin, *My Life and an Era,* ed. John Hope Franklin and John Wittington Franklin (Baton Rouge: Louisiana State University Press, 1997), xviii.

41. Ibid., 192–202.

42. John Hope Franklin described some of his early life experiences in a public television broadcast for San Francisco station KQED on August 29, 1997.

43. Interview given to Charlie Rose, public television broadcast, November 1, 1997.

44. Beth Baker, "Forcing America to Keep Faith," *AARP Bulletin* 38, no. 8 (September 1997).

45. John Hope Franklin, *From Slavery to Freedom: A History of African Americans* (New York: Alfred A. Knopf, 1967), viii.

46. Quoted in Baker, "Forcing America to Keep Faith."

47. See John Hope Franklin, *The Color Line: Legacy for the Twenty-First Century* (Columbia and London: University of Missouri Press, 1993).

48. John Hope Franklin, quoted by Steven A. Holmes, "Scholar Takes on His Toughest Study of Race," *New York Times,* September 28, 1997, sec. 1, p. 1.

49. John Hope Franklin, *From Slavery to Freedom: A History of American Negroes* (New York: Alfred A. Knopf, 1967), x.

50. Kenneth Stampp, quoted in John G. Sproat, "Kenneth M. Stampp," *Dictionary of Literary Biography* (Detroit, Mich.: Gale Research Company, 1983), 402.

51. Quoted by Sproat in ibid.

4. From Mormon Polygamy to American Monogamy

1. "An Old Timer," in "Expressions from the People," *Deseret News,* April 14, 1885, quoted in B. Carmon Hardy, *Solemn Covenant* (Urbana and Chicago: University of Illinois Press, 1992), xix. For an insightful discussion of the political implications that would underpin the making and enforcing of fictions pertaining to marriage in Mormon Utah, see Nancy Cott, "Giving Character to Our Whole Civil Polity: Marriage and the Public Order in the Late Nineteenth Century," in *U.S. History as Women's History: New Feminist Essays,* ed. Linda K. Kerber, Alice Kessler-Harris, and Kathryn Kish Sklar (Chapel Hill: University of North Carolina Press, 1995), 108–109. According to Cott, "One of the principal means that the state can use to prove its existence—to announce its sovereignty and its hold on the populace—is its authority over marriage. . . . Marriage can be better understood as a constitutive part of public order in a given time and place, in a relation subject to change."

2. Hardy, *Solemn Covenant,* 2–3. Hardy shows instances of recurrence of polygamy in the western world prior to that of Mormonism.

3. Church names of the time indicate that other sects were similarly oriented toward the past, for example, the Primitive Methodists.

4. A peep stone appears to have been an artifact found in the mountains that was believed to confer magical powers on the possessor, especially powers that could reveal what lay beneath the surface of the land.

5. Charles G. Finney's *Memoirs* consists of his recollections and observations about his career as an evangelist. The book is not an autobiography. *Memoirs of Rev. Charles G. Finney* (New York: A. S. Barnes & Company, 1876).

6. Ibid., 78.

7. Fawn M. Brodie, *No Man Knows My History: The Life of Joseph Smith, the Mormon Prophet* (New York: Alfred A. Knopf, 1946), 15.

8. 1803, 1823, 1853, 1873, and so forth. The pattern of economic downswings encompassed about twenty years; it characterized the advances of the industrial revolution.

9. See Brodie, *No Man Knows My History* for a discussion of the particular financial upheavals of the Mormons. "Andrew Jackson's bank controversy" underlay many westward adventures. Like others, the Mormons found themselves involved.

10. In Joseph Smith's official "Testimony of the Prophet Joseph Smith," which appears as a preface to *The Book of Mormon: Another Testament of Jesus Christ* (Salt Lake City, Utah: The Church of Jesus Christ of Latter-Day Saints, 1981), n. p., Smith speaks, in parentheses, of "the indigent circumstances of my father's family"; Brodie, *No Man Knows My History,* 1–15. Brodie traces the Smith family's New England background in detail. See also Alice Felt Tyler, *Freedom's Ferment* (New York: Harper & Row, 1962), 87. Tyler quotes Daniel Hendrix, a Palmyra resident who aided Smith in publishing the Book of Mormon. Brodie, *No Man Knows My History,* quotes the same passage I quote with the notation that her information comes from a "Letter of Hendrix dated February 2, 1897, published in the *St. Louis Globe Democrat,*" 26. The same passage is also quoted in Leonard J. Arrington and Davis Bitton, *The Mormon Experience: A History of the Latter-Day Saints* (Urbana and Chicago: University of Illinois Press, 1992), 9–12. In *Religion and Sexuality* (New York: Oxford University Press, 1984), 125–130, Lawrence J. Foster outlines several approaches to understanding the circumstances of Joseph Smith: Smith was "a handsome, dynamic leader with great physical and intellectual vitality—a man not afraid to break with convention." Perhaps the most revealing clues to understanding Smith's early life can be found in a book by his mother, Lucy Mack Smith: *Biographical Sketches of Joseph Smith and His Progenitors for Many Gen-*

erations (Liverpool, England, 1855). Joseph Smith ordered this book suppressed, but there have been reprints.

11. Brodie, *No Man Knows My History,* 34; Brodie cites *The Palmyra Register,* January 21, 1818, and *The Palmyra Herald,* February 19, 1823. This story appears repeatedly in various works about Joseph Smith.

12. Smith, *Biographical Sketches,* 85, as quoted in Brodie, *No Man Knows My History,* 35.

13. Tyler, *Freedom's Ferment,* 87.

14. Robert L. Millet, ed., *Joseph Smith: Selected Sermons & Writings* (New York: Paulist Press, 1989), 14–15. According to this editor, four distinct accounts of this experience were recorded by Joseph Smith and his scribes. The accounts vary.

15. If a difference between peep stone and seerstone exists in the context of this period and this chapter, it is probably that Joseph and his friends used "peep stone" in the early days of Joseph's prospecting in the mountains and "seerstone" later as he developed religious materials.

16. The most famous of Smith's revelations were preceded by other revelations and by early visions. Brodie, *No Man Knows My History,* 21.

17. Millet, ed., *Joseph Smith: Selected Sermons & Writings,* 181–182.

18. Lawrence Foster, *Religion and Sexuality: The Shakers, the Mormons, and the Oneida Community* (Urbana and Chicago: University of Illinois Press, 1984), 128–130. See also Tyler, *Freedom's Ferment,* 88–93. Accounts about the plates differ. Smith's wife and scribe describe them as wrapped in linen cloths. Smith's mother Lucy Smith recalled that they were sometimes kept in a red morocco trunk at Emma's bureau. See Jan Shipps, *Mormonism: The Story of a New Religious Tradition* (Urbana and Chicago: University of Illinois Press, 1985), 4–23.

19. Brodie, *No Man Knows My History,* 40 and n. In this biography, Brodie quotes Lucy Mack Smith's description of the stones: "Two smooth three-cornered diamonds set in glass and the glasses set in silver bows." Brodie also notes that Martin Harris, an associate, said the stones were "white, like polished marble, with a few grey streaks," while David Whitmer said they were "two small stones of a chocolate color, nearly egg shape, and perfectly smooth, but not transparent."

20. Buddy Youngreen, *Reflections of Emma* (Orem, Utah: Granden Book Company, 1982); Brodie, *No Man Knows My History,* 50–66. Brodie also discusses another and earlier scribe, farmer Martin Harris.

21. Shipps, *Mormonism: The Story of a New Religious Tradition,* 14; Brodie, *No Man Knows My History,* 61. Brodie quotes David Whitmer, a farmer, at greater length on the method of "translation: "Joseph Smith would put the seer stone into a hat, and put his face in the hat, drawing it closely around his face to exclude the light; and in the darkness the spiritual light would shine. A piece of something resembling parchment would appear, and on that appeared the writing. One character at a time would appear, and under it was the interpretation in English. Brother Joseph would read off the English to Oliver Cowdery who was his principal scribe, and when it was written down and repeated to Brother Joseph to see if it was correct, then it would disappear, and another character with the interpretation would appear. Thus the Book of Mormon was translated by the gift and power of God, and not by any power of man."

22. Youngreen, *Reflections of Emma,* 91. For another discussion of the finding of the plates that differs from that given in Arrington and Bitton or in Tyler, see Louis J. Kern, *An Ordered Love: Sex Roles and Sexuality in Victorian Utopias: The Shakers, the Mormons, and*

the Oneida Community (Chapel Hill: University of North Carolina Press, 1981), 138–139. "Translation" is the word Smith is said to have used. Many versions of these events exist.

23. For an informed study of the cultural settings of the Book of Mormon, see Philip L. Barlow, *Mormons and the Bible: The Place of the Latter-Day Saints in American Religion* (New York: Oxford University Press, 1991), 11–42. Like foundation writings of other religions, the Book of Mormon is an amalgam of stories, revelations, predictions, mystical insights, moral "sayings," and millennialism.

24. Arrington and Bitton, *The Mormon Experience*; Tyler, *Freedom's Ferment*, 68–107. These historians give different versions of the "Beginnings." Both accounts note that Smith could read but that he was educated little beyond literacy. Both accounts—and others—note the difficulty of confirming or disproving supernatural manifestations, and both suggest that their significance depends on succeeding events rather than on their authenticity.

25. This summary sketch of the clouded beginnings of American Mormonism can be filled in by consulting the chronology provided in Shipps, *Mormonism: The Story of a New Religious Tradition*, 151–168.

26. Philip L. Barlow, *Mormons and the Bible* (New York: Oxford University Press, 1991), 46. Authorities differ on details of church growth.

27. Shipps, *Mormonism: The Story of a New Religious Tradition*, 120. See Frances Richardson Keller, "The Harlem Literary Renaissance," *The North American Review*, n.s., V, no. 3 (May-June 1968): 29–34 for a discussion of the significance of the concept of the "elect" to a group.

28. Arrington and Bitton, *The Mormon Experience*, 131–132; Tyler, *Freedom's Ferment*, 94. Tyler quotes Brigham Young's biographer, M. R. Werner, as suggesting that "the shrewd and skeptical young man early discerned that the new religion might easily be made a paying proposition." *Brigham Young* (New York: Harcourt Brace, 1925), 12. Kern refers to "the frank statement of Lucy Smith (Joseph's mother's) about the breast plates [the golden plates] of Nephi: 'The whole plate was worth at least five hundred dollars.'" *An Ordered Love*, 139. Many quarrels over land deeds among professed Mormons and between apostates and Church members over property ownership took place; Mormon banks, operating according to the practice of the time, printed large amounts of unsecured currency; many debts remained unpaid as Mormons fled before persecuting villagers.

29. Gordon Shepherd and Gary Shepherd, *A Kingdom Transformed: Themes in the Development of Mormonism* (Salt Lake City: University of Utah Press, 1984), 19–34; Foster, *Religion and Sexuality*, 186–190.

30. David Whitmer, quoted in Brodie, *No Man Knows My History*, 95.

31. Ibid.

32. Foster, *Religion and Sexuality*, 95.

33. Shipps, *Mormonism: The Story of a New Religious Tradition*, 121. Shipps writes: "On the one hand there were Saints who understood the Mormon message and accepted its substance metaphorically, and on the other there were Saints who accepted the gospel quite literally." There were as well many other preachers who claimed mystic powers and divine connections.

34. Millet, ed., *Joseph Smith: Selected Sermons & Writings*, 187.

35. It has also been suggested that the Saints believed that they were reliving the ancient wanderings of the Jews, that this belief provided a mystique that drew them together. It is certainly true that without the support they provided one another, they could scarcely have survived. As one source tells it, they "saw many long years of persecutions and afflictions at the hands of their enemies."

36. For instance, in the 1840s, a debate took place about whether the priesthood was

also given to the sisters but was later taken from them. At some point, as in most religions, almost every tenet of the faith came into question. As in most religions, factions arose from time to time.

37. A. L. Morton has called this promise the "Everlasting Gospel." A. L. Morton, *The Everlasting Gospel: A Study in the Sources of William Blake* (London: Lawrence & Wishart, 1958).

38. Shipps, *Mormonism: The Story of a New Religious Tradition,* ix–x and following.

39. Shepherd and Shepherd, *A Kingdom Transformed,* 19–46; David J. Whittaker, "The 'Articles of Faith' in Early Mormon Literature and Thought," in *New Views of Mormon History: A Collection of Essays in Honor of Leonard J. Arrington,* ed. Davis Bitton and Maureen Ursenback Beecher (Salt Lake City: University of Utah Press, 1987), 63–92.

40. Kern, *An Ordered Love,* 144–157.

41. Tyler, *Freedom's Ferment,* 96.

42. Some authorities give this organizing effort as the Quorum of Seventy. An explicit summation of church organization appears in Lowell C. Bennion, "Mormon Country a Century Ago: A Geographer's View," in Alexander, ed., *The Mormon People.* See Figure One, "Priesthood Pyramid for Mormondom, 1880," 5.

43. Shepherd and Shepherd, *A Kingdom Transformed,* 139; Tyler, *Freedom's Ferment,* 103. Tyler notes that Mormon missionaries who were sent to England "found a vast reservoir of new adherents in the poorer districts of English factory towns, where discontent and superstition combined to make conversion easy."

44. A major work of Joseph's ministry was his new translation of the Hebrew Bible.

45. Breck England, *The Life and Thought of Orson Pratt* (Salt Lake City: University of Utah Press, 1985).

46. Mrs. T. B. H. Stenhouse, *A Lady's Life among the Mormons: A Record of Personal Experiences of the Wives of a Mormon Elder* (London: George Routledge and Sons, 1873), 7.

47. Ibid., 15.

48. Richard Van Wagoner, *Mormon Polygamy: A History* (Salt Lake City: Signature Books, 1989), 29–39.

49. Millet, ed., *Joseph Smith: Selected Sermons & Writings,* 100.

50. Ibid., 101.

51. Marilyn Warenski, *Patriarchs and Politics: The Plight of the Mormon Woman* (New York: McGraw-Hill Book Company, 1978), 21–53.

52. A similarity to Puritan experience, especially that of Anne Hutchinson and John Winthrop, is apparent. The debate that arose formed the substance of the antinomian controversy.

53. The religious and social turbulence in American culture in the early nineteenth century have frequently been noted; scholars have remarked their virulence in the "burned-over" district of western New York. Lillian Wellman gives a historiographical account of this scholarship in "Crossing over Cross: Whitney Cross's *Burned-Over District* as Social History," *Reviews in American History* 17 (March 1989): 159–174. Another factor may have been at work. Mormon leaders repeatedly let it be known that God had decreed the innate inferiority of the female sex. Therefore, the patriarchal plan for society demonstrated God's wisdom. This pervasive understanding would have weighed heavily in producing for women a lack of self-respect and a lack of confidence in their own worth. See Hardy, *Solemn Covenant,* 99.

54. Exclusion of women from the priesthood was typical. The only exceptions were the more radical offshoots of seventeenth-century Anabaptism. Quakers included women, but conceived priesthood, in the usual sense, as an undesirable feature of any religion.

55. Bennion's plan appears on page 5 of Alexander, ed., *The Mormon People*. To note the extent of the training of children from the early days of Mormonism, see Jill Mulvay Derr, "Sisters and Little Saints: One Hundred Years of Mormon Primaries," in Alexander, ed., *The Mormon People*, 75–102.

56. This included enterprises that were conceived to yield commercial profit, such as silk-making, from growing the worms to producing a finished product to providing grain for their communities. See *The Woman's Exponent* 5, no. 18 (December 1, 1876). In this and subsequent issues, many editorials encourage women in these and other projects.

57. All organizations, male and female, came under one specific line of authority, but this did not occur until 1972. Even as late as that, it is difficult to discern the extent of cult influences and of developing fiction-stories. See Warenski, *Patriarchs and Politics*, 135–142.

58. Van Wagoner, *Mormon Polygamy: A History*, 3–12.

59. *Book of Mormon* (Salt Lake City, Utah: Church of Jesus Christ of Latter-Day Saints, 1986), Jac. 1:15; 2:23–27; 3:5; Mos. 11:2–4; Eth. 10–5; Book of Commandments, 124.

60. Hardy, *Solemn Covenant*, 4–20.

61. Quoted in Van Wagoner, *Mormon Polygamy: A History*, 3. It should be noted, however, that Phelps wrote the letter to Young in 1861. Lawrence Foster believes that the revelation was taken down in 1831 shortly after Smith gave it orally. *Religion and Sexuality*, 299, n. 29. In any case, it followed almost immediately after the organization of the church. By the use of the word "white," Smith drew upon the believed relationship of the "red" men—Indians—to Mormon descendants.

62. Quoted in Kunz, "One Wife or Several?," 54.

63. The text of the revelation is given in the appendix of Stenhouse, *A Lady's Life among the Mormons*, 164–173.

64. Kunz, "One Wife or Several?," 55; Foster, *Religion and Sexuality*, 125–135. Smith was murdered on June 27, 1844, in Carthage, Illinois.

65. For a study of polygamy at the time of its public inception (1852), see Jessie L. Embry, *Mormon Polygamous Families: Life in the Principle* (Salt Lake City: University of Utah Press, 1987), 53–71. Embry notes the revelation stated that if the first wife refused her consent, "she then became the transgressor." On page 52, Embry gives Orson Pratt's reasons for plural marriage and provides many case studies of its ramifications.

66. Van Wagoner, *Mormon Polygamy: A History*, 15–35.

67. Even before the introduction of polygamy among the Mormon settlers, the climate in Missouri was rising to panic proportions over the issue of slavery in the territories.

68. For a discussion of the hardships that accompanied the secretive introduction of polygamy, see Maureen Ursenbach Beecher, *Eliza and Her Sisters* (Salt Lake City, Utah: Aspen Books, 1991), 75–97.

69. See Briffault, *The Mothers*, 207–233. Briffault traces an "evolution" of monogamous marriage covering many ancient lands, tribes, and customs. Since biblical Old Testament practice was the concern of the Mormon leadership, I limit the present discussion to Old Testament polygyny.

70. Shipps, *Mormonism: The Story of a New Religious Tradition*, 122.

71. Van Wagoner, *Mormon Polygamy: A History*, 3. Van Wagoner cites biblical passages in Genesis 29–30, I Samuel 1:2, II Chronicles 11:21, II Chronicles 13:21, I Chronicles 14:3, and I Kings 11:3. Verses 21–30 of Genesis 29 address the polygamy of the Old Testament patriarch Jacob.

72. *The Women's Exponent* 5, no. 13 (December 1, 1876). The editorial is titled "Our Modern Dorcas." The editorial expresses the women's doubts about the scriptural Dorcas: "In the scriptures written by the Apostles, they recorded the things which seemed most es-

sential, but the acts and characters of women were almost left out." See also Warenski, *Patriarchs and Politics,* 145.

73. Millet, ed., *Joseph Smith: Selected Sermons & Writings,* 190–191.

74. Hardy, *Solemn Covenant,* xviii, 2.

75. See Youngreen, *Reflections of Emma.* In *An Ordered Love,* Louis J. Kern suggests that Smith's revelations were tailored to the needs of his situations; see also Lawrence Foster, *Religion and Sexuality,* 125–128 for a discussion of the complexity of Smith's motivations. After the revelation, Smith seems to have become increasingly committed to polygamy. B. Carmon Hardy notes in *Solemn Covenant,* 7, that according to Smith's nephew, the sealing principle in plural relationships became "the very point-essence and culmination of [Joseph's and his brother Hyrum's] . . . life-work and mission."

76. Van Wagoner, *Mormon Polygamy: A History,* 4–7; Foster, *Religion and Sexuality,* 151–159.

77. Rumors about Smith's secret affairs and wives had proliferated from the beginning. See Van Wagoner, *Mormon Polygamy: A History,* 3–10.

78. Brodie, *No Man Knows My History,* 284–288.

79. Shipps, *Mormonism: The Story of a New Religious Tradition,* 160.

80. Hardy, *Solemn Covenant,* 97–104; Shipps, *Mormonism: The Story of a New Religious Tradition,* 61, 160. Noting that the revelation about plural marriage dates from July 12, 1843, Shipps places "the inauguration of plural marriage in the same time period as Smith's organization of a Mormon political kingdom." The concern for temporal power is not disconnected from the quest for everlasting celestial dominance. At the time of the migration from Kirtland, the center of the universe was to have been established at Nauvoo.

81. Arrington and Bitton, *The Mormon Experience,* 223. For a full account see Foster, *Religion and Sexuality,* 149–151.

82. Youngreen, *Reflections of Emma,* 32. Youngreen provides vivid descriptions of Emma Smith's mental tortures.

83. Millet, ed., *Joseph Smith: Selected Sermons and Writings,* 153–154.

84. Milo M. Quaife, *The Kingdom of Saint James: A Narrative of the Mormons* (New Haven: Yale University Press, 1930). This book offers an account of this and other factions that split from the new Mormon orthodoxy. See also Foster, *Religion and Sexuality,* 149.

85. *Woman's Exponent* (September 1, 1880), 54–55.

86. Quoted in Foster, *Religion and Sexuality,* 222.

87. Quoted in Beecher, *Eliza and Her Sisters,* 67.

88. Quoted in Hardy, *Solemn Covenant,* 103.

89. A poignant example is Annie Clark Tanner, *A Mormon Mother: An Autobiography* (Salt Lake City, Utah: Tanner Trust Fund, University of Utah Library, 1969). Other Mormon women's journals also record emotional distress, particularly the journals of women pioneers, the wartime journals of women, the journals recording slavery, and journals recording property losses.

90. Ann Eliza Young, *Wife No. 19; or, The Story of a Life in Bondage, being a Complete Exposure of Mormonism, and Revealing the Sorrows, Sacrifices and Sufferings of Women in Polygamy* (Hartford, Conn.: Dustin, Gilman & Co., 1875; reprint, New York: Arno Press, 1972). An editor's note in the later edition furnishes the information that the writer was the twenty-seventh wife of Brigham Young, who, according to some authorities, married fifty-five times. The note appears on an unnumbered page opposite the title page of this volume. Ann Young's account has been denigrated by the suggestion that her motives were economic. But economic problems *were* crucially important to many plural wives.

91. Stenhouse, *A Lady's Life among the Mormons,* 85.

92. Quoted in Julie Dunfey, "'Living the Principle' of Plural Marriage: Mormon Women, Utopia, and Female Sexuality in the Nineteenth Century," *Feminist Studies* 10, no. 3 (Fall 1984): 526.

93. Quoted in Hardy, *Solemn Covenant*, 105.

94. See Jennie Anderson Froiseth, *The Women of Mormonism, or, The Story of Polygamy as Tolerated by the Victims Themselves* (Detroit, Mich.: C. G. G. Paine, 1882), 45–46, 150–163.

95. Official Mormon post-statehood publicity indicates the number was relatively small; later studies suggest, however, that the custom penetrated Mormon society much more widely than had been thought.

96. Some women entered plural marriage because of family and community pressures. In *Wife No. 19*, Ann Young tells of the pressures her parents exerted to persuade her to become one of Brigham Young's wives.

97. Catholic women religious and others share Mormon women's views of the importance of God's truth over earthly comfort. They may also share some anxieties like those of Mormon women.

98. Joseph Smith and successors used excommunication; see Kern, *An Ordered Love*, 159, 164. Divorce was available to Mormon women in polygamy; see Embry, *Mormon Polygamous Families*, 175–186. Mormon practice could afford leniency about divorce because established religious pressures retained power over Mormon women. Not long ago Marilyn Warenski, author of *Patriarchs and Politics*, was excommunicated. In matters of compliance, God's wrath was frequently invoked in early days in a manner reminiscent of Puritan preachings.

99. I refer to American experience. In other parts of the world, polygamy was steadfastly upheld.

100. Stenhouse, *A Lady's Life among the Mormons*, 19–36.

101. The Female Relief Society, the official women's organization of the church, was founded at the behest of Joseph Smith; Emma Smith became its first president. Among Mormon women it exercised enormous influence.

102. See Hardy, *Solemn Covenant*, 84–94, for discussion of the rationales for polygamy.

103. Cheryl Thurber, "Sunday Schools and American Christian Consumer Culture," Paper presented at the American Historical Association Conference, January 7, 1996, Atlanta, Georgia. Mormons advantageously used the stream of publications emanating from the new "Christian consumerism."

104. Helen Mar Whitney, *Why We Practice Plural Marriage as Taught by the Prophet Joseph* (Salt Lake City, Utah: The Juvenile Instructor Office, 1882).

105. Warenski, *Patriarchs and Politics*, 115 n.

106. Quoted in ibid., 164.

107. "Nearly mandatory" means approved Mormon practice: children's programs, weekly gatherings of church groups, and comment and policy expressed in church publications. In modern times, it has meant the conviviality of nightly "stake-houses," recreation centers in many communities. From the beginning there were threats that "all that do wickedly shall burn as stubble." See Kern, *An Ordered Love*, 137. Smith threatened that those who demurred about his policies would be "destroyed."

108. Women as well as men were sometimes "called" for service out of the areas where they lived and were frequently depended upon for service in the local temple as well.

109. Wives *officially* accepted and supported the new cultural imperative. It is true that they knew at that time that divorce was possible and could be attained without undue stigma. See *Diary of Brigham Young, 1857* (Salt Lake City: Tanner Trust Fund, University of

Utah Library, 1980), n. 10, and other notes touching divorce, 1–90. It is also true that some women looked forward to an improved position in the celestial kingdom; this would occur because of the increased numbers of children and because of the infinite potentialities promised for life after death in the vastness of a Mormon domination of the universe.

110. Warenski, *Patriarchs and Politics,* 155–160.

111. Ibid. Probably as a reward for public approval of polygamy as well as by means of their own efforts, Mormon women gained establishment support for voting rights. Utah granted women suffrage in 1870.

112. *The Woman's Exponent* 5, no. 18 (1877), 109–110. The editorial suggests that 900,000 women in England would be unable to find husbands. It asks what was to be done for them. Would they not be better off if all were able to share husbands? This public justification in an official women's publication seems to be derived from the male rationalization that Mormon men were saviors of women who otherwise would remain single. One historian suggests that the experience of the introduction of polygamy as Mormons followed the Overland Trail from Nauvoo provided a background; it had forced women to undergo the problems polygamy raised and also introduced some of them to the possibilities in women's groups. See Beecher, *Eliza and Her Sisters,* 81–86.

113. Eliza Snow's background exemplifies this situation: She was born in Becket, in the Berkshire Hills of Massachusetts, in 1804, but soon moved with her parents to the Ohio Territory, then to the Connecticut Western Reserve. Beecher, *Eliza and Her Sisters,* 7.

114. Julie Dunfey, "'Living the Principle' of Plural Marriage," 523–536.

115. Quoted in Van Wagoner, *Mormon Polygamy: A History,* 102.

116. Joan Iversen, "Feminist Implications of Mormon Polygyny," *Feminist Studies* 10, no. 3 (Fall 1984): 505–521. While polygamy pushed women toward self-sufficiency, it also left some women in severe economic difficulties. See Peggy Pascoe, *Relations of Rescue* (New York: Oxford University Press, 1990), 87–90. See also Joan Smyth Iversen, *The Antipolygamy Controversy in U.S. Women's Movements, 1880–1925: A Debate on the American Home* (New York: Garland Publishing, 1997).

117. Ibid., 107–142. For a review of protestations asserting the wisdom of polygamy, see Hardy, *Solemn Covenant,* Chapter 3, especially "Blessings of the Abrahamic Household," 94–97.

118. Non-Mormon women, that is, the rest of American women, expected that Mormon women would use their coveted voting power to disable polygamy. They couldn't understand that Mormon women preferred to perpetuate religious hegemony in Utah. This preference became conspicuous when Utah became the second state to grant women the suffrage.

119. Warenski, *Patriarchs and Politics,* 156. It should be noted that since then, Mormon women have been developing tenets of their own. Some poignant beliefs suggest that for women the religion centers on the significance of the Temple. This is also a tradition of antiquity in which women served their lifetimes as Temple priestesses. See Carol Cornwall Madsen, "Mormon Women and the Temple: Toward a New Understanding," in *Sisters in Spirit: Mormon Women in Historical and Cultural Perspective,* ed. Maureen Ursenback Beecher and Lavinia Fielding Anderson (Urbana and Chicago: University of Illinois Press, 1987), 80–110. This is a channel of thought upheld by C. Mark Hamilton, "The Salt Lake Temple: A Symbolic Statement of Mormon Doctrine," in Alexander, ed., *The Mormon People: Their Character and Traditions,* 103–127.

120. Much of the scholarship in women's histories documents these concerns. See, for example, Nancy Woloch, *Women and the American Experience* (New York: Alfred A. Knopf, 1984), 192–197; Linda K. Kerber and Jane DeHart-Mathews, eds., *Women's America* (New

York: Oxford University Press, 1987), 323; Mary Ryan, *Womanhood in America* (New York: New Viewpoints, 1975), 83–191; Gerda Lerner, "The Political Activities of Antislavery Women," in *Women and Power in American History*, ed. Kathryn Kish Sklar and Thomas Dublin (Englewood Cliffs, N.J.: Prentice Hall, 1991), 172–184.

121. It is difficult to designate any single moment as the beginning of the struggle for women's rights in the United States. It was probably taking shape well before the founding of the republic. It expressed itself through many religious, civic, and educational endeavors. By the time of the Seneca Falls Convention in 1848 it was well underway.

122. There was some reason for resentment over the methods Mormon investors used to acquire property and over their financial maneuverings.

123. Stenhouse, *A Lady's Life among the Mormons*, 128.

124. See Nancy F. Cott, "Giving Character to Our Whole Civil Polity," 108.

125. We note interest in women's needs and those of slaves and free blacks. It is notable that abolitionist movements flourished over the early part of this period, as did efforts of women to organize for votes and for civil rights. The Granger movement, the New South movement, and the beginnings of the Populist movement also developed over the later years in which polygamy became a public question in the wider American polity.

126. For male points of view, see Embry, *Mormon Polygamous Families*, 189–190.

127. Jan Shipps, "Marketing Mormonism: The LDS Church's Use of Public Relations and Advertising Techniques to Represent Themselves and Sell Their Message to the World," paper presented at the American Historical Association, January 7, 1996, Atlanta, Georgia.

128. Hardy, *Solemn Covenant*, 206–243.

129. National Public Radio broadcast, Station KQED, national news, 11:30 a.m., August 20, 1997.

130. Cott, "Giving Character to Our Whole Civil Polity," 107.

131. Dean C. Jesse, "Walls, Grates and Screeking Iron Doors: The Prison Experience of Mormon Leaders in Missouri, 1838–1839," in Bitton and Beecher, eds., *New Views of Mormon History*, 19–42. See also Merlo J. Pusey, *Builders of the Kingdom* (Provo, Utah: Brigham Young University Press, 1981), 147–155.

132. At the same time that Mormon women attended national suffrage conferences, non-Mormon women organized anti-polygamy societies. There were, however, some eastern leaders who were sympathetic to Mormon women because of the adjustments polygamy required of them.

133. For a detailed description of these events, see Iversen, *The Antipolygamy Controversy in U. S. Women's Movements, 1880–1925*, 21–95.

134. Elizabeth Cady Stanton, *Eighty Years and More (1815–1897): Reminiscences of Elizabeth Cady Stanton* (London: T. Fisher Unwin, 1989), 285.

135. See Jean Goldzink, *Charles-Louis De Montesquieu, Lettres persanes* (Paris: Presses Universitaires de France, 1989), 40 (trans. Frances Richardson Keller).

136. Carol Cornwall Madsen, "Schism in the Sisterhood: Mormon Women and Partisan Politics, 1890–1900," in Bitton and Beecher, eds., *New Views of Mormon History*, 212–214. Madsen provides a summary of these events.

137. Utah became a state in 1896. At this time, the vote was also restored to Utah women, largely because leading Utah women had worked together tirelessly to reinstate the suffrage after the criminalizing of polygamy in 1887. The document revoking the revelation on polygamy was an "advise," not a new revelation.

138. Hardy, *Solemn Covenant*, 167–205. This chapter provides a detailed study of the practice of polygamy "Abroad and at Home" after the 1890 manifesto.

5. Eleanor Roosevelt

I intend in this chapter to show how my fictions suggest the operations of fictions in the background and living of one individual rather than to contribute and interpret biographical information about Mrs. Roosevelt; for this, I will, however, review circumstances of her life. Since it has become possible to access FBI files and to review bibliographies, etc., at the Franklin D. Roosevelt Library in Hyde Park, New York, and elsewhere, fine biographical studies have become available. I have gratefully referred to these studies and to Eleanor Roosevelt's writings to illustrate my thesis. I am especially indebted to Blanche Wiesen Cook's *Eleanor Roosevelt*, vol. 1.

1. Eleanor Roosevelt, *The Autobiography of Eleanor Roosevelt* (New York: Harper & Brothers, 1961), 4. Originally this work was published as *The Autobiography of Eleanor Roosevelt* (1961). It is a compendium of earlier works. Eleanor Roosevelt described it as "both an abbreviated and an augmented edition of my autobiography." It includes *This Is My Story* (1937), *This I Remember* (1947), and *On My Own* (1958). *The Search for Understanding* first appeared as the "augmented" section of *The Autobiography of Eleanor Roosevelt.*

2. Ibid., 4.

3. Ibid., xv–xvi.

4. Ibid., 5.

5. Eleanor Roosevelt, *You Learn by Living* (New York: Harper & Brothers, 1960), 25. Again, in *This Is My Story,* she wrote "I was always afraid of something: of the dark, of displeasing people, of failure" (*Autobiography of Eleanor Roosevelt,* 12).

6. I can suggest no better surveillance of sources for Eleanor Roosevelt's maternal forbears than those cited in Blanche Wiesen Cook, *Eleanor Roosevelt*, vol. 1, *1884–1933* (New York: Penguin Group, 1993) 504, nn. 21–22. This is the definitive work. I am indebted to this splendid biography for much of the new richness of our knowledge of Eleanor Roosevelt's life and activities. Cook used the Franklin D. Roosevelt library in Hyde Park, New York, where the Eleanor Roosevelt Family Papers and the Lorena Hickok Papers are located. The latter include the interview Eleanor Roosevelt provided to Lorena Hickok.

7. See G. William Domhoff, *The Higher Circles: The Governing Class in America* (New York: Vintage, 1971).

8. Cook, *Eleanor Roosevelt*, 56.

9. Roosevelt, *This Is My Story,* in *The Autobiography of Eleanor Roosevelt*, 9.

10. See Roosevelt, *This Is My Story,* in *The Autobiography of Eleanor Roosevelt,* esp. 14–19.

11. Quoted in Joseph Lash, *Love, Eleanor* (Garden City, N.Y.: Doubleday & Company, 1982), 5.

12. Ruby Black, *Eleanor Roosevelt: A Biography* (New York: Duell, Sloan and Pearce, 1940), 3.

13. Quoted in Lash, *Love, Eleanor,* 5.

14. The date was February 9, 1878.

15. Quoted in Cook, *Eleanor Roosevelt,* 34.

16. Alice Lee Roosevelt was President Theodore Roosevelt's first wife and Elliott's sister-in-law. She died in childbirth.

17. Black, *Eleanor Roosevelt, A Biography,* 4–5.

18. Quoted in Cook, *Eleanor Roosevelt,* 33.

19. Quoted in Lash, *Love, Eleanor,* 7.

20. Quoted in Cook, *Eleanor Roosevelt,* 58.

21. Roosevelt, *This Is My Story,* in *The Autobiography of Eleanor Roosevelt,* 8.

22. Ibid., 4.

23. Quoted in Cook, *Eleanor Roosevelt*, 59. "Bamie" was Elliott and Theodore's older sister.

24. Black, *Eleanor Roosevelt: A Biography*, 6–7.

25. Roosevelt, *You Learn by Living*, 3.

26. This incident must have deeply impressed the little girl. It is related by many authorities; it can only have been told by Eleanor herself. William Chafe, "Biographical Sketch," in *Without Precedent: The Life and Career of Eleanor Roosevelt*, ed. Joan Hoff-Wilson and Marjorie Lightman (Bloomington: Indiana University Press, 1984), 4; most recently quoted in Doris Kearns Goodwin, *No Ordinary Time* (New York: Simon & Schuster, 1994), 94.

27. See Cook, *Eleanor Roosevelt*.

28. Roosevelt, *You Learn By Living*, 25–26. See Cook, *Eleanor Roosevelt*, for an insightful discussion of this period.

29. Roosevelt, *This Is My Story*, in *The Autobiography of Eleanor Roosevelt*, 8.

30. See Cook, *Eleanor Roosevelt*, for an insightful discussion of this period.

31. Roosevelt, *You Learn by Living*, 28.

32. Roosevelt, *This Is My Story*, in *The Autobiography of Eleanor Roosevelt*, 104.

33. Cook, *Eleanor Roosevelt*, 79.

34. See *The Autobiography of Eleanor Roosevelt* for a progressive view of Eleanor Roosevelt's own assessments of her inner development.

35. Roosevelt, *You Learn by Living*, 4–5.

36. Ibid.

37. Ibid.

38. Roosevelt, *This Is My Story*, in *The Autobiography of Eleanor Roosevelt*, 35.

39. Ibid., 37.

40. Roosevelt, *You Learn by Living*, 32.

41. Quoted in Lash, *Love, Eleanor*, 31, 33–34.

42. Lois Scharf, *Eleanor Roosevelt: First Lady of American Liberalism* (Boston: Twayne Publishers, 1987), 67.

43. See Frances Richardson Keller, "The Hearsts and American Society 1820–1920," Afterword in Judith Robinson, *The Hearsts: An American Dynasty* (Newark: University of Delaware Press, 1991), 390–396.

44. Quoted in Lash, *Love, Eleanor*, 73.

45. Ibid.

46. Geoffrey C. Ward, *Before the Trumpet: Young Franklin Roosevelt, 1882–1905* (New York: Harper & Row, 1985), Chapter 6.

47. Cook, *Eleanor Roosevelt*, 149.

48. Quoted in ibid., 141.

49. Scharf, *Eleanor Roosevelt: First Lady of American Liberalism*, 37.

50. Roosevelt, *This Is My Story*, in *The Autobiography of Eleanor Roosevelt*, 63, 68.

51. Quoted in Cook, *Eleanor Roosevelt*, 150.

52. Her godmother was Mrs. Henry (Susie) Parish, sister of her grandmother.

53. Roosevelt, *This Is My Story*, in *The Autobiography of Eleanor Roosevelt*, 55.

54. Black, *Eleanor Roosevelt*, 18–19.

55. Aunt Bye was Mrs. William Sheffield Cowles. She was a loving friend and mentor to Eleanor.

56. Roosevelt, *This Is My Story*, in *The Autobiography of Eleanor Roosevelt*, 56.

57. Discussed and quoted in Cook, *Eleanor Roosevelt*, 183.

58. Ibid., 179.

59. Roosevelt, *This Is My Story*, in *The Autobiography of Eleanor Roosevelt*, 61.

60. Ibid., 65.

61. Ibid., 58.

62. Ibid., 61

63. Ibid., 68.

64. Professor Arnaldo Testi views this Roosevelt's mission as an effort to combine the strengths of both genders in a political dominance. See Arnaldo Testi, "The Gender of Reform Politics: Theodore Roosevelt and the Culture of Masculinity," *Journal of American History* 81, no. 4 (1995): 1509–1533.

65. Roosevelt, *This I Remember*, in *The Autobiography of Eleanor Roosevelt*, 141.

66. Roosevelt, *This Is My Story*, in *The Autobiography of Eleanor Roosevelt*, 65.

67. Ibid., 66, 68.

68. Roosevelt, *This I Remember*, in *The Autobiography of Eleanor Roosevelt*, 109.

69. See discussion in Cook, *Eleanor Roosevelt*, 189–197.

70. Ibid., 192.

71. Roosevelt, *This Is My Story*, in *The Autobiography of Eleanor Roosevelt*, 81.

72. Quoted in Lash, *Love, Eleanor*, 128.

73. Roosevelt, *This Is My Story*, in *The Autobiography of Eleanor Roosevelt*, 125.

74. Ibid., 75.

75. Ibid., 91.

76. Eleanor's mother had attempted to overlook her father's "indiscretions"—with disastrous consequences.

77. See Lash, *Love, Eleanor*, 71–72.

78. See ibid., 70.

79. William H. Chafe, "The Personal and the Political," in Linda K. Kerber, Alice Kessler-Harris, and Kathryn Kish Sklar, eds., *U.S. History As Women's History: New Feminist Essays* (Chapel Hill: University of North Carolina Press), 1995, 200.

80. Roosevelt, *This I Remember*, in *The Autobiography of Eleanor Roosevelt*, 161.

81. Ibid., 131.

82. Ibid., 134.

83. Roosevelt, *This Is My Story*, in *The Autobiography of Eleanor Roosevelt*, 88.

84. Ibid., 89.

85. Chafe, "Biographical Sketch," 9.

86. Quoted in Lash, *Love, Eleanor*, 116.

87. Interview with Earl Miller in Joseph Lash, *Love, Eleanor*, 116–123.

88. Roosevelt, *This Is My Story*, in *The Autobiography of Eleanor Roosevelt*, 80.

89. Ibid., 87.

90. Ibid., 91.

91. Ibid., 90.

92. Quoted in Cook, *Eleanor Roosevelt*, 219.

93. Roosevelt, *This Is My Story*, in *The Autobiography of Eleanor Roosevelt*, 104.

94. Ibid., 105.

95. See Cook, *Eleanor Roosevelt*, 280–281 for discussion of these events.

96. Roosevelt, *This Is My Story*, in *The Autobiography of Eleanor Roosevelt*, 107.

97. Roosevelt, *You Learn By Living*, 124.

98. Roosevelt, *This Is My Story*, in *The Autobiography of Eleanor Roosevelt*, 108.

99. Ibid., 112–113.

100. Ibid., 115.

101. Roosevelt, *This I Remember*, in *The Autobiography of Eleanor Roosevelt*, 142.

102. Ibid.

103. Her uncle, Theodore Roosevelt, ran against Al Smith in this 1924 race for governor of New York.

104. Roosevelt, *This I Remember*, in *The Autobiography of Eleanor Roosevelt*, 144–145.

105. Ibid., 148.

106. Ibid.

107. Ibid., 152.

108. Quoted in Lash, *Love, Eleanor*, 101. This was a letter to Marion Dickerman.

109. Roosevelt, *This I Remember*, in *The Autobiography of Eleanor Roosevelt*, 151.

110. Roosevelt, *This Is My Story*, in *The Autobiography of Eleanor Roosevelt*, 125.

111. Roosevelt, *This I Remember*, in *The Autobiography of Eleanor Roosevelt*, 148.

112. Lash, *Love, Eleanor*, 111.

113. Quoted in Scharf, *Eleanor Roosevelt: First Lady of American Liberalism*, 110.

114. Roosevelt, *This I Remember*, in *The Autobiography of Eleanor Roosevelt*, 163.

115. Lash, *Love, Eleanor*, 124–125.

116. Ibid., 125.

117. Quoted in ibid., 145.

118. Quoted in ibid., 174.

119. Carroll Smith-Rosenberg, *Disorderly Conduct: Visions of Gender in Victorian America* (New York: Oxford, 1985), 53–76; quotation, 54.

120. Quoted in Lash, *Love, Eleanor*, 211.

121. Quoted in ibid., 154, 160.

122. Allida M. Black, *Casting Her Own Shadow: Eleanor Roosevelt and the Shaping of Postwar Liberalism* (New York: Columbia University Press, 1996), 199–200. In this astute study of Eleanor Roosevelt's painful, successful, and complex political development, we see the building of fictions that determined her life and influence.

123. Quoted in Lash, *Love, Eleanor*, 163.

124. Roosevelt, *This I Remember*, in *The Autobiography of Eleanor Roosevelt*, 167.

125. Ibid., 171.

126. Ibid., 176.

127. Three quotations about the National Youth Authority in Black, *Casting Her Own Shadow*, 30–33.

128. Roosevelt, *This I Remember*, in *The Autobiography of Eleanor Roosevelt*, 182–183.

129. Ibid., 181.

130. Ibid., 278–279.

131. Cook, *Eleanor Roosevelt*, 5. The longer version of this advice is:

> You cannot take anything personally.
> You cannot bear grudges.
> You must finish the day's work when the day's work is done.
> You cannot get discouraged too easily.
> You have to take defeat over and over again and go on.
> Be sure of your facts.
> Argue the other side with a friend until you have found the answer to every point which may be brought up against you.
> Women who are willing to be leaders must stand out and be shot at. More and more women are going to enter politics and more and more they should do it.
> Above all, women in political life must develop skin as tough as rhinoceros hide.

132. Quoted in David Emblidge, ed., *My Day: The Best of Eleanor Roosevelt's Acclaimed Newspaper Columns, 1936–1962,* Vol. 2, *The Postwar Years* (New York: Pharos Books, 1990), 14.

133. Quoted in Emblidge, *My Day,* 17.

134. Quoted in ibid.

135. Quoted in ibid., 23.

136. Letter quoted in Joseph Lash, *A World of Love* (New York: Garden City, N.J.: Doubleday & Company), 240.

137. Ibid., 248.

138. Quoted in ibid., 242.

139. Quoted in ibid., 251.

Index

Abolitionist movement, 42–43, 100, 172n125
Adams, Clover, 131
Addams, Jane, 46
African American male suffrage. *See* Suffrage
Allenswood School, 112, 119, 123
Amazons, 24
Anthony, Susan B., 42–43
Anti-Semitism, 73, 111, 147
Aristotle, 34
Arthurdale, 143
Atalanta, 24
Athena (Greek goddess), 30–31. *See also* Goddess worship

Bachofen, J. J., 157n8
Baruch, Bernard, 143
Basque region, 24–25, 157n15. *See also* Etxeko-andrea; Gender roles
Bible:
   Elizabeth Cady Stanton's revision of, 42
   Joseph Smith translates, 88
   and nineteenth-century millenarianism, 80
   and oppression of women, 35, 160n57
   and polygamy, 90–92, 168nn69,71
Blackwell, Antoinette Brown, 45
Bloomer, Amelia, 43
Book of Mormon, 84–85, 90–91, 95, 165n21, 166n23
Boston marriage, 128. *See also* Victorianism; Women's sexuality
Bowers, Claude G., 66–67
Burgess, John W., 59–62, 68
Burned-over district. *See* Second Great Awakening
Burns, James MacGregor, 13

Carpetbaggers, 53, 56, 59, 64–65
Child labor, 46–47, 108, 115, 128, 136, 141
Church of Jesus Christ of Latter-Day Saints, 85. *See also* Mormon church
Civil War, 11, 34, 48, 50–51, 62
Civilian Conservation Corps (CCC), 144
Code of Hammurabi, 36
Coitcheleh (Shawnee queen), 26
Compromise of 1850, 53, 56
Congressional Reconstruction. *See* Reconstruction
Constitution of 1787, 43, 49, 53
Cook, Nancy, 128, *129*, 135
Cooper, Anna Julia, 45–46
Couverture, 43–44, 47, 160n67
Cowdery, Oliver, *84*, 86, 165n21
Cowles, Mrs. William Sheffield (Eleanor Roosevelt's Aunt Bye), 119, 123, 174n55
Cox, James M., 132

Declaration of Human Rights, 151
Declaration of Independence, 42, 50, 53
Declaration of Sentiments, 42
Dewson, Molly, 129
Diana (Roman goddess), 30. *See also* Goddess worship
Dickerman, Marion, 128, *129*, 135, 138
Direct revelation:
   Golden plates, 83–84, 165n18, 166n28
   Peepstones, 79, 83, 164n4, 165nn15,19,21
   Seer stones (Urim and Thummim), 83, 165nn15,19,21
   See also Hutchinson, Ann; Smith, Joseph
Disfellowship, 89, 95, 170n98. *See also* Mormon church, theocracy of
Divorce, 42, 170nn98,109
Dix, John Alden, 123
Dreier, Mary, 129
Droysen, Johann Gustav, 16
DuBois, W. E. B., 67–69
Dunning, William Archibald, 57–59, 62
Dunning School, 58–59, 63–66, 69

Edmunds-Tucker Bill, 103. *See also* Polygamy, opposition to
Education:
   of African Americans, 45, 67, 73
   of white men, 5, 56–58, 60, 62–63, 70, 75
   of white women, 4–5, 43, 45–46
Engels, Friedrich, 31, 158n24
Etxeko-andrea, 25. *See also* Basque region; Gender roles

Female genital mutilation, 36
Female Relief Society, 97, 156n22, 170n101. *See also* Mormon women; Smith, Emma Hale
Fictions, 7–10, 14–15. *See also* Mormon church; Myth-making; Patriarchy; Reconstruction
Fifteenth Amendment, 51–52. *See also* Suffrage
Fleming, Walter L., 59–60, 64
Foot-binding, 36
Fourteenth Amendment, 51–52
Franklin, John Hope, 72–73, *74*, 75
Free love, 45
Freedman's Bureau, 65
Freud, Sigmund, 35
Freylingshuysen University, 45
Fuller, Margaret, 44

Gender roles:
   in Basque society, 25 (*see also* Etxeko-andrea)
   in biblical times, 35
   in codes of law, 36

179

and sexuality, 12, 33, 90–92, 101
and slavery, 100
and statehood for Utah, 104
theocracy of, 78, 88, 95, 97
theology of, 79, 84–88 (*see also* Book of Mormon; Mormon Book of Commandments)
See also Direct revelation; Monogamy; Polygamy
Mormon women:
    and divorce, 170nn98,109
    economic activity of, 168n56
    and Female Relief Societies, 97, 156n22, 170n101
    opposition to Edmunds-Tucker Bill, 103
    position in Mormon theocracy, 166n36, 170n108, 171n119
    responses to polygamy:
        dissatisfaction with, 95–96
        ramifications of refusal to participate in, 168n65
        support for, 97–98, 103–104
    and suffrage, 98–100, 102–103, 171n111, 172nn132,137
    writings about polygamy, 95, 97, 169nn89,90, 170n96
    See also Reorganized Church of Jesus Christ of Latter-Day Saints; Smith, Emma Hale; Smith, Lucy Mack; Snow, Eliza Roxey; Whitney, Helen Mar; Young, Ann Eliza Webb
Moskowitz, Belle, 136
Mother-goddess, 29–30, 33, 38, 40. *See also* Goddess worship
Mott, Lucretia Coffin, 43
Myth-making, 9, 26
    and gender, 21–47
    historians and, 9, 11, 16–20, 48–77
    and religion, 78–104, 166n23

National Consumers' League, 129
National Youth Administration (NYA), 144
Native Americans, 26, 72, 100, 107, 168n61
Nativism, 111, 136
New Deal, 142–148
New York Consumers' League, 115
Ninhursag (Sumerian goddess), 29. *See also* Goddess worship
Non-Partisan Legislative Committee, 141
Nugur (Chinese goddess), 29. *See also* Goddess worship
Nut (Egyptian goddess), 29. *See also* Goddess worship

Oberlin College, 43, 45. *See also* Education
Objectivity. *See* Historians
Ovid, 27

Panic of 1873, 58
Parrish, Mrs. Henry (Susie), 115

Patriarchy:
    consequences of, 36
    defined, 11, 156n1
    and family structure, 34
    Mormonism and, 78–79, 89–90, 97, 101, 167n53
    origins of, 22–23
        economic, 32
        legal, 36, 43
        philosophical, 34
        religious, 33–34, 167n53
        social, 32
    pathologization of, 21, 40–41
    periodization of, 23
    perpetuation of by men, 32–36
    technology and, 159n40
    women's enculturation to accept, 3–5, 36–37, 40, 89–90, 97–98 (*see also* Victorianism)
    women's resistance to, 40–47, 95, 100
    See also Mormon church; Mormon women; Polygamy; Smith, Joseph; Victorianism
Peepstones. *See* Direct revelation
Polygamy:
    Brigham Young's practice of, 95, 99, 169n90
    centrality of to Mormon beliefs, 79
    criminalization of in United States, 172n137
    disavowed by Mormon church (1890), 98
    and economic hardship, 78, 95, 96, 169n90, 171n116
    facilitation of homosocial networks, 98–99, 103
    in history, 33, 92
    initiated in Mormon church (1843), 12, 169nn75,80
    Joseph Smith's practice of, 93, 95–96, 99, 169nn75,80
    Mormon women's responses to, 95–101, 103–104, 168nn65,89
    officially acknowledged by Mormon church (1852), 92, 99
    opposition to, 101–103, 171n118
        anti-polygamy petition, 103
        Anti-Polygamy Society (1878), 102, 172n132
        Edmunds-Tucker Bill, 130
        persecution of Mormons, 100, 102
    and pressure to practice among Mormons, 170n96
    See also Mormon women; Woodruff Manifesto
Pratt, Orson, 87, 92

Queen Coitcheleh, 26

Race riot (Tulsa, Oklahoma), 72
Racial terminology in U. S. history, 161n1
Racism, 111
    in historical scholarship, 58–59, 61–66, 68–69, 71, 73, 76
    Jim Crow laws, 70, 72

relationship with Sara Delano Roosevelt, 116–120, 127, 136
and sexual double standard, 126–127, 141–142
Roosevelt, Hall (Eleanor's brother), 131
Roosevelt, Sara Delano (Eleanor's mother-in-law), 116–120, 124, 127, 133, 135–136
Roosevelt, Theodore (Eleanor's uncle), 118–119, 121–122, 125, 175n64, 176n103

Scalawags, 53, 59
Schneiderman, Rose, 128
Second Great Awakening, 79–80, 167n53
Seer stones. *See* Direct revelation
Seneca Falls Women's Rights Convention, 42, 100, 172n121
Settlement house movement, 46, 115
Sexual double standard, 106
and Mormon beliefs, 91–92, 97, 101
in Roosevelt family, 109, 126–127, 133, 175n76
Sexuality. *See* Mormon church, and sexuality; Victorianism; Women's sexuality
Slavery:
and Civil War, 168n67
and Compromise of 1850, 53, 56
and Constitutional law, 49–50, 53
and democracy in United States, 53
enslavement of women, 32–34, *41*
evolution of in United States, 53
origins of human slavery, 32–33
and patriarchy, 38
religious justification of, 38
and slave trade, 53
Smith, Al, 124, 135–136, 176n103
Smith, Emma Hale, 31, 83, 87, *94,* 165n18
childbearing of, 93
forms Reorganized Church of Jesus Christ of Latter-Day Saints, 100
marriage to Joseph Smith, 93
president of Female Relief Society, 170n101
reaction to polygamy, 93–95
Smith, Joseph, *82*
background of, 80–81, 164n10
beliefs about gender roles, 91
and direct revelation, 12, 83–85, 87, 165nn15,16,18,19,21
education of, 165n24
forms Church of Jesus Christ of Latter-Day Saints, 85
leadership style of, 87, 89, 170n98
millenarian beliefs of, 86
political life of, 93
and translation of Old Testament, 88, 91
Smith, Lucy Mack, 80–81, 166n28
Snow, Eliza Roxey, 95, *96,* 97, 171n113
Social Darwinism, 58
Social reform movements, United States:
abolitionist movement, 42–43, 100, 172n125
anti–child labor movement, 46–47, 108, 115, 128, 136, 141
dress reform, 43
labor movement, 46, 115, 128–129, 132
settlement house movement, 46, 115
spiritualism, 44
temperance movement, 46, 100
woman suffrage movement, 11, 36, 43, 45, 100, 102–103, 162n7, 172n125
women's rights movement, 42–47, 100
Souvestre, Marie, 112–113, 115–116
Stampp, Kenneth, 75–77
Stanton, Elizabeth Cady, 42, 102
Stenhouse, Fanny, 95
Stone, Lucy, 43–44
Suffrage:
for African-American men, 52–53, 56, 162n7
for women, 11, 36, 43, 45, 98–100, 102–103, 134–135, 162n7, 171n118, 172n137
See also Mormon women

Tammany Hall, 124
Teapot Dome scandal, 135
Temperance movement, 43, 46, 100
Tennessee Valley Authority (TVA), 142–143, 146
Thirteenth Amendment, 51–52
Thompson, Malvina, 137
Todhunter School, 135, 140–141
Transcendentalism, 44
Truth, Sojourner, 43
Tugwell, Rexford, 143

Unemployment, 140
United Nations, 151
Urim and Thummim. *See* Direct revelation

Vanderlip, Mrs. Frank (Narcissa), 133. *See also* League of Women Voters
Victorianism, 111, 147
and childrearing, 111–112, 125
and homosocial partnerships, 139
and sexual double standard, 90, 106, 126
and women's duties, 105, 119, 121, 135
and women's public roles, 125
and women's sexuality, 112, 120–121, 126, 139
von Ranke, Leopold, 16, 58–59, 61

Whitney, Helen Mar, 97
Wilson, Woodrow, 62, *63,* 124–125, 131–132
Wobblies, 132
Woman suffrage (1920), 36, 134
and African Americans, 162n7
efforts of mainstream women's rights activists to outlaw in Utah, 102–103
and election of Franklin Roosevelt as governor of New York, 134–135
nineteenth-century woman suffrage movement, 11, 43, 45, 102–103, 172nn125,137

FRANCES RICHARDSON KELLER was educated at Sarah Lawrence College and received her Ph.D. degree from the University of Chicago. She is author and editor of numerous articles and books, including *American Crusade: The Life of Charles Waddell Chesnutt; Slavery and the French Revolutionists* by Anna Julia Cooper (editor and translator); and *Views of Women's Lives in Western Tradition.* Dr. Keller taught History and Women's Studies at San Francisco State University, and continues to lecture and publish widely on topics in women's, African-American, and U.S. history.